D1175061

LAW CLERKS
AND THE JUDICIAL PROCESS

Law Clerks
and the Judicial Process

*Perceptions of the Qualities
and Functions of Law Clerks
in American Courts*

John Bilyeu Oakley
and Robert S. Thompson

UNIVERSITY OF CALIFORNIA PRESS
Berkeley   Los Angeles   London

University of California Press
Berkeley and Los Angeles, California

University of California Press, Ltd.
London, England

1   2   3   4   5   6   7   8   9

Library of Congress Cataloging in Publication Data

Oakley, John Bilyeu.
    Law clerks and the judicial process:
Perceptions of the qualities and functions
of law clerks in American courts
    Bibliography: p.
    Includes index.
    1. Clerks of court—United States.   2. Judicial
process—United States.   I. Thompson, Robert S.,
joint author.   II. Title.
KF8771.O'2   347.73'16   80-16167
ISBN 0-520-04046-5

Contents

Preface

This brief book has only one pretension: that it may stand as a pioneering effort at inquiry into a neglected but significant part of the process of judicial decision-making. The role of the judiciary in American government has attracted a great deal of scholarly interest in the past century, but that interest has focused almost exclusively upon judges themselves, how they come to be appointed or elected to office, and how they wield their power as determined from the public record of their decisions. Judicial decision-making has been perceived as a uniquely individual process in our pluralistic society, except insofar as the power of decision has been vested in the groups of judges who constitute appellate courts. Only in recent years has the use of staff to assist judges in their decisions drawn penetrating commentary, and the best of this scholarship has been directed primarily to the structure and functions of staffs which serve courts as a whole rather than individual judges. Other than the personal accounts of idiosyncratic working habits that have occasionally been published by particular judges or their "law clerks" (as staff assistants to individual judges are generally called), virtually no literature exists which explores how judges themselves perceive the impact of judicial staff upon their decisions.

The reason for the dearth of such literature is readily apparent: the tradition of confidentiality in the relationship between judges and law clerks is as hallowed as the secrecy of impending decisions of the United States Supreme Court. As we discuss at some length in our text, this tradition has inhibited qualitative analysis of the various models for the use of judicial staff even by participants in the process of judicial decision-making, and has almost wholly insulated that process from the scrutiny of extrinsic scholarship. By demonstrating that empirical data about judicial use of personal staff can be obtained without compromising the confidentiality of the relationship between judges and staff and the decisions which they produce, we hope our efforts will make possible further research that will progress from the exploratory to the definitive.

The general theme of this book is how a fairly representative cross section of American judges uses staff assistance in making its decisions, and how its use of staff might be improved. The judges involved sit on four different types of courts: the Supreme Court of California, the United States Court of Appeals for the Ninth Circuit, the four United States district courts in California, and the five courts of appeal in the California state court system. Our analysis entails consideration of five related but somewhat distinct underlying topics, which we expect to be of varying independent interest to particular readers. We have attempted to discuss each constituent topic in sufficient detail in the text to permit a reader of the text alone to follow our theme from development to conclusion; where we have felt that additional detail might be of interest to students of particular topics, we have made liberal use of footnotes.

Our first topic is a history of the use of law clerks in American courts, by which we seek to put our subsequent data and conclusions in context. Accompanying this history is the most comprehensive bibliography yet assembled on the subject. If our experience in compiling these materials from highly scattered and frequently obscure sources is any guide, this aspect of our work alone should be of major assistance in facilitating further research; to this end we present our bibliographic data both in the standard legal form of footnoted citations and in an appended bibliography of conventional style. Our footnotes conform to *A Uniform System of Citation*, 12th edition, published by the Harvard Law Review Association. Our bibliography conforms to *A Manual of Style*, 12th edition, published by the University of Chicago Press. Our intent is that our sources will thus be readily accessible to scholars of all disciplines.

Second, we draw from our historical material an idealized model of the judge–law clerk relationship, which emphasizes the importance of law clerks being recent law school graduates of limited tenure as judicial assistants if the process of judicial decision is to be enhanced rather than impeached by staff participation.

Third, we present the central topic of the book: the results of our interviews with sixty-three federal and state judges on how they personally use (and how they fear their colleagues may abuse) the various types of staff assistance available to them.

In the course of presenting our interview data, we address a fourth topic: in both text and footnotes we present a great deal of detailed data on the structure and operation of the four types of courts, federal and state, at which we studied the use of judicial staff. Some of these data were derived from our personal experiences as judge and law clerk, more were discovered or disclosed in the course of our interviews of particular judges of the subject courts, and still more were obtained from existing published and unpublished sources. In this respect our work serves both as primary source material for future scholarship and as a compilation of source materials already extant. It casts considerable light on how American courts operate, quite apart from judicial use of law clerks. New material on the internal operation of the Supreme Court of California may prove of particular interest, not only because of that court's national stature but also because of the recent politically tinged controversy over the integrity of the court's decision-making process.

Fifth and finally, we compare the idealized model of judicial use of staff which emerged from our historical materials—and which coincided at the outset of our research with our personal attitudes about proper law clerk usage—with the realities of modern court conditions revealed in our interviews and described in our data on the structure and operation of the courts studied. We find that the basic principles embodied in the clerkship ideal are shared by most of our subject judges; we also find that substantial conformity to the clerkship ideal is to some degree unobtainable in the present circumstances of severely overworked courts. We reaffirm the importance of the clerkship ideal, compare the relative adherence to its principles among the courts we studied, and offer strategies for promoting the effectuation of these principles to the greatest extent possible, given current conditions.

The research and writing of this book took place over nearly three years, from the summer of 1976 to the spring of 1979. The use of law clerks and other judicial staff did not remain static throughout this period. Because our judicial interview data date from the summer of 1976, we have fully described the structure and operating procedures of the subject courts as of that time so that the interview data can be understood in their contemporaneous context. Where significant changes have occurred subsequent to our interviews, we have incorporated details of the changes into our text and footnotes. The book thus sets forth structural and operational data that are current through the beginning of 1979.

We expect the use of staff at the federal courts we studied to change little over the next few years, with the exception of the provision to circuit judges of a third personal law clerk. Legislation permitting circuit judges to hire a third law clerk was passed late in 1979; it is discussed at the conclusion of the Appendix, in an addendum to our *Note on Funding of Law Clerks at Lower Federal Courts*. More important, we believe, was the 1978 legislation noted in the text by which significant numbers of new judges were added to the lower federal courts. The thrust of federal judicial administration in the foreseeable future will be to attack court congestion through the efficient deployment of these new judges, rather than through innovations in the use of staff.

More immediate and fundamental changes in the use of staff may be in the offing at the California Supreme Court and courts of appeal. We describe in the book some of the changes already wrought under the stewardship of California's new Chief Justice; we expect more to follow, and hope that our work may illuminate the reexamination of staff practices which is currently under way within the judicial system of California. These developments should be of interest to other than Californians; the history we recount herein shows that in the use of law clerks as well as in social mores generally, California's trends tend to become the nation's conventions.

Portions of this book have previously appeared in substantially abridged form in the December, 1979, issue of the *California Law Review*, volume 67, at pages 1286–1317. We appreciate the consent of the University of California Press to publish this preview of our work.

Our greatest debt of gratitude is owed to the judges who consented to our interviews. We also thank for their time and interest the many law clerks and other personnel whom we interviewed with the consent of their supervising judges. Particularly helpful to us were Professor Arthur Hellman, then Supervising Staff Attorney of the United States Court of Appeals for the Ninth Circuit, and Stephen Buehl, Executive Assistant to the Chief Justice of California. We are also indebted to Mr. B. E. Witkin for his information on the early use of staff attorneys at the Supreme Court of California, and to Ms. Winifred L. Hepperle of the National Center for State Courts for her bibliographic assistance. We gratefully acknowledge the financial support provided our research by the law school of the University of California at Davis and by the Committee on Research of the Davis Division of the Academic Senate of the University of California. We also wish to acknowledge the valuable assistance provided to us by Carol Warren of the Department of Sociology of the University of Southern California, by programmers Hal Grade and Syd Springer of the Social Science Data Service of the University of California at Davis, by Carole Hinkle, who carefully typed and retyped the many drafts of our manuscript, and by the students of the law school of the University of California at Davis who provided us with research assistance: Steven Forester of the class of 1978, Adam Lewis and Bill Cunningham of the class of 1979, Allison Mendel and David Jenkins of the class of 1980, and, most of all, Marilyn McCloskey of the class of 1977. We have had the benefit of comments upon several drafts of the manuscript by Professors Floyd Feeney and Friedrich K. Juenger of the law school of the University of California at Davis; the transformation from manuscript to book has been greatly eased by the editorial assistance of Paul Weisser. Finally, we have gained much insight and constant encouragement from our spouses Fredericka Oakley and Elizabeth Thompson, doctoral candidates respectively in Anthropology at Yale University and in Sociology at the University of Southern California. We alone, of course, remain solely responsible for the content of this book.

March, 1980   J.B.O.
                                                               R.S.T.

1. INTRODUCTION

American law is far from simple, and yet Americans cling to a simplistic conception of how their courts apply, interpret, and occasionally create the law by which they live. The flaws of the conception are both ironic and paradoxical: ironic in the simplicity attributed to the process of adjudication under so complex a system of law, paradoxical in the assumption that the tasks of adjudication are more complex than is generally true. The public conceives of the judicial process as an intellectual cottage industry in which judges labor in solitude as they handcraft decisions to exquisite legal questions in the manner of Learned Hand and Oliver Wendell Holmes. To the extent that the public is aware that few current judges have such style or stature, its reaction tends toward cynicism rather than sophistication. It does not see its conception of the judicial process as naive or anachronistic, only as betrayed: an ideal unrealized but not unattainable.[1.1]

1.1. As with most scholars who comment on public conceptions of governmental processes, what we present is but our conception of the public's conception of how our courts operate. We should add that the public we have in mind is apparently a rather small segment of the citizenry as a whole. Most members of the public are not sufficiently well-informed about the operation of courts to have particular conceptions of how courts generate decisions. See Sarat, *Studying American Legal Culture: An Assessment of Survey Evidence*, 11 LAW & SOC'Y REV. 427, 438–39 (1977). Our representation of the conception of judicial decision-making on the part of those members of the public educated enough to know of Learned Hand and Oliver Wendell Holmes draws some support from evidence that a mythic conception of the United States Supreme Court, in the most general sense of a suspension of political judgment and an acceptance as legitimate of whatever decisions the Court cares to reach, is associated with above-average social status

The popular conception fails to encompass both the mortal dimensions of the typical judicial intellect and the crush of routine cases which demand only the application of settled principles to unique facts. The occasions on which judges fashion novel rules of law are exceptional, and even then the judges' creative pleasure is diminished by the constant backlog of undecided, unoriginal cases awaiting decisions of importance to the parties but to no one else.

In fact, modern American judging in all courts of national significance—the federal courts and the more prominent state appellate courts—staggers along despite the burden of bloated caseloads and the shortcomings of distinctly human judges only by the delegation of a great deal of the labor of judging to law clerks: subordinate, anonymous, but often quite powerful lawyers who function as the noncommissioned officers in the army of the judiciary.

This book continues the modern trend of treating law clerks as an institution both integral to the judicial process and worthy of separable scholarly interest. Writing about law clerks, like writing about sex, has only recently become respectable. It is only in the last few decades that, except for romanticized and highly expurgated accounts, either has been issued in volumes not sheathed in plain paper wrappers. With boldness worthy of a Grove Press, however, recent legal literature has begun to discuss the institution of the law clerk frankly for what it is: indispensable.[1.2] Judges now candidly acknowledge the role of law clerks and are willing to discuss their functions. We present the findings and con-

---

and education. *See* Casey, *The Supreme Court and Myth: An Empirical Investigation*, 8 LAW & SOC'Y REV. 385, 398–403 (1974). *See also* Dolbeare, *The Public views the Supreme Court*, in LAW, POLITICS, AND THE FEDERAL COURTS 194 (H. Jacob ed. 1967).

1.2. We credit a poet with first drawing our romantic analogy, albeit at a higher level. *See* W. H. AUDEN, *Law Like Love*, in COLLECTED SHORTER POEMS 1927–1957 154 (1966). As examples of literature on both topics from the romanticized era, *see* J. AUSTEN, PRIDE AND PREJUDICE *passim* (1813); F. BIDDLE, MR. JUSTICE HOLMES 147–52 (1942). On the contribution of the Grove Press, *see*, *e.g.*, Grove Press, Inc. v. State of Florida, 156 So. 2d 537 (Fla. 1963), *rev'd per curiam sub nom.* Grove Press, Inc. v. Gerstein, 378 U.S. 577 (1964). For fuller accounts of the adventures of Grove Press in publishing Henry Miller's *Tropic of Cancer*, see Zeitlin v. Arnebergh, 59 Cal. 2d 901, 383 P.2d 152, 31 Cal. Rptr. 800 (1963); *Henry Miller Ban to be Defied Here*, N.Y. Times, Apr. 25, 1961, at 37, col. 1; *Federal Order Lifts Ban on Importing "Tropic of Cancer,"* *id.*, Aug. 11, 1961, at 25, col. 1.

clusions on proper law clerk usage which we have drawn from personal interviews with sixty-three judges of state and federal courts within California.

Our interest in the selection, tenure, and utilization of law clerks is a reflection of—and a reaction to—the prevailing trend toward the bureaucratization of all governmental institutions, including those charged with the administration of justice.[1.3] Besides illuminating the current state of the law clerk institution in American courts, we seek to defend a two-pronged thesis on the proper use of law clerks. First, we assert that the bureaucratization of the judicial process is not a function of the use of law clerks per se. It results from a shift in the character of law clerks away from the traditional model by which freshly graduated lawyers of acknowledged brilliance were retained as law clerks for brief but finite periods to serve individual judges, and towards a new model by which generally less distinguished lawyers serve as law clerks for a career and frequently are responsible to groups of judges rather than individuals among them. Second, we assert that modern court conditions mandate not the abolition of staff bureaucracies serving judges but rather their careful exploitation, so that the profits of dealing with routine cases on a bureaucratized basis may subsidize the retention of labor-intensive but qualitatively superior law clerks of the traditional type.

A. Prior Literature

True to our earlier analogy, the first widespread yet unromanticized revelations of the use of law clerks had a salacious side, implying that judges were prey to the blandishments and biases of the law clerks with whom they dallied behind closed doors.[1.4] Freethinkers were quick to rise to the defense of law clerks, and although some conceded that law clerks were not totally bereft of

1.3. See generally Heydebrand, The Context of Public Bureaucracies: An Organizational Analysis of Federal District Courts, 11 LAW & SOC'Y REV. 759, 761–71, 792–94, 812–14 (1977).

1.4. See The Bright Young Men Behind the Bench, U.S. NEWS & WORLD REPORT, July 12, 1957, at 45; Rehnquist, Who Writes Decisions of the Supreme Court?, id., Dec. 13, 1957, at 74, reprinted in 53 BRIEF 89 (1958); Rehnquist, Another View: Clerks Might "Influence" Some Actions, U.S. NEWS & WORLD REPORT, Feb. 21, 1958, at 116. See also Kurland, Book Review, 22 U. CHI. L. REV. 297, 299 (1954) (C. PRITCHETT, CIVIL LIBERTIES AND THE VINSON COURT), in which Chief Justice Vinson and Justice Murphy are said by Professor Kurland to have been "absolutely dependent upon their law clerks for the production of their opinions."

influence, if only in an attenuated, institutional sense,[1.5] the defense generally took the tack of playing down the role of law clerks to the level of triviality by denying that such outrageous conduct as the drafting of substantially complete opinions by law clerks commonly occurred, rather than by contesting the propositions that such conduct was outrageous at all or necessarily a threat to judicial virtue.[1.6]

1.5.   See J. FRANK, THE MARBLE PALACE 115–19 (1958); Bickel, *The Court: An Indictment Analyzed*, N.Y. Times, Apr. 27, 1958, § 6 (Magazine) at 16. *See also* A. BICKEL, POLITICS AND THE WARREN COURT, at 139–45 (1965).

1.6.   *See, e.g.*, Cohen, *Justice Douglas: A Law Clerk's View*, 26 U. CHI. L. REV. 6 (1958); Cuomo, *The New York Court of Appeals: A Practical Perspective*, 34 ST. JOHN'S L. REV. 197, 211–12 (1960); Rogers, *Clerks' Work Is "Not Decisive of Ultimate Result*," U.S. NEWS & WORLD REPORT, Feb. 21, 1958, at 114, 116. *See also* Clark, *Internal Operation of the United States Supreme Court*, 43 J. AM. JUD. SOC'Y 45 (1959); Hills, *A Law Clerk at the Supreme Court of the United States*, 33 (L.A.) B. A. BULL 333 (1958); Johnson, *What Do Law Clerks Do?* 22 TEX. B. J. 229 (1959). *But see* Medina, *Some Reflections on the Judicial Function at the Appellate Level*, 1961 WASH. U. L. Q. 148, 153–55; Newland, *Personal Assistants to Supreme Court Justices: The Law Clerks*, 40 ORE. L. REV. 299, 311–16 (1961). *See also* B. Witkin, Appellate Court Opinions 34 (Syllabus for Panel Discussion at Appellate Judges' Conference, ABA Section of Judicial Administration, Montreal, Canada, Aug. 7, 1966):

> The fact that law clerks do write opinions is sometimes considered a matter too delicate for discussion. But in a day when every important executive in public and private affairs relies on skilled speech writers, report writers, and other experts to whom he delegates anything but final decisions, there is no need to seek excuses for delegation of part of the opinion writing function to talented young experts, with superior legal training, including law review or other writing or teaching experience.

The trivial view of law clerks, who supplied intellectual entertainment and perhaps an idea or two to their judges, was well supported by an accumulation of posthumous encomia to United States Supreme Court Justices by their law clerks. *See, e.g.*, Acheson, *Recollection of Service with the Federal Supreme Court*, 18 ALA. LAW. 355 (1957) (re Mr. Justice Brandeis); F. BIDDLE, *supra* note 1.2; Boskey, *Mr. Chief Justice Stone*, 59 HARV. L. REV. 1200 (1946); Brudney & Wolson, *Mr. Justice Rutledge—Law Clerks' Reflections*, 25 IND. L. J. 455 (1949–50); *Chief Justice Vinson and His Law Clerks*, 49 Nw. U. L. REV. 26 (1954); Jaffe, *An Impression of Mr. Justice Brandeis*, 8 HARV. L. SCH. BULL. 10 (1957); McCormack, *A Law Clerk's Recollections*, 46 COLUM. L. REV. 710 (1946) (re Mr. Justice Stone); Pickering, Gressman, & Tolan, *Mr. Justice Murphy—A Note of Appreciation*, 48 MICH. L. REV. 742 (1950).

Two of the most reflective articles were written not on Supreme Court Justices, who seem to have laid greater claim to mythology, but on Second Circuit judges. *See* Kurland, *Jerome N. Frank: Some Reflections and Recollections of a Law Clerk*, 24 U. OF CHI. L. REV. 661 (1957); Braden, *The Value of Law Clerks*, 24 MISS. L. J. 295 (1953) (re Judges Clark and Minton, prior to the latter's brief service on

The ensuing twenty years have brought a great deal of enlightenment about what law clerks do indeed do.[1.7] The new literature on law clerks has moved beyond the nostalgia and beatification of earlier essays to probe the institution with objective scholarly scrutiny.[1.8] By this airing, the relationship between

the Supreme Court). It is most unfortunate that Mr. Braden's elegant defense of the traditional role of law clerks was published in a relatively obscure journal and failed to figure in the subsequent uproar over allegations of law clerks' undue influence upon Supreme Court decisions. *See* note 1.4 *supra*.

1.7. *See, e.g.*, R. LEFLAR, INTERNAL OPERATING PROCEDURES OF APPELLATE COURTS 79–94 (1976); D. MEADOR, APPELLATE COURTS: STAFF AND PROCESS IN THE CRISIS OF VOLUME (1974); NATIONAL CENTER FOR STATE COURTS, THE CALIFORNIA COURTS OF APPEAL 71–118 (1974) [hereinafter cited as CAL. COURTS OF APPEAL]; M. SCHICK, LEARNED HAND'S COURT 98–99, 106–108 (1970); J. WILKINSON, SERVING JUSTICE: A SUPREME COURT CLERK'S VIEW (1974); Baier, *The Law Clerks: Profile of an Institution*, 26 VAND. L. REV. 1125 (1973); Brennan, *Justice Brennan Calls National Court of Appeals Proposal Fundamentally Ill-Advised* 59 A.B.A.J. 835, 836–37 (1973); Carrington, *Report on Group Discussions, Topic II: Responsibility for Decisions* in 5 ADVISORY COUNCIL FOR APPELLATE JUSTICE, APPELLATE JUSTICE: 1975—SUPPLEMENT, PROCEEDINGS AND CONCLUSIONS 65–67 (P. Carrington ed. 1975) (National Conference on Appellate Justice, Jan. 26–28, 1975) [hereinafter cited as 5 APPELLATE JUSTICE: 1975]; Dorsen, *Law Clerks in Appellate Courts in the United States*, 26 MOD. L. REV. 265 (1963); Fite, Potts, & Sweeney, *Law Clerkships: Three Inside Views*, 33 ALA. LAW. 156 (1972) (discusses state and federal courts in Alabama) [hereinafter cited as *Three Views*]; Francis, Post-Argument Procedures, 52 F.R.D. 51, 70, 71–73 (1971) (discusses N.J. Supreme Court); Goldberg, *Preparation for Hearing Oral Argument*, 63 F.R.D. 499, 500–504, 506 (1974) (discusses United States Court of Appeals for the Fifth Circuit); Lesinski, *Judicial Research Assistants: The Michigan Experience*, 10 TRIAL JUDGES' J. 54 (1971); Medina, *supra* note 1.6 (discusses United States Court of Appeals for the Second Circuit); Newland, *supra* note 1.6; Ragatz and Shea, *Supreme Court Law Clerks*, 35 WIS. B. BULL. 33 (1962); Rutzick, *Gerald Gunther: A Man Who Enjoys an Occasional Brief Constitutional*, HARV. L. REC., Mar. 2, 1973, at 8 (discusses clerkships with Learned Hand and Earl Warren); Tamura, *What Everyone Always Wanted to Know About the Courts of Appeal But Were Afraid to Ask*, L.A. Daily J., Oct. 17, 1973, at 25, 27 (discusses California courts of appeal); Williams, *Justices run 'nine little law firms' at Supreme Court*, SMITHSONIAN, Feb. 1977, at 84; Wright, *Observations of an Appellate Judge: The Use of Law Clerks*, 26 VAND. L. REV. 1179 (1973) (discusses United States courts of appeals); Zeigler and Hermann, *The Invisible Litigant: An Inside View of Pro Se Actions in the Federal Courts*, 47 N.Y.U.L. REV. 157, 176–77, 207–08, 238–45, 249–50 (1972); S. Flanders, District Court Studies Project Interim Report at 45–46 (Federal Judicial Center, June, 1976). *See generally* R. LEFLAR, APPELLATE JUDICIAL OPINIONS 272–291 (1974) (collecting other materials). *See also* Herman, *Law Clerking at the Supreme Court of Canada*, 13 OSGOODE HALL L. J. 279 (1975).

1.8. *See especially* D. MEADOR, *supra* note 1.7; CAL. COURTS OF APPEAL, *supra* note 1.7; Baier, *supra* note 1.7; Newland, *supra* note 1.6.

judges and law clerks has received an academic blessing akin to that given unmarried cohabitors by the California Supreme Court.[1.9]

Explicit manuals on clerking techniques are now being published,[1.10] and some judges and commentators have become convinced that courts will be better served by the well-trained professional who makes clerking a career than by the traditionally short-termed law clerk fresh from the nest of law school.[1.11] Other reformers call for commercialized law clerking of a different sort; while praising the virtues of the traditional law clerk, who comes to the court better versed in the theory than the practice of law and works at the side of a single judge, they argue that there is a low limit to the number of such handmaidens whom any one judge can usefully employ. Their cure for appellate court congestion is the "central staff": the hiring of a corps of lawyers to work for the court as a corporate whole.[1.12]

1.9.

[W]e believe that the prevalence of nonmarital relationships in modern society and the social acceptance of them, marks this as a time when our courts should by no means [continue to] apply the doctrine of the unlawfulness of the so-called meretricious relationship. . . . [T]he nonenforceability of agreements expressly providing for meretricious conduct rested upon the fact that such conduct, as the word suggests, pertained to and encompassed prostitution. To equate the nonmarital relationship of today to such a subject matter is to do violence to an accepted and wholly different practice.

Marvin v. Marvin, 18 Cal. 3d 660, 683, 557 P.2d 106, 122, 134 Cal. Rptr. 815, 831 (1976).

1.10. *See, e.g.*, Aldisert, *Duties of Law Clerks*, 26 VAND. L. REV. 1251 (1973); Hamley, *Law Clerks for Judges of the Ninth Circuit Court of Appeals*, 26 VAND. L. REV. 1241 (1973); Smith, *A Primer of Opinion Writing for Law Clerks, id.* at 1203; Wright, *Selection, Training and Use of Law Clerks in United States Courts of Appeals*, 63 F.R.D. 453, 465 (1974); A. DiLeo & A. Rubin, Law Clerk Handbook (Sept. 1977, rev'd Mar. 1978) (Federal Judicial Center FJC-M-1; looseleaf). *See also* B. WITKIN, MANUAL ON APPELLATE COURT OPINIONS 21–23 (1977).

1.11. *See* B. WITKIN, *supra* note 10, at 12–14; O'Connell, *Streamlining Appellate Procedures*, 56 JUD. 234, 236 (1973). *See generally* Thompson, *Mitigating the Damage: One Judge and No Judge Appellate Decisions*, 50 CAL. ST. B. J. 476, 513–15 (1975).

1.12. *See* P. CARRINGTON, D. MEADOR & M. ROSENBERG, JUSTICE ON APPEAL 44–48 (1976) [hereinafter cited as JUSTICE ON APPEAL]; Lesinski & Stockmeyer, *Prehearing Research and Screening in the Michigan Court of Appeals: One Court's Method for Increasing Judicial Productivity*, 26 VAND. L. REV. 1211 (1973). *See generally*, D. MEADOR, *supra* note 7, *passim*; Cameron, *The Central Staff: A New Solution to an Old Problem*, 23 U.C.L.A. L. REV. 465 (1976); Christian, *Using Prehearing*

B. *The Nature and Purpose of This Study*

Our study focuses on aspects of law clerking left largely un-discussed in the literature: (1) the comparative virtues and vices of traditional law clerks who remain with a judge for just one or two years, as opposed to the new breed of long-term career clerks; and (2) the perceptions and beliefs of judges themselves as to the im-pact upon judicial decisions of law clerks in all their incarnations, whether working for one judge or for a court in general, and whether employed for a limited or an indefinite tenure. Econ-omy, convenience, and our special interests led us to examine these aspects within the state and federal courts of California. In view of California's large and respected state court system, its many federal courts, and the heterogeneous population which both systems serve, we think our study has relevance to law clerk usage in all American courts and, insofar as it depicts the percep-tions of a broad spectrum of judges, is representative of most of them.

The study was originally motivated by a fear that the endan-gered species status of the traditional law clerk in the California courts of appeal[1.13] presented a significant threat to legal ecology, foreboding unfortunate consequences to the quality of appellate justice in California. In seeking to articulate our fears, however, we found in the literature on law clerks an almost utter lack of any qualitative, as opposed to quantitative, evaluation of law clerks' impact on a court as a function of such variables as their personal characteristics, the length of their tenure with the court, and their assignment to the court in general or to individual judges.[1.14] The

---

Procedures to Increase Productivity, 52 F.R.D. 55, 59–61 (1971); Meador, *Professional Assistance for Appellate Judges: A Central Staff of Lawyers*, 63 F.R.D. 489 (1974); *Report and Recommendations on Improvements of Appellate Practices: IV. Central Staff*, 5 APPELLATE JUSTICE: 1975, *supra* note 7, at 129; Stockmeyer, *Rx for the Certiorari Crisis: A More Professional Staff*, 59 A.B.A.J. 846 (1973). *See also* Benthall-Nietzel, *Staff Attorneys and Kentucky Courts in Transition*, 41 KY. BENCH & BAR 27, 29 (1977).

1.13. *See* Thompson, *supra* note 1.11, at 514. *See also* notes 2.77, 2.87, 5.39 *infra*.

1.14. The literature is not lacking in *quantitative* analysis of law clerks, at least insofar as central staffs of research attorneys who screen out insubstantial cases are repeatedly applauded for their efficiency and the resulting increase in per-judge dispositions of courts which employ them. *See, e.g.* Christian, *supra* note 1.12; Baier and Lesinski, *In Aid of the Judicial Process: A Proposal for Law Curricular and*

literature displayed a parallel lack of analysis attempting to compare idealized conceptions of the function and impact of law clerks with the reality of workaday courts.

Since it was evident that many judges were now willing to discuss the role of law clerks without false romanticism, we felt that it was time to attempt to study not only *how* law clerks were being used but also *how well*. We have hitherto suggested, with tongue in legal cheek, that there are parallels to be drawn between social attitudes toward law clerks and toward sex insofar as each plays a vital role in serving a higher ideal but has nonetheless become only recently (in our culture, at least) the subject of uninhibited public discussion. The analogy has purposefully been exaggerated, however, to allow us to emphasize more dramatically how fundamentally different the two subjects are. The use of law clerks may demand confidential investigation, lest the integrity of decisions in individual cases be compromised, but the institution has no intrinsic claim to privacy. Law clerks are a publicly funded institution whose use demands public scrutiny and critical appraisal. In this spirit we undertook the project of interviewing as many California judges equipped with law clerks as would consent to talk with us.

C. Outline of Presentation of Findings and Comparative Analyses of Law Clerk Usage

We begin with an historical review of the origins and evolution of law clerks and with brief sketches of several modern variants of law clerks. We then draw from these materials a "traditional" conception of the law clerk's role in the judicial process which we defend as an ideal. After explaining how our study was inspired by suspicions that current law clerk practices in California courts were considerably at odds with this ideal, we present the methodology and findings of our interviews as to whom judges in California select as their law clerks, how they put them to use, and how their use of law clerks is integrated into the use of such law

---

Student Involvement, 56 JUD. 100 (1972); Flanders and Goldman, *Screening Practices and the Use of Para-Judicial Personnel in a U.S. Court of Appeals: A Study in the Fourth Circuit* 1 JUST. SYS. J. 1 (1975). For brief references to the qualitative advantages of youthful, short-termed clerks, see K. LLEWELLYN, THE COMMON LAW TRADITION: DECIDING APPEALS 322 (1960); Baier, *supra* note 1.7, at 1141–42; Braden, *supra* note 1.6, at 298; Newland, *supra* note 1.6, at 316–17.

clerk surrogates as central staff attorneys and part-time student law clerks. We discuss seriatim our interviews with judges of each of the four courts we studied, and precede each discussion with a profile of the structure and internal operations of that court.

We conclude with comparative analyses of the courts we studied, seeking to set forth and to critically appraise (1) the contrasts between current state and federal models of law clerk selection and usage; (2) the contrasts between these models and our clerkship ideal; (3) the contrasts among the various courts in the use of law clerk surrogates; (4) the relative hospitality of the four courts to the short-term law clerks whom we hold crucial to our clerkship ideal; and (5) strategies for achieving greater affinity to the clerkship ideal.

II. THE GENESIS
AND DEVELOPMENT
OF THE USE OF LAW CLERKS

A definitive history of law clerks has yet to be produced. There are, however, some quite useful outlines of the subject which are customarily cited as the extent of the available lore.[2.1] Nothing definitive will be attempted here, although this sketch will draw upon research beyond the limits of the standard secondary sources. Because we feel that it remains the model of the "traditional" law clerkship that is in danger of extinction among the appellate judiciary of the state of California, we devote considerable attention to the use of law clerks as conceived by the founding father of the institution.

A. *Horace Gray and Samuel Williston*

Although proof of paternity is rarely conclusive, the available evidence seems indisputably to bestow the mantle upon Horace Gray of Massachusetts as the first American judge to make use of law clerks.[2.2] In the extraordinary career of Gray, it was his custom to do things sooner than his peers: he graduated from Harvard at 17;[2.3] he matriculated to the Harvard Law School at 19 after independent study abroad;[2.4] while at Harvard Law School, he developed, contemporaneously with Langdell, the case method of studying law;[2.5] and his skills in assembling cases led to his appointment, shortly after his graduation, as the Acting Reporter

2.1. Baier, *supra* note 1.7; Newland, *supra* note 1.6.

2.2. *Accord*, Fredonia Broadcasting Corp., Inc. v. RCA Corp., 569 F.2d 251, 255 (5th Cir. 1978); Baier, *supra* note 1.7, at 1132; Newland, *supra* note 1.6, at 301.

2.3. Williston, *Horace Gray*, in 8 GREAT AMERICAN LAWYERS 139–140 (W. Lewis ed. 1909) [hereinafter cited as *Gray*].

2.4. *Id*. at 141.   2.5. *Id*. at 142–44.

of Decisions of the Massachusetts Supreme Judicial Court of Errors, an appointment soon made permanent upon the death of his predecessor.[2.6] This appointment was widely regarded as a stepping-stone to the bench and was thus all the more unusual to devolve upon one barely 23 years of age;[2.7] in due course, Gray was appointed an associate justice at age 36, then the youngest in the history of the Massachusetts Supreme Court.[2.8] By age 45, in 1873, he had acceded by seniority to the Chief Justiceship of the court.[2.9] As Chief Justice, Gray took complete command of the court, writing one quarter of all the opinions of the seven-member court, as well as presiding at the many trials which were then within the court's jurisdiction.[2.10]

Always a more methodical worker than a quick one,[2.11] Gray began in the summer of 1875 to afford himself, at his own expense, the services of a highly ranked new graduate of the Harvard Law School.[2.12] Each year a new clerk would arrive from the halls of Harvard, referred to Chief Justice Gray by his half brother, the eminent jurisprudent and professor of the Harvard Law School, John Chipman Gray.[2.13] When Horace Gray was appointed in 1882 to a seat on the United States Supreme Court, he brought the use of a law clerk to that Court.[2.14]

2.6. *Id*. at 144–46.   2.7. *Id*. at 146.

2.8. *Id*. at 150.   2.9. *Id*. at 151.

2.10. *Id*. at 151–54.

2.11. *Id*. at 152–153; S. WILLISTON, LIFE AND LAW 92 (1940).

2.12. *Gray*, *supra* note 2.3, at 157–58. Professor Baier has attributed the idea of using law clerks to Horace Gray's half brother, Professor John Chipman Gray of Harvard. *See* Baier, *supra* note 1.7, at 1132, citing S. WILLISTON, *supra* note 2.11, at 87. The authority cited by Professor Baier states only that Chief Justice Gray's clerks were selected for him by Professor Gray, and does not discuss which of the Grays first conceived of the idea. We have found no evidence as to whether Professor Gray inspired or merely assisted Chief Justice Gray's innovation.

2.13. S. WILLISTON, *supra* note 2.11, at 87; *Gray*, *supra* note 2.3, at 158.

2.14. *Gray*, *supra* note 2.3, at 156, 158. Justice Gray continued to pay his clerks from his own pocket until Congress began, in 1886, to provide each Justice with a personal assistant. Act of Aug. 4, 1886, ch. 902, 24 Stat. 222.

Williston, whose year with Justice Gray began in 1888, after the commencement of federal funding of law clerks, uses the terms "secretary" and "law secretary" to refer to Gray's law clerks, both in Massachusetts and in Washington. *See* Gray, *supra* note 2.3, at 157; S. WILLISTON, *supra* note 2.11, at 87. It is not clear whether Gray himself used this term from the beginning of his use of law clerks, or if the secretarial designation accompanied the 1886 Congressional creation of a funded position of "stenographic clerk" for each Justice. Since "law clerk" was contemporaneously used to describe young associates of law firms, *see generally* S.

In many ways, Gray's use of a law clerk is strikingly similar to that of current Justices of the United States Supreme Court, nearly a century later.[2.15] Gray's lasting imprint on the traditional

WILLISTON, *supra* note 2.11, at 107, it seems probable that the term "law secretary" was an offshoot of the language of the 1886 Act.

An excellent précis of the evolution of publicly funded law clerks for United States Supreme Court Justices appears in Newland, *supra* note 1.6, at 300–05. As there recorded, the inspiration for the 1886 Act providing a "stenographic assistant" for each Justice was the 1885 annual report of the United States Attorney General, which advocated providing each Justice with "a secretary or law clerk, to be a stenographer, . . . whose duties shall be to assist in such clerical work as might be assigned to him." *Id.* at 301. Justice Gray's brethren took this job description literally and hired personnel of a paralegal nature whose bibliographic skills were secondary to stenographic ones, to the extent that they had skills at all and were not merely patronage employees. *See id*, at 306, 311; *Gray, supra* note 2.3, at 158. This may account for the general practice of referring to such assistants as secretaries until 1919, when Congress began to provide each Justice not only with a "stenographic clerk" but also with a more highly paid "law clerk." *See* Newland, *supra* note 1.6, at 302. Thus, Francis Biddle, who served with Justice Holmes for the 1911 term, uses the word "secretary," *e.g.*, F. BIDDLE, *supra* note 1.2, at 7, but Dean Acheson, who served with Justice Brandeis for the 1919 term, uses the word "clerk," Acheson, *supra* note 1.6, at 360.

The statutory and popular terminology for the assistants to lower-court federal judges has always been "law clerk," but new titles have proliferated among the state courts. *See* Baier, *supra* note 1.7, at 1130. To conform to the most standard term, and the one predominant in popular usage, this book will use "law clerk" as the generic term for a law school graduate employed as a legal assistant to a judge. When greater specificity is needed, we will refer to "elbow clerks" as the species of law clerks serving individual judges, and to "staff attorneys" as the species of law clerks serving a group of judges collectively. *See* D. MEADOR, *supra* note 1.7 at 17. *See also* note 2.75 *infra*.

2.15. *See generally* Newland, *supra* note 1.6, at 312–13. A major difference is the responsibilities of most of the current Justices' clerks for review of petitions for discretionary review by the Court. *See* J. WILKINSON, *supra* note 1.7, at 17–21. *But see* Brennan, *supra* note 1.7, at 836. In Justice Gray's time, the Court's docket was essentially mandatory. *See* text accompanying note 2.27 *infra*. Since 1925, much of the United States Supreme Court's docket has been subject to cases in which the Court has discretionarily granted a writ of certiorari. *See* Act of Feb. 13, 1925, ch. 229, 43 Stat. 936. *See generally* R. STERN & E. GRESSMAN, SUPREME COURT PRACTICE 147–93 (4th ed. 1969). The Supreme Court has come to "certiorarify" even cases ostensibly within its mandatory appellate jurisdiction by adopting the device of requiring "jurisdictional statements" in such cases, on the basis of which it denies review of many appeals on the purportedly "jurisdictional" ground that the appeal fails to present a "substantial federal question." SUP. CT. R. 15(1) (e) & (f); R. STERN & E. GRESSMAN, *supra* at 193–202. *See generally* Hellman, *The Business of the Supreme Court Under the Judiciary Act of 1925: The Plenary Docket in the 1970's*, 91 HARV. L. REV. 1709, 1721–23, 1736–37 (1978).

nature and functions of law clerks is attributable not only to his
origination of the institution but also to his personality, which
was receptive to the roles that law clerks are supposed to have
played ever since. Gray was a scholar of note, able to hold his own
intellectually with his clerks, and so to sift through their ideas and
to adopt what he felt to be useful without the development of
dependence.[2.16] Gray was a devout believer in the unimpeachable
appearance of judicial impartiality, and this led him to a state of
splendid isolation which caused him to be perceived as a stern and
remote magistrate by those who appeared before him,[2.17] though
he was capable of the greatest congeniality and intimacy towards
his clerks.[2.18] Childless, and indeed a bachelor for the greater part
of his judicial career, Gray readily adopted a parental affection for
his clerks and their progress both through the year with him and
through their later lives.[2.19] Gray was blessed with a ready and
dependable source of the finest legal talent through his half
brother's position, which freed him from the distraction of clerkship selection.[2.20] Finally, it should be noted that what we know
of Gray and his law clerks is derived almost exclusively from the
same sort of source as is most of our knowledge about the clerkship practices of subsequent Supreme Court Justices: the rose-
tinted reminiscences of a former law clerk.[2.21]

   In Gray's case, it is fortunate that the originator of the institution was served by a law clerk of such eminence as Samuel
Williston, who wrote both biographically[2.22] and autobiograph-
ically[2.23] about Justice Gray and his clerks. Williston thus left a
record of his clerkship with Gray which remains unrivalled in

   2.16. *See Gray, supra* note 2.3, at 161–62.

   2.17. S. WILLISTON, *supra* note 2.11, at 92.

   2.18. *Id.*

   2.19. As Massachusetts's Reporter of Decisions, Gray had been permitted to
practice law. His law office had been attractive to apprentices, affording them the
best possible introduction to appellate practice. Gray referred to his protégés as
"his boys" and followed their careers with interest, *Gray, supra* note 2.3, at 148, an
enthusiasm which apparently he retained as a judge, *see* S. WILLISTON, *supra* note
2.11, at 94.

   2.20. *See* text accompanying note 2.13 *supra*.

   2.21. *Compare Gray, supra* note 2.3 *and* S. WILLISTON, *supra* note 2.11, *with,*
e.g., Acheson, *supra* note 1.6 (and authorities cited thereafter in note 1.6) *and* J.
WILKINSON, *supra* note 1.7. *See generally* note 2.24 *infra*.

   2.22. *Gray, supra* note 2.3.

   2.23. S. WILLISTON, *supra* note 2.11.

substantive detail, in no small part because Williston's memoirs were written when he was nearly eighty and had the freedom to discuss confidential matters afforded by the passage of over fifty years and the demise decades before of Gray and all his brethren.[2.24]

According to Williston, Gray employed clerks exclusively as sources of inspiration and criticism.[2.25] Neither a Rasputin nor a ghostwriter, Williston served his judge as a sounding board and editor, contributing ideas but not documents to Gray's work as a judge. Gray's chambers were in his home, where Williston set up shop in a corner of the large study around which Gray had constructed his house.[2.26] The Court in its 1888 form had little control over its docket, and took what cases came within its jurisdiction.[2.27] Williston was expected to review all the newly filed cases as would a judge, and to formulate a recommended disposition which would be discussed with Justice Gray orally in advance of the Court's Saturday morning conferences.[2.28] Gray was at his best in oral colloquy, and would treat the law clerk much like a law professor would treat a student, exploring the clerk's views by cross-examination, and only inferentially revealing his own opinions.[2.29] Somewhat unusually for elders of the land in those times, Gray had genuine interest in and respect for his clerks' views,[2.30] and expected them to bring to bear on the Court's

2.24. With the exception of brief comments by two former clerks of Justice Brandeis, see Acheson, supra note 1.6; Jaffe, supra note 1.6, virtually all of the recollections of United States Supreme Court law clerks have been published while most of their mentors' colleagues, if not their mentors themselves, remained alive and sitting on the Court at which they served. As one former clerk has characterized another's attempt to serve Cleo and the Court with equal fealty, such contemporaneous memoirs of Supreme Court clerkships tend to be "panglossian." Heineman, Book Review, 88 HARV. L. REV. 678 (1975) (reviewing J. WILKINSON, SERVING JUSTICE). See, e.g. Cohen, supra note 1.6. Whatever Williston's freedom with regard to discussing cases and colleagues of Justice Gray, it is at least open to question whether Williston felt constrained by lingering loyalties to play down his importance as a law clerk.

2.25. See Gray, supra note 2.3, at 159–60.

2.26. S. WILLISTON, supra note 2.11, at 91.

2.27. See generally F. FRANKFURTER & J. LANDIS, THE BUSINESS OF THE UNITED STATES SUPREME COURT, 86–102 (1927).

2.28. See Gray, supra note 2.3, at 158–59.

2.29. S. WILLISTON, supra note 2.11, at 92.

2.30. Id. at 93; Gray, supra note 2.3, at 159.

problems the latest theories brewing at the Harvard Law School.[2.31]

Williston would frequently be asked to draft opinions in cases assigned to Justice Gray, but these drafts purportedly served only as discussion pieces to enlighten the judge in drafting his own opinion for the Court.[2.32] Williston also read opinions circulated by other justices.[2.33] Although Gray was candid and at times caustic in his comments on his colleagues,[2.34] he was careful in his relations with his brethren to show more courtesy towards their work product than would have Williston, "fresh from law school theorizing."[2.35] The level of intimacy between clerk and judge may be measured by the fact that Gray, then 60 years of age, became engaged during Williston's clerkship and sought out his clerk's advice on an engagement ring.[2.36] Williston himself was newly engaged and putting money aside toward marriage, a goal Gray advanced considerably by altering his clerkship schedule so as effectively to double young Williston's pay.[2.37]

B. *Proliferation of Law Clerks*

Notwithstanding Justice Gray's happy experiences with young Harvard graduates, his method of using law clerks was not emulated by his colleagues even after Congress assumed the cost. Indeed, it was to be nearly fifty years before it was clear that Gray's use of law clerks was the taproot of a tradition. Although all nine Justices were employing assistants by 1888, two years after federal funding was provided, the typical Justice of those years obtained a law clerk through friends or relatives or from the bar

2.31. *Gray, supra* note 2.3, at 159; S. WILLISTON, *supra* note 2.11, at 93.

2.32. S. WILLISTON, *supra* note 2.11, at 92; *Gray, supra* note 2.3, at 159.

2.33. S. WILLISTON, *supra* note 2.11, at 92.

2.34. *Id.* at 94–95.   2.35. *Id.* at 92.   2.36. *Id.* at 97.

2.37. Williston was well paid quite apart from Justice Gray's effective doubling of his rate of compensation. His government salary of $1,600 per annum, *id.* at 87; *see* Act of Aug. 4, 1886, ch. 902, 24 Stat. 222, compares quite favorably with the $600 salary he earned the year *after* his clerkship as managing clerk of a Boston law firm, a position won only through family connections, *see* S. WILLISTON, *supra* note 2.11, at 103. As a measure of his good fortune in earning even $600 as a yearling attorney, Williston noted that a generation before, it had been the custom for law graduates to pay firms to be allowed to serve as apprentices, and that to his knowledge none of his Harvard classmates had earned a salary in his first year of law practice. *Id.* at 104.

and law schools of the District of Columbia, and sought to retain him for as long as the salary level would permit.[2.38] Fortunately for the survival of Justice Gray's clerkship motif, Justice Gray's successor on the Supreme Court was another Chief Justice of the Massachusetts Supreme Judicial Court, Oliver Wendell Holmes, Jr. While it does not appear that Holmes had employed law clerks during his twenty years as a Massachusetts justice, he was an old friend of John Chipman Gray.[2.39] Within three years of taking his seat in Washington, Holmes was taking annual honor graduates of the Harvard Law School as his law clerks, selected by Professor Gray.[2.40] When Gray died in 1915, young Professor Felix Frankfurter of the Harvard Law School was asked by Holmes to take Professor Gray's place as procurer of clerks,[2.41] and Louis Brandeis made the same request when he joined the Court in 1916.[2.42] In 1919, Congress authorized each Justice of the Supreme

2.38. See Newland, *supra* note 1.6, at 306–07; *see also* note 2.14, *supra*. The initially generous $1,600 salary, *see* note 2.37 *supra*, was increased by only $400 over the next thirty-three years, Newland, *supra* note 1.6, at 301. Commencing in 1919, the Justices were each provided with a "law clerk" at $3,600 per year as well as a "stenographic assistant" at $2,000 per year, Act of July 19, 1919, ch. 24, 41 Stat. 163; Act of Mar. 1, 1919, ch. 86, 40 Stat. 1213, and since 1926, the Court itself has been authorized to set employees' salaries, *see* Newland, *supra* note 1.6, at 302–03. The current statutory provision is 28 U.S.C. § 675 (1976).

2.39. Lash, *A Brahmin of the Law: A Biographical Essay*, in FROM THE DIARIES OF FELIX FRANKFURTER 36 (J. Lash ed. 1974). Although Biddle mentions Holmes's law clerks at the United States Supreme Court throughout his biography of Holmes, F. BIDDLE, *supra* note 1.2, he makes no mention of Holmes having had assistants while on the Massachusetts Supreme Judicial Court.

2.40. Newland, *supra* note 1.6, at 306.

2.41. *Id.*; Lash, *supra* note 2.39, at 36.

2.42. Lash, *supra* note 2.39, at 36; Newland, *supra* note 6, at 306. Frankfurter continued supplying Harvard-bred law clerks to Holmes's successor, Cardozo. Frankfurter's protégés were dubbed the "happy hot dogs," *see* G. SCHUBERT, JUDICIAL POLICY MAKING: THE POLITICAL ROLE OF THE COURTS 111 (rev. ed. 1974), and the last of them became Frankfurter's own first law clerk when Frankfurter was appointed to the Court upon Cardozo's sudden death. Lash, *supra* note 2.39, at 36, 63–64. Thereafter, Frankfurter was annually supplied with new clerks by his intellectual heir at Harvard, Professor Henry Hart. *Id.* at 88.

After noting that Justices Gray and Holmes were the pioneers in using annual, highly talented law clerks, Professor Llewellyn went on to exclaim: "I should be inclined to rate it as Frankfurter's greatest contribution to our law that his vision, energy and persuasiveness turned this two-judge idiosyncrasy into what shows high possibility of becoming a pervasive American legal institution." K. LLEWELLYN, *supra* note 1.14, at 321.

Court to employ both a "law clerk" and a "stenographic clerk."[2.43] Although the shift was gradual, it became the custom of the Court over the next twenty years for each Justice to have one law clerk in the fashion of Horace Gray, and a second purely clerical assistant.[2.44] Thus when Chief Justice Taft was appointed in 1921, he retained a conventional secretary from year to year and secured a new law clerk annually from the dean of the Yale Law School.[2.45] When Harlan Fiske Stone joined the Court in 1925, the former dean of the Columbia Law School made it his practice to take a Columbia graduate each year as his clerk.[2.46] Similar clerkship practices were adopted by each of the Roosevelt appointees, so that the short-termed law professor protégé was the typical Supreme Court law clerk by 1939.[2.47]

2.43. *See* note 2.38 *supra*. *See also* Act of May 29, 1920, ch. 214, 41 Stat. 631; Newland, *supra* note 1.6, at 302–03.

2.44. Newland, *supra* note 1.6, at 302–03.

2.45. *Id.* at 303, 308.

2.46. *Id.* at 308. The late Justice Douglas recalled in vivid terms his disappointment at not being selected as Stone's first clerk: "I was so unhappy that for two weeks the sun never came out for me. The world was black and I was unspeakably depressed . . . ." W. DOUGLAS, GO EAST, YOUNG MAN 194 (1974). There is some evidence that, at least in his later years, Justice Douglas induced similar feelings in those who *were* selected as his own clerks. *See* B. WOODWARD & S. ARMSTRONG, THE BRETHREN 240–43 (1979); *Douglas: Personal View of Impersonal Judge*, Sacramento Bee, Nov. 24, 1975, at B2. *See also* Interview with William W. Oliver, Professor of Law, Indiana University, formerly law clerk to Chief Justice Vinson (1952–53) and head law clerk to Chief Justice Warren (1953–54), May 17, 1972, at pp. 17–18 (unpublished interview conducted by Professor Mortimer Schwartz, School of Law, University of California, Davis, for the Earl Warren Oral History Project of the Bancroft Library, University of California, Berkeley). *But see* Cohen, *supra* note 1.6.

At least Justice Douglas was spared the misfortune of a clerkship with Justice Stone's colleague, Mr. Justice McReynolds. It appears certain that, were all past Justices of the Court to be resurrected and reunited, Justice McReynolds would win by acclamation the designation as the Court's all-time ogre. Chief Justice Taft once wrote his son that Justice McReynolds was "inconsiderate of his colleagues and others and contemptuous of everybody." A. MASON, HARLAN FISKE STONE: PILLAR OF THE LAW 220 (1956). Chief Justice Hughes had equally acid relations with McReynolds. *See* Williams, *supra* note 1.7, at 85. Not surprisingly, in an era when the prestige of the position was insufficient recompense for persecution, McReynolds "was plagued with troubles in locating and retaining clerks. . . . Because of his strong language and asperity toward his subordinates, the atmosphere was too demanding for some of his assistants." Newland, *supra* note 1.6, at 306–07.

2.47. Newland, *supra* note 1.6, at 306.

These two decades from 1919 to 1939 also saw law clerks blossom at less exalted courts. Congress supplied a law clerk to each federal circuit judge in 1930[2.48] and to selected district judges in 1936.[2.49] By 1933, law clerks were employed by the courts of last resort of California, Illinois, Massachusetts, New Jersey, New York, Oklahoma, and Pennsylvania;[2.50] and by 1942, almost half the states provided law clerks for their courts of last resort.[2.51]

The postwar decades have seen steady growth in the use of law clerks by all courts other than state trial courts.[2.52] As of 1970,

2.48. Act of June 17, 1930, ch. 509, 46 Stat. 774. Until the 1948 revision of the Judicial Code, Act of June 25, 1948, ch. 646, 62 Stat. 869, the provision of law clerks to circuit judges was made conditional on the approval of the Attorney General. The current provision is 28 U.S.C. § 712 (1976).

2.49. The original authorization of law clerks for district judges required a certification of need by the senior circuit judge of the circuit involved, and limited the total number of district court clerks in the first year to thirty-five. Act of Feb. 17, 1936, ch. 75, 49 Stat. 1140. Subsequent appropriations acts limited district court clerks to two, Act of May 14, 1940, ch. 189, 54 Stat. 181, and then three per circuit, e.g., Act of June 28, 1941, ch. 258, 55 Stat. 265. Numerical limitations were eliminated in the 1948 revision of the Judicial Code, Act of June 25, 1948, ch. 646, 62 Stat. 869, and the requirement for certification of need for each district judge's law clerk by the chief judge of the circuit was eliminated by the Act of Sept. 1, 1959, Pub. L. No. 86-221, 73 Stat. 452. The current provision is 28 U.S.C. § 752 (1976).

2.50. Curran & Sunderland, *The Organization and Operation of Courts of Review*, in JUDICIAL COUNCIL OF MICHIGAN, THIRD REPORT, app. 51, 147–48 (1933). *See also* JUDICIAL COUNCIL OF KANSAS, SECOND ANNUAL REPORT 12 (1928) (proposing law clerks for Supreme Court); *Great Saving Through Use of Supreme Court Clerks*, 16 AM. JUD. SOC'Y J. 63 (1932) (Oklahoma Supreme Court); Kocourek, *Relief for the Appellate Courts: the Referendary System*, 7 AM. JUD. SOC'Y J. 122 (1923); *Methods of Work in the Appellate Courts of the United States*, 10 AM. JUD. SOC'Y J. 57, 61–62 (1926) (Pennsylvania Supreme Court); *Proceedings of the Thirty-Third Annual Session of the Texas Bar Association*, 1914 TEX. B.A. 1, 19–21 (Chief Justice of Texas Supreme Court proposes use of law clerks to help reduce court's backlog); *Relief for Appellate Courts*, 15 AM. JUD. SOC'Y J. 175 (1931) (Oklahoma Supreme Court; Superior Judicial Court of Massachusetts). On the origins of law clerks at the California Supreme Court and courts of appeal, see note 2.86 *infra*.

2.51. ABA SECTION OF JUDICIAL ADMINISTRATION, METHODS OF REACHING AND PREPARING APPELLATE COURT DECISIONS: REPORT OF A COMMITTEE TO GATHER INFORMATION CONCERNING METHODS OF REACHING AND PREPARING APPELLATE COURT DECISIONS 37–38 (1942).

2.52. *See* D. MEADOR, *supra* note 1.7, at 16; Baier, *supra* note 1.7, at 1133–35; P. Barnett, Law Clerks in the United States Courts and State Appellate Courts (Nov. 1973) (Am. Jud. Soc'y Research Study). Law clerk usage in California state appellate courts is discussed at notes 5.1–5.97 and accompanying text *infra*. Regarding other states' courts, see ABA SECTION OF JUDICIAL ADMINISTRATION, IN-TERNAL OPERATING PROCEDURES OF APPELLATE COURTS 43–46 (1961); COUNCIL OF STATE GOVERNMENTS, STATE COURT SYSTEMS: A STATISTICAL SUMMARY PREPARED FOR THE CONFERENCE OF CHIEF JUSTICES 81–89, Tables XIII–XIV (1974); D. KAR-LEN, APPELLATE COURTS IN THE UNITED STATES AND ENGLAND 15, 18–19, 33 (1963) (New York Court of Appeals; Appellate Division, New York Supreme Court); D. MARS AND F. KORT, ADMINISTRATION OF JUSTICE IN CONNECTICUT 66 (I. Davis ed. 1963) (Connecticut Supreme Court of Errors); T. MORRIS, THE VIRGINIA SUPREME COURT: AN INSTITUTIONAL AND POLITICAL ANALYSIS 76, 78, 84–85 (1975); Breen, *Solutions for Appellate Court Congestion*, 47 AM. JUD. SOC'Y J. 228, 230–31 (1964); Benthall-Nietzel, *supra* note 1.12 (Kentucky Court of Appeals); Cameron, *supra* note 1.12, at 470–74 (Arizona Supreme Court); Cameron, *Judges' Fears and Central Staff*, 17 JUDGES' J. 27 (1978); (Arizona Supreme Court) Cuomo, *supra* note 1.6 (New York Court of Appeals); English, *Crisis in Civil Appeals*, 50 CHI. B. REC. 231, 236 (1969) (Illinois Appellate Court); Hopkins, *The Winds of Change: New Styles in the Appellate Process*, 3 HOFSTRA L. REV. 649, 655–56 (1975) (Appellate Division, New York Supreme Court); Lee & Moloney, *The Kentucky Court of Appeals Apprentice Law Clerk Program*, 21 KY. ST. B.J. 90 (1957); Lesinski, *supra* note 1.7 (Michigan Court of Appeals); Lesinski & Stockmeyer, *supra* note 1.12 (Michigan Court of Appeals); Lilly & Scalia, *Appellate Justice: A Crisis in Virginia?* 57 VA. L. REV. 3, 28 & n.56 (1971) (Virginia Supreme Court); McCormick, *Appellate Congestion in Iowa: Dimensions and Remedies*, 25 DRAKE L. REV. 133, 140, 147 (1975) (Iowa Supreme Court); Noble, *The Law Clerk*, TRIAL JUDGES J., Oct. 1968, at 4 (New Mexico Supreme Court); Ragatz and Shea, *supra* note 1.7 (Wisconsin Supreme Court); Shapiro & Osthus, Congestion and Delay in State Appellate Courts, at 16–17 (Dec. 1974) (Research Project of the Am. Jud. Soc'y.); Spector, *Staffs of State Courts of Last Resort* (pt. 1), 34 AM. JUD. SOC'Y J. 144 (1951); Stock-meyer, Borst, Stenger, & Reid, *The Office of the Commissioner of the Michigan Court of Appeals and Its Role in the Appellate Process*, 48 F.R.D. 355 (1970); Stuart, *Iowa Supreme Court Congestion: Can We Avert a Crisis?* 55 IOWA L. REV. 594, 607 (1970); *Three Views*, *supra* note 1.7, at 156–60 (Alabama Supreme Court); Note, *Alabama Appellate Court Congestion: Observations and Suggestions from an Empirical Study*, 21 ALA. L. REV. 150, 162 (1968) (Alabama Supreme Court); Note, *Appellate Court Reform*, 45 MISS. L. J. 121, 132–35 (1974) (Mississippi Supreme Court); Alaska Judicial Council, First Annual Report (1960) (Alaska Supreme Court); American Judicature Society, Law Clerks in State Appellate Courts (Jan. 1968) (Report No. 16); American Judicature Society, Solutions for Appellate Court Congestion and Delay, Analysis and Bibliography, at 7–9 (Sept. 17, 1963) (A.J.S. Information Sheet No. 24); T. Farer & C. Jacob, The Appellate Process and Staff Research Attorneys in the Appellate Division of the New Jersey Superior Court, 1972–73 (May 1974) (Nat'l Center for St. Cts. Pub. No. W0011); J. Lake, The Appellate Process and Staff Research Attorneys in the Supreme Court of Nebraska, 1972–73 (May 1974) (Nat'l Center for St. Cts. Pub. No. W0009); G. Lilly, The Appellate Process and Staff Research Attorneys in the Supreme Court of Virginia, 1972–73 (May 1974) (Nat'l Center for St. Cts. Pub. No. W0008); J. Lucas, The Appellate Process and Staff Research Attorneys in the Illinois Appellate Court, 1972–73 (May 1974) (Nat'l Center for St. Cts. Pub. No. W0010); Memorandum by Flor-

federal circuit judges have each had two law clerks, and some circuit judges now have three.[2.53] Since 1965, federal district judges have had the option of having a second law clerk in lieu of a

---

ence Peskoe, Clerk of the New Jersey Supreme Court (c. 1975), *excerpted* in Cameron, *supra* note 1.12, at 465 n.*, 468 n.10, 478 (New Jersey Supreme Court).

As of 1973, Massachusetts was one of the few states to provide law clerk assistance for its trial courts. P. Barnett, *supra*, app. at "Massachusetts." New York provides law clerks to some of its trial courts on what was, as of 1955 at least, a sorrowfully haphazard basis; some judges had personal law clerks, some judges shared clerks, some divisions of a court would have no clerks at all, while other divisions of the same court did, and the salaries and responsibilities of the clerks varied widely. *See* ASSOCIATION OF THE BAR OF THE CITY OF NEW YORK, BAD HOUSEKEEPING: THE ADMINISTRATION OF NEW YORK COURTS 59–70, 75 (1955). Connecticut has provided for its supreme court law clerks to be assigned to assist superior court judges who request them, if such clerks can be spared. D. MARS & F. KORT, *supra* at 66. *Cf. Proceedings of the Annual Meeting of the Association*, 26 CONN. B.J. 428, 449, 451–52 (1952) (Conn. State Bar committee recommends law clerks for state trial judges based on experience of federal district court in Connecticut with assistance of law clerks). Some of the busier counties in California equip their superior courts with law clerks to assist with notions and appeals from inferior courts. *See, e.g.* CAL. GOVT. CODE § 69894.1 (West 1976) (Los Angeles County). Trial courts in California also get substantial assistance from commissioners who are appointed by the courts themselves. *See* CAL. CONST. art. VI, § 22; 1978 JUDICIAL COUNCIL OF CALIFORNIA REPORT 118–125; 1 B. WITKIN, CALIFORNIA PROCEDURE, *Courts* §§ 223–25 at 480–82 (2d ed. 1970). *See generally In re* Edgar M., 14 Cal. 3d 727, 536 P.2d 406, 122 Cal. Rptr. 574 (1975) (juvenile court referees); Rooney v. Vermont Investment Corp., 10 Cal. 3d 351, 515 P.2d 297, 110 Cal. Rptr. 353 (1973) (superior court commissioners). For discussions of other states' use of commissioners, see authorities cited in note 2.85 *infra*.

2.53. Professor Carrington, Project Director for the American Bar Foundation, recommended "two, and perhaps three, law clerks" for each circuit judge in his 1968 report. P. CARRINGTON, ACCOMMODATING THE WORKLOAD OF THE UNITED STATES COURTS OF APPEALS 2 (1968). At that time, circuit judges were held to the same staff salary limit as district court judges. See Act of Aug. 9, 1968, Pub. L. No. 90-470, § 401, 82 Stat. 666. The next year, circuit judges were given an additional salary allowance over that allowed for district judges, which was sufficient to hire a second law clerk. Act of Dec. 24, 1969, Pub. L. No. 91-153, § 401, 83 Stat. 403. The differential between circuit and district judges' staff salary allowances has since been doubled, Act of Oct. 5, 1974, Pub. L. No. 93-433, § 401, 88 Stat. 1187, and this level of differential has been maintained since. The relevant appropriations acts are usefully collected in *Historical and Revision Notes*, following 28 U.S.C.A. § 604 (West 1968 & Supp. 1979). Since 1974, circuit judges have been able to hire up to three clerks at somewhat reduced rates of pay. *See* note 5.110 *infra*. As had been true for many years, each of the previously cited acts provided an additional staff salary allowance differential for the chief judge of each circuit and of each district court having five or more judges; such chief judges have three

court crier.[2.54] Meanwhile, the number of law clerks at the United States Supreme Court has steadily increased too, with the associate Justices generally having two law clerks after 1947,[2.55] and the Chief Justice three, and with all Justices having at least three law clerks since 1970.[2.56] As of 1973, there were law clerks at the highest courts of all but six states, and at the intermediate appellate courts of all but three of the states having such courts.[2.57] The

---

law clerks as a matter of course. *See also* Wright, *supra* note 1.7, at 1179; Flanders & Goldman, *supra* note 1.14, at 3,4.

2.54. This option was created by adding a further Byzantine twist to the already convoluted administrative constraints on the employment of staff by lower federal courts. We have attempted to unravel the system for funding the law clerks of federal circuit and district judges in an appended note. *See* Appendix, *Note on Funding of Law Clerks at Lower Federal Courts*, p. 150 *infra* [hereinafter cited as *Federal Funding Note*].

2.55. Newland, *supra* note 1.6, at 303–04.

2.56. See H. ABRAHAM, THE JUDICIAL PROCESS: AN INTRODUCTORY ANALYSIS OF THE COURTS OF THE UNITED STATES, ENGLAND AND FRANCE 239 (3d ed. 1975); G. CASPER & R. POSNER, THE WORKLOAD OF THE SUPREME COURT 72 (1976); J. WILKINSON, *supra* note 1.7, at 48; *Report of the Study Group on the Caseload of the Supreme Court*, 57 F.R.D. 573, 609 (1973) [hereinafter cited as *Freund Report*]. The late Justice Douglas sometimes employed one fewer law clerk than authorized. *See* B. WOODWARD & S. ARMSTRONG, *supra* note 2.46, at 240 (2 clerks for 1972 term); *id.* at 346 (3 clerks for 1974 term). Since 1974, Chief Justice Burger and Mr. Justice White have been experimenting with use of a long-term law clerk in lieu of one of their short-term law clerks; the other Justices have apparently resisted general adoption of this practice. H. ABRAHAM, *supra*, at 239. The Chief Justice and some of the associate Justices now have four law clerks. *See* G. CASPER & R. POSNER, *supra*, at 109.

The most comprehensive contemporary account of United States Supreme Court law clerk practices has appeared in the magazine of the Smithsonian Institution, of which the Chief Justice is a Regent, 20 U.S.C. § 42 (1976). It was there reported that, as of February 1977, "the current crop of Supreme Court law clerks is the largest yet, 36." Williams, *supra* note 1.7, at 88. It is unclear whether this number includes the two "legal officers" whom the Court employs on a long-term basis ("for four years or more") *id.* at 86, the similarly semi-permanent lawyer employed as "special assistant" to the Chief Justice, *id.* at 87, or the law clerks whom the Court has historically provided to retired Justices such as the late Justices Clark, Douglas, and Reed while they continued to maintain chambers at the Supreme Court, *id.* at 85; G. CASPER & R. POSNER, *supra* at 72 n.15. The article states that besides two secretaries (three for the Chief Justice) and a messenger, each Justice has "three to four law clerks," Williams, *supra* note 1.7, at 85, and it describes Mr. Justice Stewart as having three law clerks and sharing a fourth, *id.* at 91.

2.57. P. Barnett, *supra* note 2.52, at 1.

most law clerks present at any court were the thirty-one then working at the Supreme Court of California.[2.58]

C. *Corporate Clerks: The Advent of Central Staff*

A major modern innovation in clerkship practice involves the use at appellate courts of "central staff," a corps of court-employed lawyers responsible indirectly to the court as a whole and directly to a supervising staff attorney rather than a particular judge. The central staff is designed to meet the greatly increased volume of appeals which has accompanied the modern liberality of appellate procedure; its function is to identify matters of a routine nature and to process them in some expediting fashion, generally to the point of recommended dispositions suitable for pro forma adoption by the court.[2.59]

The scope of routine decision-making spans the spectrum of appellate court operation. In intermediate appellate courts such as the California courts of appeal and the federal circuit courts of appeals, most appeals may be taken as a matter of right, and the courts have discretion over their dockets only with respect to the "extraordinary" or "prerogative" writs which they may choose to grant as means of reviewing otherwise nonappealable orders of trial courts. Where appeals are allowed as a matter of right, many will be taken without regard to their merit, creating a sizeable reservoir of routine cases. In courts of "last resort," that is, in the United States Supreme Court and its counterpart at the pinnacle of each state's own court system, plenary decision on the merits of an appeal is frequently as discretionary as is review by extraordinary writ. The greater the scope of discretion in granting or denying review and the greater the number of cases competing for review, the greater will be the frequency of denials on grounds extraneous to the correctness of the lower court decisions submitted for review, and thus the greater will be the percentage of cases regarded as routine for administrative purposes regardless of the difficulty of the issues raised on appeal.[2.60]

2.58. *Id*. at 8.

2.59. *See generally* authorities cited in note 1.12 *supra*.

2.60. For details of the jurisdiction of the appellate courts we studied, see notes 5.17 & 5.19 and accompanying text *infra* (California courts of appeal); note 5.60 and accompanying text *infra* (Supreme Court of California); note 5.100 and accompanying text *infra* (Ninth Circuit). Comparative details on the processing of

Most central staffs "screen" all or part of the flow of incoming cases to identify those which fit their courts' classifications of "routine." [2.61] After the screening process, the work product of the typical central staff consists principally of proposed opinions or orders disposing of, or expediting the disposition of, the routine cases sifted out of the docket at the screening stage. The court's decision to adopt, reject, or modify the proposed order or opinion is usually made by a panel of three judges which reviews the appeal with less care than in cases not deemed routine; frequently oral argument is omitted, with or without the consent of the parties, in cases prepared for disposition by the central staff. At a few courts, the central staff's function is limited to reviewing subordinate or preliminary issues, such as whether the case has become moot since filing, or whether the appellate court has jurisdiction, and if the court has a choice, whether it ought to exercise its jurisdiction.

Some courts use central staffs for the preparation not of proposed dispositions but of "bench memoranda" which assist judges in advance of oral argument by summarizing the issues in the cases to be argued; at these courts, the central staff either routinely prepares the bench memoranda in all cases, or screens out the routine cases in which it will prepare the bench memoranda, leaving pre-argument preparation of the more complicated cases to individual judges and their personal law clerks. It bears emphasis that all courts which employ central staff also provide their individual judges with personal law clerks. In principle, central staff processing of routine cases—or of all cases on a routine basis—is intended to enhance the time available for judges to devote to novel cases in collaboration with their personal law clerks, thereby improving the quality of decision-making in cases of true public significance.

While isolated examples of utilization of a centralized pool of legal assistants to a court have existed for some years, it was the creation of a central staff at the Michigan Court of Appeals a dec-

---

petitions for discretionary review at the United States Supreme Court and the Supreme Court of California appear in notes 5.82 & 6.48 and accompanying text *infra*.

2.61. This summary of the function and procedures of central staffs is drawn from our own research, as set forth in Chapter V *infra*, as well as from the authorities cited in note 1.12 *supra*.

ade ago that "gave impetus and focus to the contemporary development" of the process.[2.62] Since then the concept of central staff has become the totem of prominent court reformers who promote it as the savior of appellate justice from the "crisis of volume" and the sins of inefficiency and delay.[2.63]

The use of a central staff of lawyers responsible to the court in general is now firmly entrenched at the California courts of appeal and at the appellate courts of a number of other states,[2.64] and a central staff exists de facto at the Supreme Court of California.[2.65] While the United States Supreme Court has shown little inclination for the institution,[2.66] all of the federal courts of appeals are now making use of central staff.[2.67]

Although central staffs compete with traditional law clerks for

2.62. D. MEADOR, *supra* note 1.7, at 17.

2.63. *See generally* P. CARRINGTON, D. MEADOR, & M. ROSENBERG, *supra* note 1.12, at 227–28; D. MEADOR, *supra* note 1.7, at 191; Christian, *supra* note 1.12, *passim*; Cameron, *supra* note 1.12, *passim*.

2.64. *See, e.g.*, D. MEADOR, *supra* note 1.7, at 23; Cameron, *supra* note 1.12, at 48 n.10, 470. The use of central staff at the California courts of appeal is described at text accompanying notes 5.29–5.34 *infra*.

2.65. *See* note 5.77 and accompanying text *infra*.

2.66. The United States Supreme Court does employ two semi-permanent "legal officers" to review applications for extraordinary relief, *see* Williams, *supra* note 1.7, at 86, and at least five of the present Justices pool their law clerks for the purpose of preparing a single memorandum on each certiorari petition for the collective use of all the participating Justices. *See* G. CASPER & R. POSNER, *supra* note 2.56, at 72–73; Cameron, *supra* note 1.12, at 469; Freund, *Why We Need the National Court of Appeals*, 59 A.B.A.J. 247, 250 (1973). *See also* A. BICKEL, THE CASELOAD OF THE SUPREME COURT—AND WHAT, IF ANYTHING, TO DO ABOUT IT 10 n.15 (1973).

2.67. *See* Federal Judicial Center, Central Legal Staffs in the United States Courts of Appeals (FJC-R-78-3, April 1978) [hereinafter cited as Central Staffs Report]. *See generally* D. MEADOR, *supra* note 1.7, at 231; Haworth, *Screening and Summary Procedures in the United States Courts of Appeals*, 1973 WASH. U.L.Q. 257, 263–64 (Fifth Circuit); Hufstedler, *The Appellate Process Inside Out*, 50 CAL. ST. B.J. 20, 21–22 (1975) (Ninth Circuit); Kaufman, *The Pre-Argument Conference: An Appellate Procedural Reform*, 74 COLUM. L. REV. 1094, 1096–98 (1974) (Second Circuit); Shafroth, *Survey of the United States Courts of Appeals*, 42 F.R.D. 243, 273–74 (1968); United States Court of Appeals for the Third Circuit, *Internal Operating Procedures*, 63 F.R.D. 319, 343–44 (1974); Zeigler & Hermann, *supra* note 1.7, at 233–46 (concentrates on Second Circuit); Note, *Screening of Criminal Cases in the Federal Courts of Appeals: Practice and Proposals*, 73 COLUM. L. REV. 77, 94, 97 (1973) (concentrates on Second, Fifth, and District of Columbia Circuits). *Cf.* Isbell Enterprises, Inc. v. Citizens Casualty Co., 431 F.2d 409, 410–414 (5th Cir. 1970); Huth v. Southern Pacific Co., 417 F.2d 526, 527–30 (5th Cir. 1969):

allocation of the scarce resources available to fund judicial staff, our purpose in this book is not to address the desirability of central staff as an institution separable from and alternative to the use of law clerks by individual judges.[2.68] Even in the eyes of their

Murphy v. Houma Well Service, 409 F.2d 804, 805–08 (5th Cir. 1969) (statistical summaries of screened cases).

With the exception of statutory provision for the chief judge of each circuit to appoint "a senior staff attorney to the court," Act of Oct. 10, 1978, Pub. L. No. 95-431, § 401, 92 Stat. 1021, the funding of central staffs has been accomplished from within the general budget for the judiciary. See generally Central Staffs Report, supra, at 2. See also note 5.111 infra. The provision of a senior staff attorney for each circuit originated with the appropriations act for fiscal 1975, Act of Oct. 5, 1974, Pub. L. No. 93-433, § 401, 88 Stat. 1187.

2.68. The advent of central staff as an essential aspect of the appellate process has engendered "considerable uneasiness" in the minds of many judges and other officials involved in that process. E. Barrett, F. Feeney, & L. Mayhew, The National Conference on Appellate Justice: An Evaluation, at 15 (June 1976) (Report to the National Center for State Courts). Although 84 percent of the participants in the National Conference on Appellate Justice disagreed that any use of central staff was objectionable, and 81 percent agreed that increased use of central staff was more or less inevitable because of increased workload, roughly a third of the participants considered it unacceptable for central staff to draft opinions or to recommend the final disposition of cases. Indeed, nearly a third of the participants objected to the central staff performing even the screening function of recommending cases to be disposed of without full-dress published opinions. See id. at 16, Table 6. See generally ADVISORY COUNCIL FOR APPELLATE JUSTICE, 1 APPELLATE JUSTICE: 1975—SUMMARY AND BACKGROUND (P. Carrington et al., 1974) (National Conference on Appellate Justice, Jan. 26–28, 1975).

Enthusiasm for central staff was particularly restrained among participants oriented toward the federal courts, nearly half of whom opposed the use of central staff to draft opinions, and more than half of whom opposed the making of recommendations as to final disposition by central staff. Over half of the federally oriented participants preferred a central staff composed of attorneys limited to two or three years' tenure; by contrast, two-thirds of the participants oriented towards state courts preferred a central staff composed of permanent employees. See E. Barrett, F. Feeney, & L. Mayhew, supra, at 18.

The "uneasiness" of the conference participants was reflected in the Conference's Report and Recommendations on Improvements of Appellate Practices, which noted that high-volume courts needed "staff assistance additional to that provided by the personal research aides of the judges," and delineated the functions of such staff assistance as: the making of purely advisory screening recommendations, with the implementation of such recommendations reserved to judges; the writing of prehearing memoranda "from an impartial viewpoint, presumably not in the form of a draft opinion; and the general monitoring and facilitation of pre-argument stages of the appellate process by "senior members" of the central staff. 5 APPELLATE JUSTICE: 1975, supra note 1.7, at 129 (emphasis added).

For other expressions of uneasiness over the use—or the overuse—of central

most fervent promoters, central staff are seen as complementary to the personal staff of individual judges. The major proponents of central staff universally recommend that although the growth in numbers of individual law clerks per judge should be limited, such law clerks should not be eliminated.[2.69]

---

staff, see ABA COMMISSION ON STANDARDS OF JUDICIAL ADMINISTRATION, STAN-DARDS RELATING TO APPELLATE COURTS 98–99 (1977) (commentary on § 3.62(b): Central Legal Staff); Bird, *The Hidden Judiciary*, 17 JUDGES' J. 4 (1978); Johnson, *The Supreme Court of California, 1975–1976—Foreword: The Accidental Decision and How It Happens*, 65 CAL. L. REV. 231, 248–54 (1977); Schroeder, *Judicial Administration and Invisible Justice*, 11 (U. MICH. J.L. REF. 322, 329–31 (1978); Thompson, *supra* note 1.11, at 513–16. *But see* Cameron, *Judges' Fears and Central Staff*, *supra* note 2.52.

2.69. *See* JUSTICE ON APPEAL, *supra* note 1.12, at 46, 48; D. MEADOR, *supra* note 1.7, at 118. *See generally* note 2.68 *supra* and authorities cited in note 1.12 *supra*. It is noteworthy that the central staff of the Michigan Court of Appeals, whose effectiveness sparked the modern spread of the central staff concept, *see* D. MEADOR, *supra* note 1.7, at 9, 17, was created by pooling law clerk positions which had previously been allocated to individual justices to provide them each with a second elbow clerk. *See id.* at 9; Lesinski & Stockmeyer, *supra* note 1.12, at 1213. *See generally* D. MEADOR, *supra* note 1.12, at 198–208; Lesinski & Stockmeyer, *supra* note 1.12, at 1213–30. This did not reflect dissatisfaction with the characteristics of individual law clerks of the traditional, newly graduated, short-term type. As the Chief Judge and the Research Director of that court have written:

> In the tradition of law clerkships, the tenure of a prehearing research attorney is generally one to two years. . . .
> It was initially envisioned that the prehearing staff would consist largely of career employees; however, this has not occurred. Indeed, the court is satisfied that the same considerations which have led the overwhelming majority of appellate courts to opt for short-term law clerks who have recently graduated from law school apply equally to the prehearing staff. Turnover can intensify administrative problems, but avoids the more subtle adverse effects of institutionalism. Recent law school graduates seem to make up in freshness of thought and purpose what they may lack in practical experience.

Id. at 1221. Indeed, at the Michigan Court of Appeals the central staff attorneys are recruited from the same pool as law clerks for individual judges, with the judges given first pick from the short list of prospects interviewed by a team of one judge and the Research Director or other senior staff member. *Id.* at 1220. Staff attorneys and law clerks are paid the same, *id.* at 1220 n.26, and staff attorneys are occasionally assigned as personal law clerks for temporary judges, *id.* at 1222 n.28. Such an arrangement for using short-term staff attorneys cast in the traditional law clerk mold and supervised by a career employee has been endorsed by Judge Leflar. R. LEFLAR, *supra* note 1.7, at 83–84. This has been the model followed by a number of the federal courts of appeals, including the Ninth Circuit, which announced that, effective in the fall of 1977, several additional central staff members, called "court law clerks," would be hired for terms of one or two years, commenc-

D. *Quasi Clerks: The Advent of Extern Programs*

The central staff explosion over the past decade has been echoed by the contemporaneous popularization among courts of the use of law students as quasi law clerks to individual judges.[2.70] These students work either part-time for their judges while carrying a reduced load of current law school classes, or they are given academic leave from their law schools to work full-time for their judges for one academic term. In either case, the student is unpaid but receives academic credit from his or her law school, allowing the student to continue normal progress toward a law degree.[2.71] Because no public resources are involved beyond space in the chambers of participating judges, the use of student law clerks has

---

ing upon graduation from law school. Court law clerks are hired as JSP-11 employees, and are promoted after one year to JSP-12. Letter from John M. Naff, Jr., Supervising Staff Attorney, United States Court of Appeals for the Ninth Circuit, to "All Placement Directors" (undated, circa summer 1976).

2.70. *See generally* Weinstein, *Proper and Improper Interactions Between Bench and Law School: Law Student Practice, Law Student Clerkships, and Rules for Admission to the Federal Bar*, 50 St. John's L. Rev. 441, 444–50 (1976); Weinstein & Bonvillian, *A Part-Time Clerkship Program in Federal Courts for Law Students*, 68 F.R.D. 265 (1975), *reprinted sub nom. Law Students as Part-Time Court Law Clerks*, 15 Judges' J. 58 (1976) (shortened version). *See also* Baier & Lesinski, *supra* note 1.14.

2.71. *See* Simonson v. General Motors Corp., 425 F. Supp. 575, 576 (E.D. Pa. 1976); Goodman & Seaton, *The Supreme Court of California, 1972–73—Foreword: Ripe for Decision, Internal Workings and Current Concerns of the California Supreme Court*, 62 Cal. L. Rev. 309, 312 n.8 (1974).

At the Supreme Court of California, "externs" are appointed for the fall semester, the spring semester, or for the summer. Some law schools allow academic credit for a summer extern position, but most do not, out of concern that they might become obligated in fairness to afford academic credit for all manner of other summer clinical activities that could be said to contribute towards a student's legal education. Summer externs at the Supreme Court of California are invariably students between their second and third years of law school. *Accord*, Cal. Courts of Appeal, *supra* note 1.7, at 82. This is a period in which a student qualified for an extern position can almost certainly earn between $1,000 and $1,500 a month as "law clerk" in a major metropolitan law firm. This opportunity cost for an unpaid position that does not afford academic credit tends to limit summer externships to students of some wealth or with extreme interest in the judicial process.

There has been at least one instance of the Supreme Court of California having a postgraduate extern. Marilyn McCloskey, the 1977 graduate of the law school of the University of California at Davis who assisted us in interviewing some of our subject judges, *see* note 4.23 and accompanying text *infra*, was asked by a judge of the Supreme Court of California to serve as an extern in the fall of 1977.

generally been left to the initiative of particular judges and law schools.

Although the word has not gained currency nationwide, the generic term applied to student law clerks throughout California, at both state and federal courts, is *extern*.[2.72] The etymology of the term has not been documented, but the word appears to have been coined at the California Supreme Court, circa 1970, as a play on the word *intern*. Student law clerks are interns in the conventional sense of unpaid aides rewarded only by experience, yet they are also law students learning law externally from their law schools.

The law schools themselves have played an active role in the growth of extern programs.[2.73] A law school's success in placing externs with judges is seen as a token of prestige comparable to, if of lesser magnitude than, its success in securing paid postgraduate clerkships for its students. Law schools actively cultivate interest in their extern candidates, with faculty members often performing a screening and nominating function. Some judges have continuing extern programs with particular law schools, and delegate all administrative matters, including the final selection process, to law school personnel.

Externs are generally third-year students who have performed with distinction during the first two years of law school and who have enjoyed discovering tangible evidence of their skill as lawyers in the course of jobs with commercial law firms during the summer after their second year. After this invigorating experience, the third year of law school often seems redundant; service as an extern offers escape from these doldrums, as well as valuable exposure to the internal operations of courts and an attractive addition to a résumé.

Because more openings for externs are generally available than paid positions for law clerks, and because the very best law students often have law review responsibilities or curricular desires which preclude service as externs, it is generally somewhat easier

2.72. *See* CAL. COURTS OF APPEAL, *supra* note 1.7 at 81–82; B. WITKIN, *supra* note 1.10, at 23; Goodman & Seaton, *supra* note 2.71, at 309 n.*, 312 n.8; Johnson, *supra* note 2.68, at 249 & n.64; Wold, *Going through the motions: the monotony of appellate court decisionmaking*, 62 JUDICATURE 58, 63 (1978).

2.73. *See* Smith v. Pepsico, Inc., 434 F. Supp. 524, 525 (S.D. Fla. 1977); Simonson v. General Motors Corp., 425 F. Supp. 575, 576 (E.D. Pa. 1976); Weinstein & Bonvillian, *supra* note 2.70, 68 F.R.D. at 268.

to become an extern than a law clerk. Outstanding academic performance is still the normal threshold criterion for an extern candidate, however, and selection as an extern is considered a legitimate source of pride among law students. Some externs become law clerks to the judges they have served, more become law clerks to other judges, but most eschew further court experience and go directly into the practice of law after graduation.[2.74]

E. *Career Clerks: A California Trend*

There is a direct relationship between the advent of central staffs and extern programs and the development, at the state appellate courts of California, of a pronounced trend toward retaining for indefinite periods the law clerks to individual justices. The transformation of these "elbow clerks"[2.75] from recent law graduates who remained with a judge for no more than a year or two to lifelong court attachés who are hired after several years of other

2.74. The co-author of Judge Weinstein's survey of federal court extern usage was Judge Weinstein's law clerk and former extern. Weinstein & Bonvillian, *supra* note 2.70, at 265 n.**. William Goodman, a former extern of Chief Justice Wright of the California Supreme Court, *see* Goodman & Seaton, *supra* note 2.71, at 309 n.*, spent the year following his graduation as a formally employed law clerk to Chief Justice Wright. Although Chief Justice Wright made it a rule not to consider his externs for law clerk positions, in order to forestall competition between externs, this was not his invariable practice. To our knowledge, two other former externs of Chief Justice Wright were later employed by him as law clerks. In addition, one of his law clerks had been an extern at one of the California courts of appeal, and one of his externs later worked as a law clerk for another judge of the California Supreme Court.

Externs at the California Supreme Court seem more likely than externs elsewhere to go on to postgraduate clerkships—generally at other courts. Of the six U.C. Davis law students who were externs at the California Supreme Court in 1976–1978, three later clerked at federal district courts. Two of the law clerks whom we interviewed, *see* text accompanying notes 4.22–4.23 *infra*, had served as externs at the Supreme Court of California.

Several of the judges whom we interviewed indicated that they regarded successful externs in their chambers as prime candidates to be hired as their law clerks. The National Center for State Courts found the use of externs in the California courts of appeal to be "a successful recruiting and training device." CAL. COURTS OF APPEAL, *supra* note 1.7, at 82.

2.75. Professor Meador attributes to the Federal Judicial Center the coinage of this useful phrase for distinguishing the personal law clerk of an individual judge from staff attorneys working collectively for that judge's court. *See* D. MEADOR, *supra* note 1.7, at 17 and n.45.

legal experience and come to the court as a career has been encouraged both by the legitimation of career employees on central staffs[2.76] and by the availability of externs to act as surrogates for fresh-faced but inefficient clerks of the traditional type.[2.77]

Staff attorneys share a common institutional history with law clerks, they serve coordinate purposes, and to many judges they are functionally indistinct from law clerks.[2.78] Central staffs have frequently,[2.79] if not inevitably,[2.80] been composed of more experienced personnel than the law clerks of individual judges; their

2.76. *See, e.g.*, CAL. COURTS OF APPEAL, *supra* note 1.7, at 88–89. The tendency to view central staff and permanent clerks for individual judges as birds of a feather is apparent in recent comments of California's new Chief Justice:

> At the appellate level, the confluence of two factors—the development of large, impersonal central staffs and the application of a "non-publication" rule—raises some concerns that should be addressed.
> In California's appellate courts, the recently graduated, one-year law clerk is becoming the exception rather than the rule. The law clerk has given way to the research attorney whose position is permanent.
> The theory underlying this trend is that a professional staff with the continuity of service can develop expertise, thereby saving time in the preparation of cases for the justices' decision. In turn, the justices' time is to be used more efficiently with the preliminary work of research and summarization already completed.
> Central staff functions may differ somewhat from one appellate court to another, but the potential for mischief in this bureaucratic structure remains the same—the lack of *public accountability*.

Bird, *supra* note 2.68, at 4 (emphasis in original).

2.77. When author Oakley was a law clerk at the Supreme Court of California in 1972–73, the court's thirty-one research attorneys consisted of twenty-one permanent employees and ten temporary employees. As of November 30, 1978, the court's thirty-three research attorneys consisted of twenty-seven permanent employees and only six temporary employees. *See* note 5.79 *infra*. The percentage of law clerks employed on a short-term basis thus declined in six years from just over 32 percent to just over 22 percent. During this period, extern use had grown to the point where, by an unwritten and frequently unobserved rule born of a lack of office and library space, each justice was allowed to have "up to three" externs, but no more. *See* Johnson, *supra* note 2.68, at 249 n.64. In fact, some justices have as many as five externs at one time, and three waves of externs—spring, summer, and fall—wash over the court each year. This easily doubles the use made of externs in 1972, and establishes a positive inverse correlation between the declining use of short-term law clerks and the rising use of externs at the Supreme Court of California.

2.78. *See* D. MEADOR, *supra* note 1.7, at 112–13.

2.79. *See id.* at 82; CAL. COURTS OF APPEAL, *supra* note 1.7, at 93–94.

2.80. *See* note 2.68 *supra*.

job, after all, is to counteract the "crisis of volume" by being expedient rather than stimulating. Especially in California, the popularization of experienced central staff attorneys and the siege mentality produced by the unrelenting increase in the volume of appellate filings have served to legitimate the hiring of indefinitely tenured "career" law clerks—not as staff attorneys but as the personal assistants of individual judges.[2.81] The experience and efficiency of such clerks, and a sense of the liveliness lost for lack of short-term clerks, may in turn induce an otherwise uninterested judge to participate in an extern program. The upshot is that the externs generally become the law clerks of the career clerk, and within their more severe constraints of time and talent perform that role of law clerk in more or less the traditional fashion.

The trend toward the use of career law clerks, not as a supplement to short-termed law clerks in the form of central staff or supervisory attorneys but to the virtual exclusion of short-termed law clerks, is apparently unique to California. It should be emphasized, however, that it is the trend which is unique to California, not the phenomenon of indefinitely tenured law clerks to individual judges.[2.82] Indefinitely tenured assistants were the norm at the United States Supreme Court until Horace Gray's clerkship practices, as adopted by Holmes and Brandeis, spread to the rest of the Court in the early decades of this century.[2.83] Oklahoma's first provision of law clerks to its supreme court justices in 1931 expressly required the hiring of experienced attorneys, who presumably were expected to remain indefinitely with the court;[2.84] and other states that provide more explicitly parajudicial assistance to their courts in the form of "commissioners" have historically employed experienced, career-minded attorneys in such

2.81. See CAL. COURTS OF APPEAL, *supra* note 1.7, at 77–78; B. WITKIN, *supra* note 1.10, at 12–17.

2.82. In a survey completed in 1959, out of forty-four American appellate courts reporting use of law clerks, six indicated that their clerks served for long periods of time. At twenty of the courts the usual tenure of clerks was one year, and at the rest the period varied from one to three years. Law clerks were exclusively recent law graduates at twenty-four of the reporting courts, predominantly so at six more, and about half were recent law graduates at two more. At ten reporting courts only experienced lawyers were hired as law clerks. ABA SECTION OF JUDICIAL ADMINISTRATION, *supra* note 2.52, at 45.

2.83. See Newland, *supra* note 1.6, at 306–08; Williams, *supra* note 1.7, at 87.

2.84. Curran & Sunderland, *supra* note 2.50, at 149.

posts.[2.85] Indefinitely tenured law clerks have been found at California's state appellate courts since at least 1930, and in substantial numbers since 1950.[2.86] Nonetheless, it is only recently, and apparently only in California, that by a process of accretion unaccompanied by any express change of law or policy the short-

---

2.85. *See* R. LEFLAR, *supra* note 1.7, at 82–83. *See generally* COUNCIL OF STATE GOVERNMENTS, *supra* note 2.52, at 81–84, Table XIII; D. MEADOR, note 1.7, at 14–15, 225–29; NATIONAL CENTER FOR STATE COURTS, PARAJUDGES: THEIR ROLE IN TODAY'S COURT SYSTEMS 6–7, 30–71 (1976); Curran & Sunderland, *supra* note 2.50, at 69–95; Spector, *supra* note 2.52, at 146–48; Stockmeyer, Borst, Stenger, & Reid, *supra* note 2.52; J. Parness, The Expanding Role of the Parajudge in the United States 38 (prelim. draft, 1973) (Am. Jud. Soc'y. Research Report). *See also* Kaufman, *The Judicial Crisis, Court Delay, and the Parajudge*, 54 JUDICATURE 145 (1970).

2.86. It was reported in 1933, on information obtained from Chief Justice William H. Waste, that "[f]or a number of years the Supreme Court and District Courts of Appeal of California have had appropriated a sufficient sum to permit securing the services, for each of the justices, of a competent legal secretary. In addition the Supreme Court has had the services of a supervising law secretary. . . ." Curran & Sunderland, *supra* note 2.50, at 148–49. This report indicated merely that "[t]he term of service of these assistants is at the pleasure of the justice who made the appointment." *Id.* at 149. However, it happens that two of the court's most famous former law clerks began their work at the Supreme Court of California in 1930. Raymond E. Peters, then 27 and three years out of law school, was appointed to the newly created position of "chief law secretary" in 1930, and served there until his appointment to the First District Court of Appeal in 1939. Justice Peters returned to the Supreme Court of California as an associate justice in 1959, and remained on the court until his death in 1973. *See* Traynor, *Justice Raymond E. Peters*, 57 CAL. L. REV. 559, 560 (1969); *Dedication*, 46 SO. CAL. L. REV. 227 (1973). Also arriving at the court in 1930 was 26-year-old Bernard E. Witkin, who had already begun two years earlier, by publication of his own bar examination review notes, the series of summaries of California law which was to establish him as California's leading legal writer and lecturer. Witkin served as law clerk to Justice W. H. Langdon until the latter's death in 1939, and stayed on as law clerk to Justice Langdon's replacement, Justice Phil S. Gibson. The following year, Chief Justice Waste died and Justice Gibson was elevated to Chief Justice, being replaced as an associate justice by Peters' classmate and Gibson's successor as Chief Justice, Roger J. Traynor. When the court's Reporter of Decisions retired at the end of November, 1940, Witkin was appointed his successor, and remained Reporter of Decisions until resigning in 1949 to devote himself fully to his legal writing. Interview with Bernard E. Witkin, in Davis, California, November 20, 1978. *See also* the notations of dates of appointment appearing in the frontispieces to *California Reports*, 14 Cal. 2d iii; 15 Cal. 2d iii; 16 Cal. 2d iii; 34 Cal. 2d i. The experiences of Justice Peters and Mr. Witkin as long-term law clerks apparently left them with differing perceptions of the value of short-term law clerks. At the time of his

termed law clerk has been largely excluded from the chambers of the state's appellate judges.[2.87]

Despite the historical precedents for career clerks, the California trend is profoundly in conflict with the character of the law clerk as traditionally conceived and as commonly employed in other jurisdictions. The "traditional" conception is the product of a literature which makes virtually no mention of permanent law clerks whatsoever, and it is the very shortness of tenure of this traditional law clerk that is the cardinal virtue relied upon to justify the institution against concern over undue influence upon the appointed judiciary. The common element that emerges from a review of the literature of law clerking from the days of Horace Gray to the present is the dialectic between the brashness of youth and the restraint of age, between the theories of the classroom and the pragmatism of bench and bar—a dialectic that is repeated year after year as brilliant but naive law clerks work in earnest intimacy with indulgent but independently minded judges. Some judges

---

death, Justice Peters was the only member of the Supreme Court of California still using two short-term law clerks and only one long-term law clerk. Mr. Witkin, however, has been an ardent champion of career law clerks, and indeed is the only prominent spokesman on judicial administration to recommend that judges hire *only* career clerks. *See* B. WITKIN, *supra* note 1.10, at 12–14, 17; B. Witkin, *supra* note 1.6, at 32–33.

By 1950, each justice of the California Supreme Court was equipped with one "research attorney" and one "research assistant," the latter term apparently designating newly graduated law clerks who at the beginning of their employment had yet to be admitted to the bar. *See* COUNCIL OF STATE GOVERNMENTS, THE COURTS OF LAST RESORT OF THE FORTY-EIGHT STATES: A REPORT TO THE CONFERENCE OF CHIEF JUSTICES 37 & Table 8 (1950); Spector, *supra* note 2.52, at 145–46. Several of the senior law clerks currently at the California Supreme Court began their careers at the court prior to 1950. One "research assistant" has since eclipsed Justice Peters and Mr. Witkin as the court's most famous former law clerk: California Governor Edmund G. Brown, Jr., who in 1964–65 clerked for his father's appointee, Justice Mathew O. Tobriner.

2.87. For the proportion of short-term law clerks at the California Supreme Court, *see* note 2.77 *supra*. For the proportion of short-term law clerks serving individual judges of the California courts of appeal at the time of our interviews, *see* note 5.39 *infra*. A senior research attorney with one of the California courts of appeal has provided us with a copy of her own unofficial survey of the tenure of all research attorneys of the California courts of appeal. Her figures, which included both staff attorneys and elbow clerks, showed that, as of September 1977, there were a total of ninety-two attorneys employed by the courts of appeal, of which eighty (87 percent) were permanent employees.

have never let a law clerk pen a word of opinion,[2.88] others have graciously delegated footnotes,[2.89] some have made as much use of a law clerk's language as its merit has justified,[2.90] and doubtless some have delegated opinion writing to the point of dependence.[2.91] But the central feature of every reported clerkship has been its limited tenure in relation to that of the judge, with this fundamental fact serving to keep the roles of clerk and judge in proper perspective.[2.92]

The qualities and motivation of law clerks differ markedly with their tenure.[2.93] A short-term clerk is chosen primarily for outstanding law school achievement and compatibility of personality with the judge and his or her method of operation. The emphasis is on those qualities, so lauded in the traditional literature, that will contribute most to the creative dialogue between judge and law clerk. Career clerks are chosen for reasons of efficiency rather than creativity; practical legal experience and evidence of productivity in a bureaucratic environment count for more than legal scholarship. The traditional law clerk is expected to bring to the court the flair of a novelist; the career clerk is cast in a role more akin to a newspaper's night editor. The goals of short-term

2.88. See, e.g., Edwards, The Avoidance of Appellate Delay, 52 F.R.D. 51, 68 (1971); Medina, The Decisional Process, 20 B. BULL. 94, 99 (1962) (N.Y. County Lawyers' Assoc.) (describing Judge Learned Hand); W. Leach, Recollections of a Holmes Secretary (Sept. 1940) (unpublished manuscript in Archival Collection, Harvard Law School Library).

2.89. See, e.g., A. Mason, supra note 2.46, at 513 & n.*; Acheson, supra note 1.6, at 364–65 (describing Justice Brandeis).

2.90. See, e.g., J. FRANK, supra note 1.5, at 117; J. FRANK, MR. JUSTICE BLACK: THE MAN AND HIS OPINIONS 135–36 (1949); Chilton, Appellate Court Reform: The Premature Scalpel, 48 CAL. ST. B.J. 392, 474 (1973) (California Supreme Court); Cohen, supra note 1.6, at 7; Meador, Justice Black and His Law Clerks, 15 ALA. L. REV. 57, 60 (1962); Kidney, Anonymous Clerks Serve Justices, Gain Experience, Wash. Post, June 16, 1974, § L, at 6, col. 1 (Philip Elman re Mr. Justice Frankfurter).

2.91. See J. FRANK, supra note 1.5, at 117–18; Frank, Fred Vinson and the Chief Justiceship, 21 U. CHI. L. REV. 212, 224, & 244–46 (1954); Roche, The Utopian Pilgrimage of Mr. Justice Murphy, 10 VAND. L. REV. 369, 370–72 (1957). See also note 1.4 supra.

2.92. See, e.g., J. WILKINSON, supra note 1.7, at 59; Chilton, supra note 98, at 466; Newland, supra note 1.6, at 316.

2.93. These conclusions are drawn from our own research, as presented and analyzed in Chapters V and VI infra.

and career clerks also differ greatly. The short-term clerk prizes his or her appointment for its prestige and its training in the psychology of judging; it has been won after vigorous competition and will serve as an entrée into virtually any variant of the practice of law. The long-term clerk values the job more in the present tense, as one that offers security of employment at satisfactory compensation, free of the pressures of a conventional law practice and full of a genuine sense of public service.

III. IN DEFENSE OF TRADITION: THE CLERKSHIP IDEAL

It would be fatuous to maintain that every judge, even of the United States Supreme Court, has had the powers of intellect of a Gray, a Holmes, a Brandeis, or a Learned Hand. Because judges of this caliber attract the clerks most likely to go on to their own distinction (and by the very bestowal of a clerkship add considerable impetus to that end), much of the literature of law clerks is indeed by disciples of such demigods.[3.1] But what is remarkable is that the recollections of those who served judges of a clearly lesser order show the same degree of respect and deference, if not of outright hero worship, as the testaments of those whose mentors were touched by genius.[3.2]

Of course, the dignity of the office and the self-interest of a former clerk in contributing to the reputation of his or her benefactor will color clerkship recollections, not to mention the common circumstance that such recollections are published as memo-

3.1. For an example of how bedazzled a disciple can be in the presence of the almighty, *see* Jaffe, *supra* note 1.6, in which a former Brandeis clerk recalls musing with fellow clerks over whether his mentor or Mr. Justice Holmes had the "most wonderful eyes." We do not mean to deprecate such reverence but only to point out that most law clerks work with less charismatic mentors than did some of the more prolific writers about law clerks, such as Mr. Frank and Professor Meador (Justice Black), the late Professor Bickel (Justice Frankfurter), and Professor Kurland (Justice Frankfurter, and previously Judge Frank).

3.2. *See, e.g.*, Baier, *supra* note 1.7, at 1127–28, 1153–55, 1161–63 (Michigan Court of Appeals); Ragatz and Shea, *supra* note 1.7, at 38 (Wisconsin Supreme Court); *Three Views, supra* note 1.7, at 157–60 (Alabama Supreme Court). *Compare Chief Justice Vinson and His Law Clerks, supra* note 1.6; *and* Pickering, Gressman, & Tolan, *supra* note 1.6, *with* Kurland, *supra* note 1.4.

rials to the recently departed, at a time when it is natural to applaud the positive and omit the negative aspects of a personality past changing. It is possible that some law clerks to lesser judges have been co-opted into paying lip service to a traditional law clerk's role which they did not in fact fulfill. If so, it is interesting to note the direction in which the distortion of history occurs.

The traditional model of the relationship between law clerk and judge has acquired the status of an ideal,[3.3] for while we are quite happy to have the mental processes of our judges tested by the best and brightest scions of our law schools, we are uncomfortable if testing leads to besting and the substitution of the judgments of law clerks for those of judges. Indeed, it seems to have been the fear of just such an appearance of undue influence that long inhibited discussion of law clerks and allowed the burst of debate on the topic two decades ago to assume such a lurid tone. The ideal is composed of two factors and works in practice because the traditional model of a law clerkship promotes both factors without regard to the relative intellect of the judge or the law clerk. First, the judge must retain responsibility for decision-making. Second, the clerk must carry the adversary process into the chambers, forcing the judge to justify each step of the decision-making process. The institutional features of the traditional clerkship which promote these factors are the youth and recent affinity to academia of the law clerk and the predetermined tenure of the clerkship.[3.4]

Whatever inherent deference youth may owe to age is reinforced by the manifestly satellite status of a clerk who makes only one orbit of the judge before making way for a successor. In such a system, no one's eyes can confuse the brightest of moons with the body about which it revolves. At the same time, the judge is in-

3.3. *See* Fredonia Broadcasting Corp. v. RCA Corp., 569 F.2d 251, 255–56 (5th Cir. 1978):

> A judicial clerkship provides the fledgling lawyer insight into the law, the judicial process, and the legal practice. The association with law clerks is also valuable to the judge; in addition to relieving him of many clerical and administrative chores, law clerks may serve as sounding boards for ideas, often affording a different perspective, may perform research, and may aid in drafting memoranda, orders and opinions.

3.4. *See* A. BICKEL, *supra* note 1.5, at 142–45; J. WILKINSON, *supra* note 1.7, at 66–67. *See also* J. FRANK, *supra* note 1.5, at 116.

stitutionally on notice of the dangers of undue dependence or delegation: there will be darkness in the future when only the dim
light of a new moon exists to enlighten the task of making new
decisions and justifying old ones.

To bring both clerk and our metaphor back to earth, however,
the judge's natural resistance to the influence of a young and fleet-
ing law clerk will be opposed by the clerk's incentive, precisely
because of his or her limited tenure, to fight the judge for every
inch of fair ground.[3.5] The soil of decision may be the judge's
garden, but the clerk knows that immortality lies in the seeds to be
sown therein, and the time for planting will not return in that
clerk's season. The clerk cannot afford to curry favor by agreement in hopes of someday gaining a hand on the plow; instead,
driven to immediacy by the setting sun, the clerk will seek to seed
the law at once with the manifold ideas of a fertile intellect.[3.6] Out
of such conflict are bred the best-considered decisions, for the
judge, who must weather storms long after the clerk's departure,

3.5. *See* Sacks, *Felix Frankfurter*, in 3 THE JUSTICES OF THE UNITED STATES
SUPREME COURT 1789–1969, at 2403–04 (L. Friedman & F. Israel ed. 1969):

> [V]ery early in my year as his law clerk, he [Justice Frankfurter] asked me what
> I thought of a certain case before the Court, and I stated my conclusion, of
> which he obviously approved. In making my point, I questioned the sound-
> ness of a related case decided by the Court the year before, 5–4, in which the
> Justice had voted in the majority. He had an immediate and overwhelming
> reaction. I was wrong and he was going to prove it to me. Our exchange lasted
> over an hour, and the Justice brought to bear every pressure available to verbal
> man. Anger, scorn, sarcasm, humor buttressed straightforward argument. At
> times I was hit by the sledge, and at others cut by the rapier. He did not shrink
> from using the rank of his experience, his age, and his office, and yet as he was
> more and more drawn into the ecstasy of combat, he placed us—as I now
> realize—on an equal footing. I sought to hold my ground, and I emerged, I
> think, bloodied and bent but not bowed or broken. . . . The following morn-
> ing, the Justice bounced into his office, called me in, and made it clear by his
> manner that, far from leaving any scars, our exchange had drawn us closer
> together.

3.6. *See* Baier, *supra* note 1.7, at 1156–57 & nn. 116–17; Braden, *supra* note
1.6, at 297; Hazard, *After the Trial Court—the Realities of Appellate Review*, in THE
COURTS, THE PUBLIC, AND THE LAW EXPLOSION 60, 65 (H. Jones ed. 1965); Kurland, *supra* note 1.6, at 662–63. More than one commentator has suggested that it
is this very tendency of law clerks which accounts for ever longer appellate opinions. *See* Baier, *supra* note 1.7, at 1154–55; Griswold, *Appellate Advocacy, With
Particular Reference to the United States Supreme Court*, 26 THE RECORD 342, 354
(1971) (Association of the Bar of the City of New York).

will tend to resist the premature planting of any idea not native to the judge's intelligence, however attractively packaged by the espousing clerk. Indeed, the judge has the irrefutable answer to a clerk's cry for action—that the idea should be tested against the clerk's impending replacement.

IV. A STUDY OF CLERKSHIP PRACTICES IN CALIFORNIA

A. *Origin and Methodology*

The characteristics of the ideal relationship between judge and law clerk which we have recited above are more than mere abstractions culled from the literature on law clerks. Although fully consistent with that literature, our idealized clerkship is also an embodiment of the values, concerns, and constraints derived from some years of personal experience. One of us spent more than a decade in the company of short-term law clerks as an associate justice of a California court of appeal;[4.1] the other spent three years as an itinerant law clerk of both annual and indefinite tenure at the Supreme Court of California and a federal district court.[4.2] Our collaboration developed as a result of an arrow let fly by one

4.1. Author Thompson was appointed to the California Court of Appeal for the Second Appellate District in 1968, and resigned from the court in 1979 to join the law faculty of the University of Southern California. During his eleven years on the court of appeal, Thompson employed seven clerks for one-year periods and two others for two-year periods. In both instances, the decision to retain a clerk for a second year accommodated the personal circumstances of the clerk as well as the convenience of the judge.

4.2. Upon graduation from law school in 1972, author Oakley was employed for one year as one of four short-term law clerks to Chief Justice Donald Wright of the Supreme Court of California. *Cf.* notes 5.76–5.77 and accompanying text *infra* (number and function of law clerks of Chief Justice of California). Oakley spent the following year as one of two law clerks to Chief Judge M. Joseph Blumenfeld of the United States District Court for the District of Connecticut, thereby accommodating a personal need to reside that year in New England. The next year, 1974–75, Oakley rejoined the staff of Chief Justice Wright as an indefinitely tenured law clerk, one of two working exclusively on cases assigned to the Chief Justice after the grant of a hearing or other exercise of jurisdiction. Oakley

of us at decision-making procedures of the California courts of appeal;[4.3] one feather on this shaft expressed regret over the trend at those courts away from short-termed clerks to parajudicial careerists.[4.4] The shot seemed on target to the other of us, who had become no less regretful in the course of discovering, while promoting student clerkship candidates, how few California judges remained interested in the services of young Williston's heirs and assigns.

This convergence of views made for an easy but unpromising collaboration. For lack of any conflict between collaborators or anything novel to add to a collation of existing literature, we feared that an immediate essay celebrating short-term law clerks would have little persuasive value for the judges with whom we wished most to communicate—those who had adopted long-term law clerks. Given the systematic rejection of short-term law clerks by most of the members of the California courts of appeal[4.5] (and, subsequent to the start of our study, by most of the members of the California Supreme Court),[4.6] it was obvious that the virtues we perceived in short-term clerks were being outweighed in others' eyes by advantages of career clerks of which we might be taking inadequate account. We accordingly resolved to test our views against as broad a sampling of judicial opinion as we could feasibly undertake. In the subsequent words of California's new Chief Justice, we felt it was time for "a wide-ranging dialogue that explores all ideas and challenges all assumptions," including our own.[4.7]

The resulting study of law clerk usage in California, however empirical, bears no pretensions of perfection. While our techniques are not without scientific sanction, our professional training is in law, not sociology.[4.8] What we learned has validity inso-

---

left the staff of Chief Justice Wright the following year to join the law faculty of the University of California at Davis.

4.3. Thompson, *supra* note 1.11.   4.4. *Id.* at 514–16.

4.5. *See* note 2.87 *supra*; note 5.39 *infra*.

4.6. *See* note 2.77 *supra*.   4.7. Bird, *supra* note 2.68, at 46.

4.8. *See* notes 4.11 & 4.13 *infra*. *See also* R. BOGDAN & S. TAYLOR, INTRODUCTION TO QUALITATIVE RESEARCH METHODS 83–84 (1975) (justifying field research designed to generate theories of social behavior rather than to test pre-existing hypotheses of social behavior); L. SCHATZMAN & A. STRAUSS, FIELD RESEARCH: STRATEGIES FOR A NATURAL SOCIOLOGY 61 (1973) (justifying use and advantages of observation of social behavior by participants in the behavior); *id.* at 72–73 (justifying qualitative research by open and unstructured interviews).

far as we have accurately observed, recorded, and reported the attitudes and habits of sixty-three state and federal judges in California who use law clerks to assist them in their judicial functions. The observational and recording functions were performed in a relatively unsystematic way, causing a sacrifice of accuracy that we felt was necessary in order to gain access to the confidences of a significant number of judges. Because our sample of judges was self-selected by the subjects themselves, because our techniques of investigation and interviewing tended to be impressionistic, and because our concern was with states of mind not easily quantified, our data cannot and do not purport to be statistically significant or to be rigorously representative of any class of judges other than the sixty-three individuals we interviewed. We do think that our results, however rough-hewn, have general qualitative validity—that they reflect perceptions of law clerk usage commonly held by similarly situated judges at other courts nationwide.[4.9]

Even as to our sixty-three subjects, it should be borne in mind that their views are being reported by investigators who, although they have attempted to function impartially, undertook the study with an announced bias.[4.10] The departures from this

4.9. See note 4.8 supra; notes 4.11 & 4.13 infra. See also Professor Kurland's denunciation of such "errors of not uncommon occurrence in modern research" as the beliefs that "those matters which are translatable into numbers are worth consideration; those matters which are not translatable into numbers are not worth consideration. Therefore you must assign numerical equivalents to all matters with which you wish to deal." Kurland, supra note 1.4, at 301. To quote two of the authorities cited by Professor Kurland in debunking such beliefs: "It must never be forgotten that the hard certainty, the calm objectivity which make a statistical table so convincing are to a considerable extent illusory. Actually, subjective judgments of the analyst . . . play a great part in producing the 'objective' evidence of the box score." C. PRITCHETT, CIVIL LIBERTIES AND THE VINSON COURT 275 n.5 (1954). "The Higher Statistician breaks down truth and falsity into such fine particles that we cannot tell the difference between them. By the costly rigor of their methods, they succeed in trivializing men and society, and in the process, their own minds as well." Mills, IBM plus Reality plus Humanism-Sociology, The Saturday Review, May 1, 1954, at 22. We trust that, however lacking in rigor our methods, we have avoided trivializing either ourselves or our subjects.

4.10. The solicitation letter was written over Oakley's signature, and commenced as follows:

Dear Judge:
    The purpose of this letter is to solicit your participation in a comprehensive study of law clerk usage by state and federal judges in California. This study, which we believe to be the first of its kind ever undertaken, is an outgrowth of

bias which appear in our evaluations and recommendations are some evidence that we were not immutably wed to our views on the proper use of law clerks, but we can offer no meaningful assurances that our data are entirely free from distortions introduced by our preconceptions.

These disclaimers are not offered as an apologia; we believe that the study we conducted and the results we derived were well suited to our purposes and to the environment within which we operated.[4.11] Notwithstanding the trend noted in our introduc-

---

my collaboration with Associate Justice Robert S. Thompson of the Court of Appeal of California on a proposed article concerning the appropriate tenure of judicial clerkships.

In seeking your cooperation we feel it incumbent upon us to disclose that we are not without pre-existing personal views on the subject to be studied. Judge Thompson and I share the belief, at least at the outset of this project, that law clerks who spend no more than one or two years with their judges before entering on their own careers are preferable in most instances and at most levels to law clerks who remain permanently in the service of particular judges. Specifically, we question the institutional desirability of the permanent law clerks which now prevail, almost universally, among the judges of the California Court of Appeal.

There are, of course, different opinions extant among judges. Early in our collaboration, Judge Thompson and I concluded that there was little to be gained by merely stating and supporting our mutual views through appeal to abstract principle. Accordingly, we have launched this survey in order to gather as much empirical data as possible by which to test, and perhaps to change, our existing beliefs as to optimal law clerk usage. We are confident that the opinions we bring to the project have not hardened into blind bias.

See also notes 1.13 & 4.4 and accompanying text *supra*.

The letter concluded with paragraphs on the methodology of the interviews, *see* note 4.14 *infra*, the biographical background of the investigators, and how to respond to the solicitation.

4.11. It should be noted that while we undertook our study with personal preferences for the use of short-term law clerks, our study was designed not to vindicate our preferences but to help us account for the divergent preferences of the increasing number of judges favoring long-term law clerks. *See* text accompanying notes 4.4–4.7 *supra*. Our survey was thus oriented to discovering the perceived advantages of long-term law clerks rather than proving our still inchoate hypotheses about the disadvantages of such clerks. As two of the leading proponents of qualitative sociological research have written:

We believe that the discovery of theory from data—which we call *grounded theory*—is a major task confronting sociology today, for, as we shall try to show, such a theory fits empirical situations, and is understandable to sociologists and layman alike. Most important, it works—provides us with relevant predictions, explanations, interpretations and applications.

B. GLASER & A. STRAUSS, THE DISCOVERY OF GROUNDED THEORY 1 (1967) (emphasis in original).

tion towards greater visibility for law clerks as a judicial institution,[4.12] many judges remain jealous of their relationships with
their law clerks and are uneasy about discussing them in any but
the most discreet manner. Our investigative techniques were dictated by this atmosphere of privacy—which we think unwar-
ranted but which we were obliged to respect—and by our own
lack of advance knowledge as to the most useful lines of inquiry.[4.13]

As our solicitation letter made clear,[4.14] we deliberately de-

---

4.12. *See* text accompanying notes 1.7–1.12 *supra*.

4.13. On the merits of research designed to discover rather than to prove sociological theories, see note 4.11 *supra*. On the interviewing techniques appropriate to such a research strategy, *see* J. LOFLAND, ANALYZING SOCIAL SETTINGS—A
GUIDE TO QUALITATIVE OBSERVATION AND ANALYSIS, 75–76 (1971) (emphasis in
original):

> [A]s developed in quantitative research, the activity of interviewing has in-
> creasingly reduced itself to forcing a choice between rigidly formulated alter-
> native answers attached to rigidly formulated questions. . . . An interview
> constructed of such questions and preformed answers is often called a "struc-
> tured interview." Appropriately, such a device is also known as a "question-
> naire" or "schedule." An activity of this kind necessarily assumes knowledge
> of what the important questions are and, more importantly, what the main
> kinds of answers can be. Insofar as the investigator wants to impose his ques-
> tions on others and/or knows what is happening with people he is interview-
> ing, this is a legitimate strategy. But insofar as he does not want to make such
> an imposition nor assume he already knows a great deal about his respondents'
> lives, a different strategy of interviewing is required—a flexible strategy of
> *discovery*.
>
> One such flexible strategy of discovery is termed the "unstructured inter-
> view" or "intensive interviewing with an interview guide." Its object is not to
> elicit choices between alternative answers to pre-formed questions but, rather,
> to elicit from the interviewee what he considers to be important questions
> relative to a given topic, his descriptions of some situation being explored. Its
> object is to carry on a guided conversation and to elicit rich, detailed materials
> that can be used in qualitative analysis.

4.14. The solicitation letter described the methodology of our proposed interviews as follows:

> The methodology of the study is to conduct personal interviews with as
> many judges as consent to be interviewed. Although direct quotations as well
> as generalizations based upon the interviews as a whole may be used in litera-
> ture arising from the study, no statements will be attributed to a named indi-
> vidual; rather, a description of the type of court on which he or she serves (and
> possibly a general description of his or her years of experience) will be offered.
> Each interview will be conducted by a single interviewer: either myself or my
> research assistant, Ms. Marilyn McCloskey. A basic set of general questions
> will be covered, but the format of the interview will be open-ended. The
> length of the interview will depend primarily upon the inclination of the judge

cided to conduct our research in as unstructured a fashion as possible. We were unsure at the outset what the relevant questions of detail were which would best explain judicial preferences for career law clerks. We also felt it imperative to adopt an impressionistic research posture in order to elicit the maximum number of cooperative responses. Three factors were critical here: minimizing the demands on the judge's time, assuring the judge absolute confidentiality, and being sensitive to the unique conditions which obtain in each judge's chambers. Although we announced in advance the bias we held,[4.15] we wanted to present ourselves—truly, we hope—as open and receptive to the views of our subjects, whether factually or philosophically based, whether complementary or contrary to our own. These considerations all mitigated against making a quantitative survey, either by submitting to judges an attitudinal questionnaire with the familiar spectrum from "agree strongly" to "disagree strongly" or by demanding oral responses to identical questions dictated from a script. Our tactics proved successful, and it is our hope that by our efforts the path will have been charted for a more rigorous study of law clerk usage by means of the best techniques of survey research applied to a fully representative sample of judges. If we have succeeded, the judiciary should feel sufficiently assured of the confidentiality of its responses and the probity of its participation to permit investigation of law clerk usage to continue in a more sophisticated fashion.

B. *Solicitations and Responses*

Using the lists of judges appearing in the frontispieces of the *Federal Reporter* and the *California Reports*, we identified 105 sitting judges in California whom we knew to have law clerks.[4.16]

---

being interviewed to offer such opinions and information as may be brought to mind by the interviewer's questions.

4.15. *See* note 4.10 *supra*.

4.16. These were all the justices of the Supreme Court of California and the California courts of appeal, every active and senior judge of the United States Court of Appeals for the Ninth Circuit maintaining chambers in California, and every active and senior judge of the four United States District Courts within California, as listed in Volume 525 of *Federal Reporter, 2d*, and Volume 15 of *California Reports, 3d*. The only respect in which the reporters' listing of judges required modification for our purposes was with regard to Ninth Circuit judges who maintained chambers in California. Since the headquarters of the Ninth Cir-

As far as we can determine, those 105 judges included every judge in California as of June 1, 1976 (excepting some superior court judges)[4.17] who was authorized by law to employ a law clerk.[4.18] Included in this number were not only state appellate judges, whose affinity for long-term law clerks prompted the study, but also federal judges whose budgetary constraints we knew made long-term clerkships impracticable. Thus we could, by incorporation of the federal judges, include within our study a primitive form of control group of judges who had short-term clerks out of necessity if not by choice.

Supported by research funds from the Davis campus of the University of California and from that campus's law school, we solicited interviews with each of the 105 judges. The mailings were made from June 18 through July 2, 1976. Each letter set forth in detail our reasons for soliciting the interview and our proposed format;[4.19] each letter included a reply postcard by which the judge could conveniently extend or deny an invitation for an interview.

We were surprised by the rate of response to our solicitation letter. We had expected to receive responses from 50 to 60 percent of the judges contacted, and hoped that about half of these, or 25 to 30 percent of the total, would consent to participate in our study. In fact, eighty-one judges responded directly, for an initial response rate of 77 percent. In addition, in the course of conducting our interviews we encountered seven judges who had failed to respond directly but who, when asked again orally whether they wished to participate, agreed to do so. Thus the overall response rate was 88 judges out of 105, or 84 percent. Of these, 64 judges were willing to be interviewed and 63 actually were interviewed.[4.20] Our findings are accordingly based on interviews with 60 percent of the entire group under study.

---

cuit is in San Francisco, we ascertained from officials there which judges maintained their working chambers in California as opposed to their cities of residence as listed in *Federal Reporter, 2d*.

4.17. *See* note 2.52 *supra*.

4.18. Several judges were appointed to courts within the scope of our survey during the period of our research. *See* note 5.12 *infra*. We limited our interviews to those judges sitting on June 1, 1976.

4.19. *See* notes 4.10 & 4.14 *supra*.

4.20. Because of persistent conflicts in our schedules, we were unable to arrange an interview with one senior federal district judge who left California for an

As the accompanying table shows, we obtained a particularly impressive rate of participation by the subgroup most directly concerned with our study: California state appellate judges. As of June 1, 1976, there were forty-eight sitting judges of the California courts of appeal; we were permitted to interview thirty-eight of them, or 79 percent. In addition, we interviewed five of the seven judges then sitting on the Supreme Court of California, so that overall our subjects included 78 percent of the judges then sitting on the appellate courts of California. Two years later, our subjects still constituted nearly two-thirds of all California state appellate judges.

The table also shows, as one would expect, lesser interest in participation by our "control group" of federal judges, who have little choice in the tenure of their law clerks.

Nearly half of these federal circuit (appellate) and district (trial) judges participated in the study. We were particularly grateful for the very high level of interest on the part of active circuit judges. The least interest was shown by the semi-retired "senior" judges of the federal courts, less than one-quarter of whom participated.[4.21]

---

extended period before a mutually convenient time for an interview could be arranged. Included among the sixty-three judges whom we count as having been interviewed are two special cases. One senior federal district judge who authorized his law clerk to answer all our questions was counted as having been interviewed. *See* text accompanying note 4.22 *infra*. As a rough device for testing the accuracy of our interviewing technique, author Thompson was himself interviewed by author Oakley on August 6, 1976, approximately halfway through the period in which the interviews were conducted. The Thompson interview was conducted in the normally formal circumstances of the other interviews, and extended to many areas of clerkship usage not previously discussed between the authors. The data obtained in this fashion were processed normally and later reviewed in processed form by Thompson, who found them to present an accurate encapsulation of his clerkship practices and philosophy. Because Thompson was a sitting judge of a California court of appeal and otherwise within the scope of our survey, represented an important minority view among his colleagues regarding proper clerkship usage, and would certainly have consented to an interview of this sort independently of his participation in the underlying study, we decided that our study would be more representative with his interview included than excluded. It should be noted that during the pendency of the interviews, the authors were rarely in contact. At the time he was interviewed, Thompson had seen none of the results of the previous interviews, and had discussed the progress of the interviewing schedule in only the most general terms.

4.21. *See* note 5.101 *infra*.

Table of Judges Solicited, Respondents, and Subjects

	Number of sitting judges 6/1/76[a]	Number of Respondents (% of sitting judges)	Number of Subjects (% of sitting judges)	Number of sitting judges 6/1/78[b]	Number of subjects still sitting 6/1/78[b]	Percent of subjects among sitting judges 6/1/78
Judges of Supreme Court of California	7	7 (100%)	5 (71%)	7	—[c]	—[c]
Judges of California courts of appeal	48	41 (85%)	38 (79%)	50	—[c]	—[c]
Subtotals: California state appellate judges	55	48 (87%)	43 (78%)	57	36	63%
Active federal circuit judges in California	7	7 (100%)	5 (71%)	6	5	83%
Active federal district judges in California	30	24 (80%)	12 (40%)	34	12	35%
Subtotals: active federal judges	37	31 (84%)	17 (46%)	40	17	43%
Senior federal circuit judges in California	4	4 (100%)	1 (25%)	5	1	20%
Senior district judges in California	9	5 (56%)	2[d] (22%)	9	1	11%
Subtotals: senior federal judges	13	9 (69%)	3 (23%)	14	2	14%
TOTALS	105	88 (84%)	63 (60%)	111	55	50%

[a] Per 525 F.2d; 15 Cal. 3d.
[b] Per 573 F.2d; 145 Cal. Rptr.
[c] Numbers withheld to preserve confidentiality.
[d] One more senior federal district judge consented to be interviewed but could not be interviewed on account of schedule conflicts.

C. *Interview Procedures and Results*

The interviewing process began on July 13, 1976, and continued intensively through August, 1976. Sporadic interviews were conducted thereafter with subjects whose schedules had prevented earlier contact. The final interview was conducted on October 26, 1976. All of the interviews were conducted in person at the judge's chambers, with the following exceptions: one judge was interviewed at his vacation home; two judges of the same court were interviewed jointly in one of their chambers; three judges were interviewed by telephone call to their chambers; one judge was unwilling to take time himself for an interview but authorized his law clerk to act as his proxy, and the law clerk was interviewed fully about the judge's law clerk usage. Because of the scope of the latter interview and the intent of the judge that the law clerk speak for him, we have counted the judge involved as one of our sixty-three subjects.[4.22]

We routinely asked permission to speak with the law clerks of the judges we had interviewed; in only one case was permission flatly denied. In many instances the clerk was unavailable for an interview at the conclusion of the interview with the judge, or our schedule otherwise precluded interviewing the clerk. Not counting the interview of the clerk who acted as spokesman for his judge, we interviewed the law clerks of twenty-seven of our subjects. Again not counting the spokesman clerk, we interviewed a total of thirty clerks, since twice we interviewed two clerks of a single judge, and once we interviewed the director of the central staff of one of the California courts of appeal. We also interviewed one federal magistrate whom we had encountered in the chambers of one of our subjects.

Author Thompson did not conduct any of the interviews, for fear that his judicial presence might color the responses obtained. Author Oakley conducted forty of the judge interviews, fourteen of the clerk interviews, and the one magistrate interview; the remaining twenty-three judge interviews and sixteen clerk interviews were conducted by Oakley's research assistant.[4.23]

4.22. *See* note 4.20 *supra*.

4.23. Marilyn Ruth McCloskey, A.B., 1972, Bryn Mawr College; M.A., 1974, McGill University; J.D., 1977, University of California, Davis. Ms. McCloskey's specialty as a graduate student was legal anthropology.

The interviewing process proved unexpectedly labor-intensive. The interviews themselves averaged over an hour in length per judge, and about half that per clerk, but by far the greatest amount of time was consumed in coordinating schedules, travelling to the many different courthouses, and dictating interview memoranda from handwritten interview notes.[4.24] Not counting the secretarial time required for the transcription of interview memoranda and the research time required to analyze the data, the mere accumulation and recordation of the data proved to be more than a full-time task for two people working for two months.

It has proven to be an even more demanding task to devise a satisfactory format for the presentation of our data. Our overriding concern must be to preserve the confidentiality of our sources, so that further research in this area is not jeopardized by our subjects coming to regret their participation in our study. We cannot candidly retreat behind a veil of statistics, however, because the intentionally loose structure of our interviews makes highly specific interpersonal comparisons impractical.

Our subjects do possess some "hard" characteristics, of course, such as age, political affiliation, and time as a judge; we also sought to derive retrospectively, on the basis of our interview notes, somewhat softer but nonetheless defensible value rankings for each judge with regard to what seemed, in the aftermath of the

4.24. We believed, in the fashion of some journalists, that our subjects would be most frank and candid if we abstained from any attempt at recording the interviews verbatim. While this method entails some cost to the accuracy of the record of the interview, it reduces the risk that the subject will suffer from having made a careless remark, and thereby encourages the subject to speak freely. The subject knows that even in the event of an accurate report of words which by breach of faith or confidence are attributed to him, he can simply deny having said what he later regrets. This interviewing technique acknowledges that words which are not mechanically recorded have a fragile kind of reality, especially in the mind of the speaker. If remarks attributed to the person prove embarrassing, and if there are no means of determining indisputably just what was said, human psychology and the ego of most public figures combine to allow the subject to deny the accuracy of the quotation with all the conviction of one who has convinced himself of what he wishes to convince others of: that he would never have said anything of the sort. Our subjects told us nothing that we think any would want to retract, even if their identities were revealed, but they did speak freely on what many clearly felt to be a sensitive subject; we doubt they would have been as candid had our "off-the-record" interviews nonetheless been captured on a tape recording.

interviews, to be crucial attitudes towards law clerks and their functions. When the data were thus put in quantitative form and manipulated by computer according to the statistical and cross-tabulation subprograms of the Statistical Package for the Social Sciences,[4.25] we found that the only significant correlations between and among judicial characteristics and attitudes toward law clerks were those which were apparent on the face of the interviews themselves. We were thus satisfied that nothing of egregious importance in accounting for law clerk practices was lurking latent in our interview memoranda. We were also convinced that converting the interview data to attitudes quantified after the fact threatened to convey the very illusions of precision which influenced our original choice of nonquantitative interview questions, and we therefore decided to pattern the presentation of our findings primarily on the structure of the interviews themselves, relegating our derived quantitative data to a secondary, corroboratory role.

Publication of the details of the interviews with individual judges, even in the absence of the names of the judges, would pose too great a risk of a breach of confidentiality. We have dealt with a relatively small group of strong-minded individualists whose views and styles of expression are well known to their colleagues and the appellate bar. Our solution, in the name of confidentiality but at some sacrifice in specificity, has been to construct profiles of hypothetical judges whose attitudes and characteristics are those which typify the aggregate of the judges of each of the courts we have studied.[4.26] Our findings are thus presented in the form of composite profiles setting forth the circumstances and opinions of a representative judge of each court, and contrasting the composites with significantly varying characteristics manifested by the composites' atypical colleagues. We preface each such profile with a sketch of the relevant court and its business,

---

4.25. *See generally* N. NIE, C. HULL, J. JENKINS, K. STEINBRENNER, & D. BENT, SPSS: STATISTICAL PACKAGE FOR THE SOCIAL SCIENCES 181–248 (2d ed. 1975). For assistance in understanding the SPSS program and its functions, see W. KLECKA, N. NIE, & C. HULL, SPSS PRIMER (1975). The subprograms we used for analyzing our data are described in *id.* at 60–81.

4.26. On the use of "constructed types" for the presentation of sociological data, see G. THEODORSON & A. THEODORSON, MODERN DICTIONARY OF SOCIOLOGY 74 (1969).

into which we incorporate pertinent facts learned in our interviews. We append a selected set of tables which we feel, when viewed with the caution appropriate to a quantitative presentation of our data, offer some comparative insights into the courts we studied, and offer some corroboration of the attitudes with which we have endowed our composite judges.

v. PROFILES OF COURTS AND COMPOSITE JUDGES

A. Courts of Appeal of California

1. Jurisdiction and Organization

Appeals from the superior court, California's trial court of general jurisdiction, lie initially in one of the courts of appeal.[5.1] Under the rather haphazard organization of these courts, there is one for each of five districts defined geographically by the counties within each district's jurisdiction.[5.2] Reflecting the gross disparity of the populations served by the five districts, the number of judges[5.3] statutorily authorized for each court ranges from the twenty judges of the Court of Appeal for the Second Appellate

---

5.1. CAL. CONST. art. VI, § 11.

5.2. CAL. GOV'T CODE § 69102 (West 1976). *See generally* CAL. COURTS OF APPEAL, *supra* note 1.7, at 25–29. *See also* Blume, *California Courts in Historical Perspective*, 22 HAST. L. REV. 121, 173–75 (1970).

5.3. Except for consistently referring to the "Chief Justice" of the supreme court and the "presiding justice" of each division of the courts of appeal, CAL. CONST. art. VI, §§ 2–3, the California Constitution is utterly inconsistent in its designation of the members of the supreme court and the courts of appeal sometimes as "justices" *e.g.*, CAL. CONST. art. VI, §§ 2–3, and sometimes as "judges," *e.g.*, *id.*, art. VI, §§ 6, 16. The myriad California statutes relating to courts and judicial officers are no more consistent. We will refer to the "Chief Justice," to a "presiding justice," and, except where the context seems to warrant otherwise, to the "judges" of both courts. This follows, as nearly as we can determine from our personal experience, the conventional forms of address used in California. Outside of oral argument and formal written documents, members of the supreme court and the courts of appeal commonly refer to themselves, and are commonly addressed by others, as "Judge" Doe, Roe, or whatever.

District in Los Angeles[5.4] and the sixteen judges of the Court of Appeal for the First Appellate District in San Francisco[5.5] to the seven judges of the Court of Appeal for the Third Appellate District in Sacramento[5.6] and the four judges of the Court of Appeal for the Fifth Appellate District in Fresno.[5.7] The Court of Appeal for the Fourth Appellate District is further segmented into two divisions of four and five judges each, which sit in San Diego and San Bernardino, respectively.[5.8] The First and Second Districts are organized into geographically indistinct divisions of four judges each.[5.9]

Only the Court of Appeal for the Second Appellate District has generally operated in recent years with the full number of its authorized judges.[5.10] Apparently as a matter of gubernatorial policy,[5.11] some of the judgeships authorized by statute for the other courts of appeal have either been left vacant or filled only after prolonged delays.[5.12] These vacant positions are filled on an ad

5.4. CAL. GOV'T CODE § 69102 (West 1976).

5.5. *Id.*, § 69101.   5.6. *Id.*, § 69103.   5.7. *Id.*, § 69105.

5.8. *Id.*, § 69104.   5.9. *Id.*, §§ 69101–02.

5.10. Data on the dates of deaths or retirements of court of appeals judges and the dates of the appointments of new judges appear in the frontispieces of *California Reports 3d* and, on a somewhat more haphazard but more quickly available basis, in the frontispieces of *California Reporter*. As ascertained by comparison of the rosters of judges and annotations regarding dates of vacancies and appointments, vacancies on the Court of Appeal for the Second Appellate District have generally been filled by the current Governor within six or seven months.

5.11. *See* Blubaugh, *Brown's court legacy—a new breed on the bench*, 7 CAL. J. 52 (1976).

5.12. Although vacancies created by the death or retirement of sitting judges of the Court of Appeal for the First Appellate District have been filled by the current Governor at about the same pace as similar vacancies in the Second District, the first of the four additional First District judgeships created by statute in 1975, *see* CAL. GOV'T CODE § 69101 (West 1976), was not filled until June 12, 1978, *see* 145 Cal. Rptr. VI n.1 (1978). As of April, 1979, the other three divisions of the First District were still operating with only three rather than the four authorized justices per division. *See* 150 Cal. Rptr. VI (1979). Since 1975, the Court of Appeal for the Third Appellate District has had seven authorized judgeships, *see* CAL. GOV'T CODE § 69103 (West 1976), but the seventh judge was not appointed until June 16, 1976, *see* 17 Cal. 3d vi n. 1 (1977), and a Third District vacancy created by a retirement in May of 1978 remained unfilled as of April, 1979. Although a vacancy in Division Two of the Court of Appeal for the Fourth Appellate District was filled seven months later on July 1, 1976, *see* 17 Cal. 3d vi n.2 (1977), the vacancies filled in Division One of that district on November 17, 1976, *see* 18 Cal. 3d vi n.* (1977), and May 26, 1978, *see* 145 Cal. Rptr. VIII n.2 (1978), had re-

hoc basis by pro tem judges appointed by the Chief Justice of California.[5.13] Each of the various divisions within districts has its

---

mained unfilled for twenty-one months and fourteen months, respectively. The fourth authorized judgeship for the Court of Appeal for the Fifth Appellate District was created in 1975, see CAL. GOV'T CODE § 69105 (West 1976), but was not filled until December 28, 1976, see 18 Cal. 3d vii n.* (1977), and a vacancy created by retirement at the end of 1977, see 20 Cal. 3d viii n.1 (1978), remained unfilled as of April, 1979.

Had all authorized vacancies been filled on June 1, 1976, there would have been fifty-six sitting judges of the California courts of appeal. See CAL. GOV'T CODE §§ 69101–05 (West 1976). No new court of appeal judgeships have been created since 1975.

5.13. CAL. CONST. art. VI, § 6. As revised to its current text in 1974, the California Constitution vests the assignment power directly in the "Chief Justice." The California Constitution had previously specified that the Chief Justice was the "chairman" of the Judicial Council, and it had vested the assignment power in the Chief Justice qua chairman of the Judicial Council. CAL. CONST. art. VI, § 6 (1966, amended 1974). The 1974 amendments merely inserted gender-neutral terminology into the California Constitution without substantive change, at least as to article VI, section 6. Somewhat anomalously, the current Chief Justice and her advisers on the Judicial Council's staff are apparently unaware of this change, which preceded her appointment by three years. The official text of reported decisions routinely refers to temporary judicial personnel as having been assigned "by the Chairperson of the Judicial Council," e.g., Schmier v. Board of Trustees, 74 Cal. App. 3d 314, 316, 141 Cal. Rptr. 472 (1977), and the same error occurs in the Judicial Council's annual reports, e.g., 1978 JUDICIAL COUNCIL OF CALIFORNIA REPORT 70: "The Courts of Appeal, as in past years, received substantial assistance from retired judges and superior court judges sitting on assignment by the Chairperson of the Judicial Council." It is, of course, necessary that there be a "Chair" or "Chairperson" of the Judicial Council, not only for administrative convenience but also because the 1974 constitutional amendments did not wipe California's legislative slate clean of gender-based terminology. Many statutory provisions continue to vest substantial powers in the "chairman of the Judicial Council," e.g., CAL. GOV'T CODE §§ 68115–17 (West 1976) (extraordinary powers in judicial emergency); CAL. GOV'T CODE § 68509 (West 1976) (call meetings of Judicial Council), and at least one statute passed after the 1974 constitutional amendment nonetheless referred to judges sitting under assignment by California's constitutional nonperson, "the Chairman of the Judicial Council." CAL. GOV'T CODE § 68541 (West 1976). Presumably, the "Chairman" or "Chairperson" of the Judicial Council is now decided by vote or rule of the Council, which by tradition and common sense should have the Chief Justice as its presiding officer, since article VI, section 6, in creating the Council, gives the Chief Justice the power of appointment over fourteen of the twenty members of the Council other than herself.

We recommend that henceforth temporary assignments of judges be made by the Chief Justice qua Chief Justice, and that the statutory powers now vested in the

own presiding justice;[5.14] all court of appeal judges operate exclusively and autonomously within the divisions to which they
were appointed, unless there is an ad hoc reassignment by the
Chief Justice.[5.15] Every case in the California courts of appeal is
heard by a panel of three judges; and the division system means
that in districts with divisions, the composition of the panel is
largely determined by the initial assignment of a case to a particular division.[5.16]

2. Workload

Appeal to the intermediate court is a matter of right.[5.17] A
provision of the California Constitution requires that a court of
appeal issue a written opinion stating the reasons for its decision in

---

anachronistic office of "Chairman of the Judicial Council" be transferred, in the
spirit of the California Constitution, simply to the Chief Justice. We do not mean
to suggest, of course, that the powers of the present Chief Justice are in any sense
diminished by being exercised under the wrong name. Certainly, this is a context
in which Shakespeare's famous couplet has legal as well as literary force: "What's in
a name? That which we call a rose. . . ." W. SHAKESPEARE, ROMEO AND JULIET, act
2, sc. 2, line 120.

5.14. CAL. CONST. art. VI, § 3.

5.15. In courts of appeal having more than one division, the Chief Justice has
been authorized to designate one division's presiding justice as the "Administrative Presiding Justice" of that district's entire court of appeal. See CAL. R. COURT
75–76. Nonetheless, the powers of the administrative presiding justice are quite
limited, and each division "operates as a legally autonomous unit. . . . Consequently, there are 13 different Court of Appeal operations in California. Attorneys, court clerks, reporters, research attorneys and others who come in contact
with these Courts are required to orient themselves and their own procedures
accordingly." CAL. COURTS OF APPEAL, supra note 1.7, at 196–97.

5.16. See CAL. CONST. art VI, § 3. The assignment of cases filed in courts of
appeal with more than one division is regulated by CAL. R. COURT 47, which
provides for equal distribution of the business of a court of appeal among its divisions, with responsibility for assignments rotated for one year at a time among the
presiding justices unless a majority of the court's judges decide otherwise. To this
extent, Rule 47 qualifies the courtwide powers of the administrative presiding
justice. See CAL. R. COURT 76(2); note 132 supra. See also CAL. COURTS OF APPEAL,
supra note 1.7, at 202–04 (attorneys orient arguments to the membership of the
division to which the case is assigned and believe that divisional assignments can
affect the outcome of cases).

5.17. See generally CAL. CODE CIV. PROC. § 904.1 (Deering's 1973); CAL. PEN.
CODE §§ 1235, 1237, 1237.5 (Deering's 1971). The general right to appeal is the
result of a comprehensive scheme of statutory rights to appeal, and is not guaran-
teed by the California Constitution. See CAL. COURTS OF APPEAL, supra note 1.7, at
29.

all cases appealed to it.[5.18] Original proceedings in the court, such as petitions for mandate, prohibition, or habeas corpus, may be denied summarily; once a hearing of such a petition is allowed, however, the court must issue a written opinion with specifications of reasons for its disposition of the petition.[5.19]

In the fiscal year 1976–77, the courts of appeal filed 5,626 written opinions in cases appealed to them.[5.20] They acted upon 4,140 petitions calling upon their original jurisdiction,[5.21] of which 377 (9.1 percent) resulted in written opinions.[5.22] The total business of the courts was well over twice that of ten years earlier,[5.23] during which period the authorized number of judges increased by only 44 percent.[5.24] Despite much greater productivity per judge-

5.18. CAL. CONST. art. VI, § 14, provides in pertinent part: "Decisions of the Supreme Court and courts of appeal that determine causes shall be in writing with reasons stated."

5.19. The relationship of procedures for considering petitions for original writs in California appellate courts and the California Constitution's requirement of written opinions, see note 5.18 supra, has been succinctly summarized in CAL. COURTS OF APPEAL, supra note 1.7, at 138 (footnote omitted):

> Writs are assigned immediately to a division and requests for emergency relief are given prompt attention. A petition may be denied without further briefing or argument. Writs are not considered to be within the definition of "causes"; therefore, the constitutional mandate requiring a written opinion is inapplicable to summary denials.
>
> When the Court decides that the petition may have merit, an alternative writ or an order to show cause is issued requiring respondent to file a "return." The case is then normally scheduled for oral argument and a written opinion prepared either discharging the alternative writ or issuing the peremptory writ. A peremptory writ may issue without oral argument if the parties have been given due notice, the remedy is clear, and the usual procedure would only cause delay.

5.20. 1978 JUDICIAL COUNCIL OF CALIFORNIA REPORT 70.

5.21. Derived from id., at 71, Table VIII.

5.22. Id. at 70.

5.23. The "total business transacted" by the courts of appeal, a figure including all dispositions of appeals, petitions for original writs, motions, and miscellaneous matters, rose from 10, 293 in the year ending June 30, 1967, to 22,223 for the year ending June 30, 1977. Id. at 71, Table VIII.

5.24. The authorized membership of the courts of appeal totalled thirty-nine on June 30, 1967. See Historical Note[s], following CAL. GOV'T CODE §§ 69101–105 (West 1976). As of June 30, 1977, the authorized membership was fifty-six judges, see text accompanying notes 5.4–5.8 supra, but six positions had been intentionally left unfilled by the current Governor, see notes 5.11–5.12 supra. Since all authorized positions were filled as a matter of course in 1967, see, e.g., 65 Cal.2d iv–vii (1967), the effective increase in full-time membership of the courts of appeal over the ten-year period was only 28 percent, from thirty-nine to fifty judges.

position than ten years earlier,[5.25] the courts' backlog of pending appeals increased by 13.6 percent in the 1976–77 fiscal year.[5.26] The year's filings amounted to more than 390 appeals and 220 petitions for original writs for every three judges of the court of appeal, a total of 610 matters to be considered per judge.[5.27]

3. Staff and Internal Procedures

In California, approximately two-thirds of contested felony convictions are appealed.[5.28] In most of these cases, the relevant

5.25. Dividing the "total business transacted" figures for fiscal 1967 and fiscal 1977, see note 5.23 supra, by the authorized numbers of judges for those years—thirty-nine in fiscal 1967 and fifty-six in fiscal 1977, see note 5.24 supra—yields figures of total business transacted per judge-position for fiscal 1967 of 263.9, and for fiscal 1977 of 396.8. Thus, even assuming all the unfilled judge-positions of fiscal 1977 were staffed by temporarily assigned judges, see text accompanying note 5.13 supra; 1978 JUDICIAL COUNCIL OF CALIFORNIA REPORT 70, 72, Table IX ("full-time judge equivalents" of courts of appeal for fiscal 1977 equalled 55.9 judges), the productivity of courts of appeal per judge-position increased 50.4 percent over the ten-year period.

5.26. 1978 JUDICIAL COUNCIL OF CALIFORNIA REPORT 70.

5.27. These figures were derived by dividing the total numbers of appeals filed and petitions filed in fiscal 1977, see id. at 65, Table VI, by 56 (the number of authorized judge-positions for fiscal 1977, see notes 5.25–5.26 supra) and multiplying the resulting quotient by 3, to approximate the workload facing any given judge over the course of the year. Since "a court of appeal . . . shall conduct itself as a 3-judge-court," CAL. CONST., art. VI, § 3, the number of filings per judge must be tripled to reflect the real workload that results if each filing is in fact reviewed by three judges prior to disposition. Cf. ADMINISTRATIVE OFFICE OF THE UNITED STATES COURTS, 1978 ANNUAL REPORT OF THE DIRECTOR 45 (endorsing multiplication by three of per judgeship filings in United States courts of appeals "to reflect a more realistic measure of the workload borne by individual judges") [hereinafter cited as 1978 AOC REPORT]. A similar figure for the Ninth Circuit appears at note 5.106 and accompanying text infra.

One unfortunate result of the crushing workload of the California courts of appeal may be that some dispositions are not in fact reviewed by three judges in any meaningful sense, and are announced by what amount to "one–judge" or "no–judge" opinions. "One–judge" opinions have been carefully considered only by the judges assigned to write them; "no–judge" opinions are the product of law clerks alone, with no substantive supervision from the responsible judges. These labels are, of course, wholly unofficial; no opinion admits on its face to such suspect parentage. See Thompson, supra note 1.11, at 478, 480, 515. See also note 5.53 infra. For additional insight into the effect such an overwhelming workload has on the morale of the judges of the California courts of appeal and on the psychology of their decision-making, see Wold, supra note 2.72, at 61–65 (summarizing interviews with forty-one California court of appeal judges).

5.28. In fiscal 1977, there were 6,133 "superior court contested dispositions"

law is settled by the precedent of a higher court and the relevant facts have been determined conclusively by the court below. For the courts of appeal, then, such cases are ripe for routine disposition. This climate has proved conducive to development—with considerable local variation—of a central staff for each of the courts.[5.29]

Our research shows that the principal function of these central staffs is the "screening" of appeals, that is, the sifting through of fully briefed cases in advance of oral argument to see if any are appropriate for some form of routine disposition. All criminal appeals are initially routed to a central staff attorney for review and analysis. In some districts, civil appeals are also screened.[5.30]

---

in criminal cases, and 4,040 appeals filed in these cases. The Administrative Office of the California Courts derives an appeal rate of 65.9 percent from these figures, with the qualification that "this does not necessarily reflect the precise percentage of appealable dispositions actually appealed. For example, 'superior court contested dispositions' include nonappealable acquittals and excludes [sic] convictions on pleas of guilty, a few of which are appealable." Nonetheless, the Judicial Council believes the figures "show the general relationship between appellate workload and superior court dispositions." 1978 JUDICIAL COUNCIL OF CALIFORNIA REPORT 67, Table VII & n.**. By statute, the superior court has exclusive jurisdiction over felonies, see CAL. PEN. CODE § 1462 (Deering's 1971), and it has been held that the superior court has "pendent" jurisdiction over misdemeanor counts joined to felony counts, see People v. Clark, 17 Cal. App. 3d 890, 895–98, 95 Cal. Rptr. 411, 414–16 (1971). See generally B. WITKIN, CALIFORNIA CRIMINAL PROCEDURE § 31, at 59–60 (Supp. 1978). Thus all "superior court contested dispositions" in criminal cases arise out of what were, at least initially, felony charges. By contrast to the 65.9 percent rate of appeal of contested criminal cases in superior court, only 13.9 percent of contested civil cases in superior court are appealed. 1978 JUDICIAL COUNCIL OF CALIFORNIA REPORT 67, Table VII. Of all criminal cases appealed to the courts of appeal, 81.6 percent are affirmed in full and another 10.8 percent are affirmed with modifications. Id. at 72, Table X-A. (Parallel data regarding disposition on appeal of civil cases are not currently published by the Administrative Office of the California Courts, which compiles the judicial statistics appearing in the annual reports of the Judicial Council of California.)

5.29. See Christian, supra note 1.12, at 58; Christian, Delay in Criminal Appeals: A Functional Analysis of One Court's Work, 23 STAN. L. REV. 676, 700–02 (1971).

5.30. See generally CAL. COURTS OF APPEAL, supra note 7, at 93–107 (descriptions of central staffs in each district); D. MEADOR, supra note 1.7, at 11–12. See also id. at 209–16 (detailed description of central staff at California Court of Appeal for the First Appellate District); Lesinski & Stockmeyer, supra note 1.12, at 1233 (detailed description of central staff at California Court of Appeal for the Third Appellate District). For a rather loosely edited collection of comments on decision-making practices at the California Court of Appeal for the First Appellate

If the screening staff attorney decides that an appeal is routine and subject to only one reasonable result, a memorandum or oral report explicating that fact is given to the panel of judges charged with deciding the case. If the judges agree with the staff report, the case is usually decided by a very brief per curiam opinion.[5.31] If not, the case is withdrawn from the routine disposition track and treated as a case requiring full-blown treatment by the court.

The central staff is supervised by a principal attorney who, in turn, is accountable to the court's presiding justice or, if there is more than one division to the court, to a presiding justice of one of the divisions who is designated the district's "Administrative Presiding Justice" by the Chief Justice of California.[5.32] In the 1976–

District, with particular reference to that district's use of central staff, see Summary of Comments Received by the Chief Justice's Special Committee to Study the Appellate Practices and Procedures in the First Appellate District, at 144–82 (Aug. 21, 1978) (Supreme Court of California) [hereinafter cited as First District Report].

5.31. "The draft per curiam opinion is usually from one to three pages in length. It indicates very briefly the nature of the case, the issues presented, and the reasons for deciding them as the Court does, including a few citations of authority." D. MEADOR, supra note 1.7, at 211 (describing procedures at California Court of Appeal for the First Appellate District).

Generally, the procedure allows any of the three judges who are asked to adopt a proposed per curiam opinion drafted by the central staff, to request that the case be taken off the routine disposition track and be assigned to a single judge for conventional prehearing review. However, once summary treatment has been deemed justified by the principal attorney and the presiding justice (who generally reviews such opinions first), a second or third judge who has reservations about summary disposition will feel considerable pressure to provide specific and articulable reasons for causing the staff work to go for naught. See generally Wold, supra note 2.72, at 62. The traditional role of a law clerk is to help a judge work from vague intuitions born of experience to reasoned opinions bred from the law, and such assistance might well be determinative of whether a judge, bothered by his or her colleagues' proposed summary treatment of an appeal, will feel justified in dissenting from such treatment. Yet, not one of the court of appeal judges we interviewed could afford to use his single law clerk for consultation over proposed per curiam opinions, despite the widely shared sentiment that this would be an appropriate function for a law clerk were a second elbow clerk provided to each court of appeal judge. See text accompanying note 5.56 infra.

5.32. See 1970 JUDICIAL COUNCIL OF CALIFORNIA REPORT 25–26. See also note 5.15 supra; Gustafson, Some Observations About California Courts of Appeal, 19 U.C.L.A. L. REV. 167, 188 (1971). At the Court of Appeal for the Fourth Appellate District (whose divisions are geographically separate, see text accompanying note 5.8 supra), no administrative presiding justice has been appointed. In one

77 year, 1,792 of the courts' written opinions, about thirty-two percent, were in the per curiam form, a good approximation of the cases disposed of by central staff treatment.[5.33]

In addition to appeals, petitions for original writs are universally routed to a staff attorney for review and recommendation.[5.34] Since no opinion is demanded of the court when a petition is summarily denied,[5.35] oral reports by staff attorneys are more common regarding petitions than appeals. Typically, staff recommendations of denial are reported to the presiding justice of the responsible division; if the presiding justice concurs in the recommendation of denial, the concurrence of two other judges follows almost pro forma.[5.36] Where the staff attorney finds possible merit in a petition, a memorandum is generally prepared. Once a hearing on a petition is ordered, by issuance of an alternative writ or order to show cause, the petition becomes a docketed case to be argued orally and decided by written opinion. Unless the central staff has performed extensive work on the petition prior to the granting of a hearing, further research and writing are generally referred to the personal staff of the judge to whom the case has been assigned.

The California courts of appeal uniformly adopt the "hot bench" approach to oral argument.[5.37] Sitting in panels of three judges, the courts hear counsel while armed with a calendar mem-

---

division of that court, the central staff is run by a principal attorney, who reports to that division's presiding justice. In the other division, the presiding justice personally supervises the central staff without a principal attorney or a personal law clerk.

5.33. See 1978 JUDICIAL COUNCIL OF CALIFORNIA REPORT 72, Table X. See also Wold, supra note 2.72, at 62.

5.34. There is considerable variation among the courts of appeal as to the status and supervision of "writ clerks" vis-à-vis the judges and the rest of the central staff.

5.35. See note 5.19 supra.

5.36. Since the denial of such petitions not only need not be explained by opinion but also is generally thought to be largely discretionary, with the possible exception of rare cases of habeas corpus, see 5 B. WITKIN, CALIFORNIA PROCEDURE, Extraordinary Writs §§ 123–25, at 3899–3903 (2d ed. 1971); B. WITKIN, CALIFORNIA CRIMINAL PROCEDURE §§ 795–97, at 767–770 (1963), the pressure on judges to uncritically accept staff recommendations of denial of petitions for original writs is even greater than the pressure on them to acquiesce in staff recommendations that appeals be disposed of summarily by per curiam opinions, see note 5.31 supra.

5.37. See Thompson, supra note 1.11, at 478. See also Baier, supra note 1.7, at 1159 n.724, 1160 n.127; Hufstedler, supra note 2.67, at 23.

orandum which fully discusses the case and with a varying degree of individual judge precalendar preparation beyond the memorandum. In each case one of the three judges will have been assigned the responsibility for the "calendar memorandum" in that case. If the case has been selected for routine treatment, the judge's responsibility is limited to reviewing the calendar memorandum prepared by the central staff. Otherwise the judge is responsible for personally preparing the calendar memorandum, with the assistance of his law clerk.

About one-half of the calendar memoranda in criminal cases are the product of the central staff. In some divisions an oral report sometimes substitutes for a written memorandum.

The personal staff of the judges is used principally in the preparation of calendar memoranda in civil cases and the harder criminal cases. Each judge is allotted a single personal law clerk;[5.38] about two-thirds of the judges have filled this position with a

5.38. At the instigation of the Chief Justice, the Judicial Council of California asked for and received an additional appropriation for fiscal 1979 to initiate a "two-year pilot project to add Graduate Legal Assistants who will be assigned to individual justices in lieu of additional central staff attorneys." 1978–79 CALIFORNIA GOVERNOR'S BUDGET 8. Six such positions were funded for fiscal 1979. *Id.* at 8, line 37; at 11, lines 54–55. "Graduate Legal Assistant" is California's fiscal jargon for a newly graduated law clerk. *See* note 5.41 *infra*.

We have been informed by a spokesman for the Chief Justice that the project is intended to test the cost-effectiveness of giving court of appeals judges a second short-term law clerk. The inauguration of the project was delayed until October 1, 1978, so that the appropriation of twelve months' salary for six law clerks could cover nine months' salary for eight law clerks, with the intention of seeking an additional year's funding for eight positions in the fiscal 1980 budget. The eight additional law clerks were assigned to Division Three of the First District and Division Five of the Second District, each division having four judges, and each judge receiving one additional clerk. Interview with Stephen T. Buehl, Executive Assistant to the Chief Justice, Supreme Court of California, in San Francisco, November 30, 1978 [hereinafter cited as Buehl Interview].

5.39. This figure was somewhat lower than we had anticipated. Indeed, out of our thirty-eight subjects, some sixteen (42.1 percent) had short-term law clerks. However, information obtained collaterally as to the clerkship practices of the ten court of appeal judges who chose not to participate in our study establishes that nine out of those judges had career clerks, so that the overall proportion of judges using short-term clerks on the courts of appeal as of June 1, 1976, was seventeen out of forty-eight (35.4 percent). (These figures treat judges who use career staff attorneys for in-chambers research and writing assignments, and who have no personal law clerk of their own, as using long-term clerks. Seven of the forty-eight judges fall in this category: the six then sitting on the Court of Appeal for the Third

permanent employee.[5.39] Roughly two-thirds of the judges make some use of externs.[5.40]

Annual salaries of law clerks and staff attorneys ranged in 1978–79 from $17,000 to nearly $44,000, depending on the person's legal experience before joining the court and his or her years of service at the court.[5.41] Increases in pay officially tied to merit

Appellate District, *see* Lesinski & Stockmeyer, *supra* note 1.12, at 1233, and the presiding justice of one of the divisions of the Court of Appeal for the Fourth Appellate District, *see* note 5.32 *supra*.)

Although there remained more short-term law clerks at the courts of appeal than we had expected, nothing in our data contradicts our impression, since confirmed by others, *see* notes 2.76 & 2.87 *supra*, that there is a pronounced trend towards career elbow clerks at the California courts of appeal. The judges of the courts of appeal were equally divided in their personal preferences for long-term or short-term elbow clerks as a matter of sound judicial policy, aside from budgetary and caseload constraints. *See* Appendix, Table A. Nonetheless, some of the judges favoring short-term clerks had acquiesced in staff arrangements which forced career clerks upon them, as in the Third District, and others had reluctantly shifted in recent years to the use of a long-term clerk on account of increasing caseload pressures. None of the judges we interviewed had changed the tenure of his law clerk in the opposite way, from a career clerk to a short-term clerk. *But see* note 5.38 *supra*.

5.40. *See* Appendix, Table C.

5.41. The salary of the highest-paid law clerk in the state, the Principal Attorney of the Supreme Court of California, has traditionally been held just below that of a judge of the municipal court. In fiscal 1979, the annual salary of a municipal court judge was $47,497, *see* CAL. GOV'T CODE §§ 68202–03 (West 1976). The supreme court's principal attorney had a fiscal 1979 salary of $46,044 ("Principal Attorney III"). The principal attorneys of the courts of appeal received up to $43,884 per year ("Principal Attorney II"). The ten most senior law clerks at the supreme court, other than the principal attorney, received up to $41,844 per year ("Senior Attorney IV"); the thirty-three most senior law clerks at the courts of appeal, other than the principal attorneys, received up to $36,972 per year ("Senior Attorney III"). Newly graduated law clerks at both the Supreme Court and the courts of appeal started at $1,323 per month ($15,876 per year) as "graduate legal assistants," rising to $1,450 per month ($17,400 per year) as "research attorneys" after they were admitted to the bar, typically at the end of their first three months of clerking. *See* 1978–79 CALIFORNIA GOVERNOR'S BUDGET, SALARIES AND WAGES SUPPLEMENT 2–3. By way of comparison, judges of the courts of appeal received 1978–79 salaries of $59,002; judges of the supreme court received $62,935; and the Chief Justice received $66,869. *Id.* at 2. Staff attorneys and elbow clerks are paid according to the same schedule of experience and seniority, which is issued by the California Administrative Office of the Courts, an adjunct of the Judicial Council of California; this schedule roughly tracks the job classifications and salary schedules of the attorneys in the California Department of Justice. For the text of the classification applicable to the most senior law clerks, *see* Thompson, *supra* note

are in practice awarded as a function of seniority. Roughly half of the staff attorneys and career law clerks at the courts of appeal are women; the proportion of women among short-term clerks and externs is lower, and appears to approximate the proportion of women in law school graduating classes.[5.42]

4. Composite Profile: Judge Alpha

The thirty-eight judges of the California courts of appeal whom we interviewed were drawn from all districts and every division.[5.43] They included presiding justices of divisions and administrative presiding justices of multi-division districts. Both a general composite and disparate exceptions emerge from the interviews.

For the sake of convenience, we will refer to our composite judge as "Judge Alpha." He has been on the bench for close to ten years, most of the time on the court of appeal and the rest on a trial court. Prior to becoming a judge, he had practiced law for fifteen to twenty years, either in private practice or as a prosecuting attorney. He finds the relative routine of judicial work to be a welcome relief from the stressful life of a trial attorney.

As a law student, Judge Alpha was not aware that law clerkships existed except at the United States Supreme Court.[5.44] He now believes that a clerkship is a valuable experience and wishes that one had been available to him. He believes equally that supporting staff are invaluable and that, given its present caseload, the court could not operate without them. Alpha accepts the existence and use of central staff with reservations. He would prefer

---

1.11, at 514 n.26. For fiscal 1980 California state salaries were increased by an average of 14.5 percent. *See generally* Salzman, *Why Brown Jumped into the Budget Inferno*, 10 CAL. J. 289, 290 (1979).

5.42. As of 1977, women constituted 27 percent of total law school student enrollment. ASSOCIATION OF AMERICAN LAW SCHOOLS & LAW SCHOOL ADMISSION COUNCIL, 1978–79 PRE-LAW HANDBOOK 12 (1978).

5.43. We also interviewed nineteen law clerks at the courts of appeal.

5.44. Those judges who had been aware of clerkships at lower courts had tended to regard them, then, as of too little prestige to be worth pursuing. A few judges had been aware, as graduating law students, of clerkships at the California Supreme Court. The judges' lack of knowledge of clerkship opportunities when they graduated from law school may be attributable to the fact that very few would have qualified academically for serious clerkship consideration, since law review membership is the traditional threshold qualification for a clerkship. *See* Appendix, Table K.

the alternative of an additional personal clerk. Atypical judges believe in the central staff concept without reservation or, at the opposite extreme, resist its use.

Judge Alpha employs a career law clerk. Although he believes that such a law clerk is, on balance, advantageous to him, his selection of a career law clerk resulted more from drift than from conscious decision. The judge originally had short-term law clerks, as was the custom when he joined the court. One of his clerks stayed over for several years, however, and eventually settled into a career at the court. The judge has some rather vague misgivings about the role of permanent law clerks in the best of all possible judicial worlds, but he is aware that his judicial world puts a premium on productivity. For him, as for most judges of intermediate appellate state courts, the day of the handcrafted opinion is over. He must strive not for perfection but for the best quality obtainable without halting the assembly line of appellate justice.[5.45] The less time he must spend seeking out and training new law clerks, the more time he has to exercise control over the quality of the work product of his chambers and of the central staff.

One factor which influenced Alpha to give up short-term clerks, and which many of those judges retaining short-term clerks also remarked upon, is the comparative difficulty of inducing the very best recent law graduates to clerk for the courts of appeal.[5.46] In the past, Judge Alpha had rarely secured his top clerkship candidate, who if given the choice would opt for a position with another court. Although this had always been true with regard to competing offers from manifestly more prestigious courts, such as the California Supreme Court or the Ninth Circuit, a recent development was the increased appeal of federal district court clerkships. Judge Alpha tends to agree that clerkships at his court are less exciting than clerkships elsewhere, and the risk that a short-term clerk would be disappointed has influenced his decision to retain his present clerk indefinitely.

A declining minority of court of appeal judges continue to use

5.45. *Accord*, Wold, *supra* note 2.72, at 62. *See also* Gustafson, *supra* note 5.32, at 202–03.

5.46. It is noteworthy in this regard that the district with the largest concentration of short-term clerks was the Court of Appeal for the First Appellate District, which sits in the especially attractive clerkship venue of San Francisco.

short-term "rotating" clerks whom they replace every one or two years. These judges include four of the five court of appeal judges who themselves served as law clerks, but the minority judges do not display dramatically different attitudes toward the demands of their job or the function of clerks than does Judge Alpha. They are somewhat quicker studies than Alpha (at least in Alpha's opinion) and do not find personnel decisions to be particularly difficult or painful. Were they to find competent short-term clerks difficult to procure, or were they to find, to their surprise, that some of their successful clerks actually would consider the stultifying (in the judges' opinion) work of a career clerk, they might well retain permanent clerks too. They recognize the burden of training new clerks, but consider it the price they must pay for clerks of the intellectual acumen they demand. Were they allowed two clerks, they would either have the clerks serve staggered two-year terms, so that one experienced clerk would also be available to help train the neophyte, or they would hire one clerk annually and retain the other indefinitely. The latter option is the one that Judge Alpha himself would exercise were he given two law clerk positions, which he thinks is the optimal number for his court.[5.47]

There is thus substantial agreement among the judges of the courts of appeal, regardless of their personal clerkship practices, on the pros and cons of career clerks and rotating clerks. Career clerks are known quantities whose strengths can be exploited and whose weaknesses are apparent enough to be avoided. They offer the advantages of practical experience, maturity, knowledge of their employers' personal styles of judging, and a dedication to their judges born of the identity of interests between the professional standing of their judges and their own success in their careers. In exceptional cases, career clerks are superior clerks by any standards, combining the above assets with a keen and aggressive intellect. Some career clerks are more aware than are their judges of the dangers of bureaucratized judging, and take it upon themselves to replicate the vigor and fractiousness of short-term clerks notwithstanding their long-term status. But on the whole, career clerks are more passive and unassertive than short-term clerks, and they present dangers of undue deference, boredom, and stale routine which may depreciate the overall quality of their judges' work.

5.47. *See* Appendix, Table B.

Short-term clerks are generally of a higher intellectual capacity and more aggressively pursue their ideals and their ambitions; for this reason, almost all the judges identify more closely with them than with the permanent staff. In addition, the fresh approach to recurrent problems which a new law school graduate will bring to the court is a significant asset.

The clerkship tenure choices of individual judges do not reflect differing perceptions of the distinctive qualities of rotating and career clerks so much as the differing weights particular judges assign to the acknowledged characteristics of short-term and permanent law clerks and to the bother of repetitive hiring and training of short-term clerks. For Judge Alpha there is some regret but little doubt as to which way the balance tips.

Whatever their differences in tenure and personality, the law clerks to judges of the courts of appeal are required to possess essentially similar legal skills. Most important are meticulousness and analytical ability; desirable but less important are excellent grammar and a concise and lucid writing style. Felicitous phrasemaking and a talent for persuasive argument count for little in an intermediate court whose opinions are generally not published.[5.48] Judge Alpha believes that his law clerk's effective communication with him, not with posterity, is the measure of the clerk's success in analyzing a case. The clerk's first task is to make sure the judge understands any complications in the case.

Aside from occasional special assignments requiring factual analysis of a lengthy lower-court record, or research and explication of particularly difficult points of law, Judge Alpha uses his clerk principally to review cases set for the next calendar of oral arguments before the court.[5.49] Other than the demand that clerks prepare these calendar memoranda with considerably more care than the general run of counsel who file briefs before the court,[5.50] however, there is little consensus on the style or contents of calendar memoranda. There are polar extremes and many intermediate variations in the contents of the calendar memoranda produced for particular judges.

The most important variables are the amount of instruction that accompanies an assignment of a case to a clerk for preparation

5.48. *Accord*, Wold, *supra* note 2.72, at 63.
5.49. *See* Appendix, Table F.
5.50. *See* Gustafson, *supra* note 5.32, at 202.

of a calendar memorandum,[5.51] and the degree to which the calendar memorandum is intended to anticipate the form and content of the opinion of the court.[5.52] At one extreme of the spectrum of instruction, the judge reviews the briefs in each of the four or five cases assigned to his chambers (rather than to central staff) for precalendar preparation. He instructs his clerk to compose a memorandum reaching a particular conclusion or addressing designated issues. These judges tend to brook argument only as to technical points of law. At the other pole, there are judges who assign some proportion of their precalendar case load to their clerks without any guidance at all and expect their clerks to prepare draft opinions setting forth both the result to be reached in a case and the language by which that result is to be announced. These judges generally treat the clerk's draft as setting the stage, in event of disagreement by the judge, for vigorous argument between judge and clerk.

It is interesting that there is only a partial correlation between judicial control over the calendar memorandum and judicial preferences for law clerk tenure. Some judges who encourage assertiveness in their law clerks by giving them free rein in the preparation of calendar memoranda are convinced that long-term clerks are more assertive than short-term law clerks; these judges feel that the experience and maturity of long-term law clerks may put them on a more equal footing in arguments with their judges, and make them less likely to be cowed when their employers make erroneous arguments. Judges who retain short-term law clerks generally believe the opposite, and justify the administrative burdens of short-term clerks by pointing to their greater assertiveness. Finally, almost all judges who do *not* consider assertiveness to be a valuable law clerk quality have long-term law clerks, whom they think tend to be less assertive—or at least less argumentative—than their short-term counterparts.[5.53]

5.51. We felt able to classify the attitudes of half of our thirty-eight court of appeal subjects regarding the frequency of their input into pre-argument memoranda prepared for them by their law clerks. The values we derived are as follows:

Never	3
Occasionally	3
Frequently	5
Extensively	8

5.52. *See* Appendix, Table G.

5.53. Some judges who employ "passive" career clerks also follow the prac-

With regard to the style of the calendar memorandum, the poles feature a memorandum which offers little more than a summary of facts and contentions checked against the record, and a memorandum in the form of a full-blown opinion written in the first-person-plural. Although few court of appeals judges routinely operate at either pole, the great majority have their calendar memoranda prepared in a format which, if not completely that of an opinion, allows for an easy metamorphosis by means of minor rephrasing and an infusion of the first-person-plural. Either directly or indirectly, the law clerks' calendar memoranda have a significant impact on the content of their judges' written opinions.[5.54]

Despite the differences in manner and format of preparation, there is substantial uniformity in the subsequent use of calendar memoranda. They are exchanged with other members of the panel which will hear the calendared cases, and generally are discussed at pre-argument conferences of the judges.[5.55] In most cases, the calendar memorandum will significantly color, if it does not directly become, the opinion of the court.

Nonetheless, Judge Alpha's law clerk is kept too busy prepar-

---

tice of assigning precalendar cases without instruction for the clerk's preparation of draft opinions. Since these judges encourage their clerks to mimic their patterns of thought as well as their writing style, and abhor argument, the paradoxical result can be that the "passive" clerk becomes the very powerful alter ego of the judge, producing "no-judge" opinions which go forth with very little review by their nominal author or, given the pressures of their own work, his colleagues on the bench. See Thompson, *supra* note 1.11, at 478, 480, 514–15. See also Wold, *supra* note 2.72, at 64; First District Report, *supra* note 5.30, at 146 (comments by court of appeal staff attorney).

Most judges recognized that substitution of career staff for traditional clerks poses a risk of undue delegation of judicial prerogatives to staff, although none perceived the risk as a reality in his own operation. See text accompanying notes 5.58–5.59 *infra*. Some who did not perceive the personal risk, however, had adopted a method of operation by which their first impression of a proposed decision was imposed upon a career law clerk, who was expected and conditioned to accept it without question and forthwith to articulate reasons for the conclusion. Such judges failed to recognize that such a process removes from appellate decision-making the traditional discipline of personal efforts at articulation of reasons for a decision as a test of the validity of first impressions as to the proper outcome of cases.

5.54. See Appendix, Table H.

5.55. See generally CAL. COURTS OF APPEAL, *supra* note 1.7, at 119–23; Molinari, *The Decisionmaking Conference of the California Court of Appeal*, 57 Cal. L. Rev. 606, 610–12 (1969).

ing memoranda and subsequent opinions in the cases assigned to Alpha to have time to review the memoranda and proposed opinions circulated to Alpha by other judges. Judge Alpha thinks that the single most useful new task which an additional law clerk could perform in his chambers would be the review of the work product of other chambers and the central staff.[5.56]

Occasionally, when he has need of some special factual or legal research which his regular law clerk cannot perform without falling behind in the preparation of calendar memoranda, Judge Alpha will secure the services of a central staff attorney or writ clerk. These ad hoc assignments are arranged through the presiding justice of his division and the principal attorney of the court. Judge Alpha also uses externs more or less regularly through a program organized and administered by the presiding justice and a local law school. With his distaste for personnel matters and his lack of time for training staff, Alpha is happy with the extern program only so long as it is run by others and does not disrupt the regular functions of his law clerk. Judge Alpha is satisfied with externs if the net productivity of his chambers with externs is no lower than without: if he can break even, he is happy to have fresh faces and ideas around.[5.57] He does not deal directly with externs very often, however, preferring to have their work coordinated by his law clerk. Nevertheless, he has occasionally worked directly with an extern, and has been surprised at the quality of work produced. Although he has heard externs argue heatedly with his law clerk, he is pleased that they are sufficiently awed by his judicial status to abstain from arguing with him personally.

Judge Alpha's extern practices are representative of the court as a whole in only an attenuated sense. Roughly a third of the judges make no use of externs at all.[5.58] Some of these judges feel variously that externs have little or nothing to contribute to the work of their chambers, that externs are likely to be politicized in their approach to law, and that externs are overly argumentative and insufficiently deferential. Others, like Judge Alpha, are not opposed to externs but await the initiative of some other judge in starting an extern program at their court. These indifferent judges would use externs occasionally if it were convenient to do so.

5.56. *See* note 5.31 *supra*.
5.57. *See* Appendix, Tables D & E.
5.58. See *id.*, Table C.

Roughly another third of the judges are active boosters of extern programs. These judges include most of the judges using short-term clerks. They often recruit externs for the use of other judges as well as for themselves. Such judges welcome the additional assistance of externs, and have created extern programs with the assistance of cooperating law schools. They tend to deal directly with their externs as if the externs were full-fledged law clerks. The remaining third of the judges are those represented by Judge Alpha: although indifferent to externs, they take them when they are available for the asking. For these judges, externs possess both the virtues and the vices of short-term clerks; they are bright and enthusiastic, and as long as the vices are mitigated by the administration of the program by someone else and the supervision of the externs by regular law clerks, the externs remain welcome.

Judge Alpha is aware of the potential usurpation of judicial functions by both central staff and personal clerks. He is firmly convinced that the danger can be exaggerated, and in any event that harm can be averted by a conscientious judge. Judge Alpha is confident that his own performance is not unduly influenced by his staff; he feels that both central staff and elbow clerks are indispensable to the work of the court, but that in his case, at least, they are essentially technicians who implement decisions he makes personally. He is aware, however, of colleagues on the courts of appeal who abdicate much of their function to their assistants, and he thinks the problem is worse at the Supreme Court of California.

Indeed, a significant number of the judges represented by Judge Alpha feel that the Supreme Court of California frequently gets out of step with the state because of the undue influence of short-term law clerks at that court. This view, ironic in light of the great numerical predominance of career clerks at the California Supreme Court, is indicative of a lack of consensus among judges of the courts of appeal as to whether short-term or long-term law clerks pose a greater threat of usurpation. Judges who use career law clerks reject any degree of usurpation in their own chambers but recognize the problem in others, including their colleagues using short-term clerks. Judges using short-term law clerks tend to agree, however, that an important factor which inhibits them from hiring career clerks is the fear that the longer they worked with a clerk, the more they would come to rely on his or her judgment, and the greater the risk that they might inadvertently cross the line of undue delegation of their judicial responsibilities.

B. *Supreme Court of California*

1. Jurisdiction

The Supreme Court of California is the state's court of last resort.[5.59] Except for capital punishment cases, it is a court of discretionary jurisdiction.[5.60] The prerequisite to supreme court action on the merits is the vote of at least four of the court's seven judges to grant a "Petition for Hearing" in a case before a court of appeal, or to accept jurisdiction of a proceeding within the original jurisdiction of the supreme court.[5.61]

5.59. CAL. CONST. art. 6, § 1.

5.60. CAL. CONST. art. 6, § 11. It has been stated that the California Supreme Court's jurisdiction is also "mandatory" in disciplinary proceedings against judges and attorneys. Goodman & Seaton, *supra* note 2.71, at 310 n.2 (1974). Although this overstates the effect of the cited rules of court, CAL. R. OF COURT 919 (formerly 920), 952, which appear to contemplate possible denial of review by the supreme court, as a practical matter the supreme court always does accept jurisdiction to review such disciplinary recommendations. In the absence of the supreme court's review and concurrence, a recommendation for the suspension or disbarment of an attorney or the suspension, retirement, censure, or removal of a judge has no legal effect. CAL. CONST. art. VI, § 18(b)–(c); CAL. BUS. & PROF. CODE. § 6102 (West 1974).

Even in capital cases, the supreme court's consideration of the merits of an appeal is discretionary. Prior to 1966, under former article 6, section 4 of the California Constitution, the supreme court had jurisdiction over direct appeals in several categories of civil cases as well as capital cases. Nonetheless, most such direct appeals were routinely transferred to the courts of appeal. *See* 1968 JUDICIAL COUNCIL OF CALIFORNIA REPORT 62. *See generally* Witkin, *New California Rules on Appeal* (pt.2), 17 So. Cal. L. Rev. 232, 236–37 (1944). *See also* text accompanying note 5.68 *infra*. This power to transfer remains with the supreme court, *Cal. Const.* art. 6, § 12: CAL. R. OF COURT 20, and was recently exercised to transfer to the courts of appeal all pending direct appeals which were controlled by the invalidation of California's death penalty law in Rockwell v. Superior Court, 18 Cal. 3d 420, 556 P.2d 1101, 134 Cal. Rptr. 650 (1976). *See* 1978 JUDICIAL COUNCIL OF CALIFORNIA REPORT 65.

5.61. CAL. R. OF COURT 27(e). *See generally* Mosk, *The Supreme Court of California, 1973–1974—Foreword: The Rule of Four in California*, 63 CALIF. L. REV. 2 (1975).

By rule of court, a hearing "will be ordered" where: (1) it is necessary to secure "uniformity of decision" or "the settlement of important questions of law"; (2) the court of appeal acted without jurisdiction; or (3) for some reason, the court of appeal could not generate a majority for a particular decision.[5.62] In practice, the California Supreme Court occasionally denies petitions for hearing that present novel issues[5.63] or create a conflict among the courts of appeal,[5.64] and occasionally the supreme court grants petitions for hearing simply to correct serious court of appeal errors which create no conflict of published precedent and pose no issues of significance to anyone other than the parties.[5.65] To assist itself in disposing of unimportant cases which create conflicts among the courts of appeal or which reach erroneous results, the supreme court has developed two techniques of decision ancillary to the granting or denying of a hearing. The court may deny a hearing but order that the opinion of a court of appeal not be published in the official reports,[5.66] thereby stripping it of precedential effect,[5.67] or the court may grant a hearing and then without further action retransfer the case to the court of appeal[5.68] for its reconsideration, sometimes in light of certain authorities cryp-

5.62. CAL. R. OF COURT 29(a).

5.63. *See generally* Note, *To Hear or Not to Hear: A Question for the California Supreme Court*, 3 STAN. L. REV. 243, 247–50 (1951).

5.64. *See e.g.*, California State Auto. Assn. Inter-Ins. Bureau v. Hoffman, 77 Cal. App. 3d 768, 143 Cal. Rptr. 835 (1978), in which the court of appeal expressly refused to follow Juzefski v. Western Cas. & Surety Co., 173 Cal. App. 2d 118, 342 P.2d 928 (1959), notwithstanding its recognition that the holding of *Juzefski*, if followed, would be determinative of the case. The supreme court denied a hearing on April 20, 1978, over the dissent of three justices. 77 Cal. App. 3d at 776, 143 Cal. Rptr. at 839. *See also* Kelleher v. Empresa Hondurena de Vapores, S.A., 57 Cal. App. 3d 52, 129 Cal. Rptr. 32 (1976), refusing to follow Johnson v. Canadian Transport Co., 54 Cal. App. 3d 827, 127 Cal. Rptr. 72 (1976). A hearing had been denied in *Johnson*, 54 Cal. App. 3d at 839, 127 Cal. Rptr. at 72, and was also denied in *Kelleher*, this time over the dissent of one justice, 57 Cal. App. 3d at 64, 129 Cal. Rptr. at 32.

5.65. In an appended note, we present a detailed examination of the policy and practice of the Supreme Court of California in granting petitions for hearing. *See* Appendix, *Note on the Supreme Court of California's Exercise of Discretionary Appellate Jurisdiction*, p. 145 *infra* [hereinafter cited as *Discretionary Jurisdiction Note*].

5.66. CAL. R. OF COURT 976(c).

5.67. CAL. R. OF COURT 977.

5.68. CAL. CONST. art. VI, § 12.

tically but pointedly set forth in the minute order retransferring the case.[5.69]

2. Workload

A review of statistics for the fiscal years ending June 30, 1957, 1967, and 1977 reveals the "crisis of volume" at the Supreme Court of California.[5.70] Total filings for these three years were 1,329 in 1957, 2,716 in 1967, and 3,665 in 1977. The figures for 1957 and 1967 were inflated, however, by appeals filed directly in the supreme court prior to the constitutional amendment of November, 1966, which abolished appeals directly to the supreme court except in cases in which the death penalty has been imposed.[5.71] In 1957 there were 290 appeals filed directly in the supreme court, and in 1967 there were 211. However, pursuant to its internal policy, the court transferred 273 of the direct appeals of 1957 to the courts of appeal; 175 of the direct appeals of 1967 were similarly transferred.[5.72] Thus the direct appeals actually considered by the court in 1957 and 1967 were virtually equal in number to the twenty-seven direct appeals in capital punishment cases filed with the court in 1977. More accurate indications of the rising workload of the court are provided by the statistics relating to petitions for hearings and original writs filed with the court in the selected years. Fiscal 1957 saw 780 petitions for hearing filed, of which 146 (18.7 percent) were granted. Fiscal 1967 saw 1,379 petitions for hearing filed, of which 157 (11.4 percent) were granted. Fiscal 1977 saw 2,927 petitions for hearing filed, of which 231 (7.9 percent) were granted. Thus petitions for hearing increased fairly steadily over the twenty years, to a volume in 1977 which was 375 percent of that in 1957. During the same period, the number of hearings granted increased only 158 percent. Petitions for original

5.69. *See*, *e.g.*, the orders retransferring Perez on Habeas Corpus, Crim. No. 19400, and People v. Murray, Crim. No. 20459, filed on July 19, 1978, and printed in Supreme Court Minutes, at 1, 1978 Cal. Official Reports Adv. Sh. No. 22 (Aug. 17, 1978). *See also* the retransferred cases cited in *Discretionary Jurisdiction Note*, *supra* note 5.65.

5.70. All of the following statistics are derived from 1978 JUDICIAL COUNCIL OF CALIFORNIA REPORT 61–65; and 1968 JUDICIAL COUNCIL OF CALIFORNIA REPORT 61–64.

5.71. *See* CAL. CONST. art. VI, § 4 (as amended 1928, repealed 1966); and CAL. CONST. art. VI, § 11.

5.72. *See* 1968 JUDICIAL COUNCIL OF CALIFORNIA REPORT 62.

writs showed a less constant increase. There were 237 such petitions filed in 1957, but an explosion in petitions for writs of habeas corpus resulted in 1,117 filings for original writs in 1967. By 1977, the court's policy of requiring habeas corpus petitioners to go first to the courts of appeal had led to a reduction in filing of petitions for original writs to 711.[5.73] Combining these figures to show the filings in the two most important sectors of the court's discretionary docket, the court was asked to decide whether to accept jurisdiction by petition for hearing or original writ in 1,017 cases in fiscal 1957, in 2,496 cases in fiscal 1967, and in 3,638 cases in fiscal 1977.

This 358 percent increase in petitions for hearings and original writs in the twenty years between 1957 and 1977 has not been matched by an increase in the ability of the court to produce written opinions. In fiscal 1957 it produced 174; in fiscal 1967 it produced 198; and in fiscal 1977 it produced 144. These data of intake and output disclose a high court immersed in its task of intelligently determining what matters it is to decide and sorely

5.73. Although the general rule that a petitioner for habeas corpus should have first sought relief from any available lower court is of long standing in California, see B. WITKIN, CALIFORNIA CRIMINAL PROCEDURE, supra note 5.34, (§ 795, at 768), it has not always been firmly applied by the supreme court. Compare In re Gonsalves, 48 Cal. 2d 638, 642, 311 P.2d 483, 486 (1957) with In re Hochberg, 2 Cal. 3d 870, 873 n.2, 471 P.2d 1, 3 n.2, 87 Cal. Rptr. 681, 683 n.2 (1970). Item 20 of the Form for Petitions for Release from or Modification to Custody prescribed by the Judicial Council pursuant to CAL. R. OF COURT 56 emphasizes the exhaustion requirement by stating: "If this petition might lawfully have been made to a lower court, state the circumstances justifying an application to this court." As explained in In re Hochberg, supra, even when the supreme court asserts jurisdiction by issuing an order to show cause why a writ of habeas corpus should not be granted, it may make the order returnable before the superior court. See, e.g., Coleman on Habeas Corpus, Crim. No. 20635 (Aug. 31, 1978), Supreme Court Minutes, at 10, in 1978 Cal. Official Reports Adv. Sh. No. 25 (Sept. 19, 1978). The superior court then proceeds to compile an evidentiary record as if it had issued the order to show cause itself. If the superior court denies relief, that order is not appealable and the petitioner must again seek habeas corpus from a court of appeal or the supreme court, which will now have an evidentiary record available from the proceedings before the superior court. As these procedures have become familiar to California prisoners, the number of petitions for habeas corpus filed directly with the supreme court has declined. Many of these matters are still ultimately presented to the supreme court, however, by the alternative route of a petition for hearing after the court of appeal has denied a petition for writ of habeas corpus. See 1978 JUDICIAL COUNCIL OF CALIFORNIA REPORT 64.

pressed to serve its vital institutional function by crafting opinions establishing the jurisprudential policy and expounding the common law of the state. One member of the court, while proposing greater liberality in the granting of hearings, has characterized the selection process as the court's "most difficult task."[5.74] This difficulty moved one of the judges with whom we talked to lament the irony that the court must now spend more time selecting its cases than attending to their disposition.

3. Staff

The California Supreme Court carries its burden with the help of a supporting staff exceeded in size only by that of the United States Supreme Court.[5.75] At the time of our survey, the court had thirty-three "research attorneys" in its employ: three serving each of the six associate justices, and fourteen serving the Chief Justice,[5.76] with one "principal attorney" nominally serving the entire court as the senior staff attorney. Most of the Chief Justice's staff functioned as a de facto central staff for the screening of petitions for hearing in criminal cases and applications for original writs of habeas corpus, reviewing these matters with little direct supervision from the Chief Justice and making recommendations on their disposition to the court as a whole.[5.77] The staffs of the

5.74. See Mosk, supra note 5.61, at 8.

5.75. For the latest available figures on the size of the legal staff of the United States Supreme Court, see note 2.56 supra.

5.76. Professor Baier has reported a telephone conversation with Chief Justice Wright of the Supreme Court of California on October 5, 1972, in which the Chief Justice described his twelve clerks, eight of them career employees, and added, "I need them all, and more!" Baier, supra note 1.7, at 1134 n.43 (emphasis in original). Two years later, the Chief Justice changed one of his explicitly short-term positions to an indefinitely tenured position. See note 5.77 infra. Two persons held this position prior to Chief Justice Wright's retirement (one of them being Author Oakley). Neither took the position with aspirations of remaining for a career, however, and neither remained as long as two years. The four "short-term" law clerks of the present Chief Justice appear to have similar expectations of two years' or less tenure with the court. See note 5.79 infra.

5.77. See generally, Chilton, supra note 2.90, at 464–65; Goodman & Seaton, supra note 2.71, at 312–13. Until 1974, with the exception of the most senior of the career clerks on the staff of the Chief Justice, all of his permanent staff worked primarily on petitions for hearing or habeas corpus. Some of these staff members worked occasionally on calendar memoranda or post-argument opinions by ad hoc assignment of the Chief Justice; some never worked on anything but petitions. The short-term clerks generally worked initially on petitions for hearing or

associate justices performed an analogous function with regard to civil petitions, although they generally operated under closer supervision by the responsible justice. Civil petitions were distributed for screening equally among the six associate justices. All but one of the judges used externs at the time of our survey, employing them principally in the screening process.[5.78] The staffing arrangements today are essentially the same, except that all the current judges now use externs.[5.79] The gender mix of the court's staff is similar to that of the California courts of appeal, with only slightly fewer women among the career clerks.

4. Internal Procedures

Because the court still cares about correcting mere error in order to avoid injustice, the process of picking and choosing from petitions "is thorough and therefore time consuming."[5.80] The

habeas corpus under the supervision of senior staff members, and "graduated" according to ability and productivity to occasional assignments of calendar memoranda and opinions. When Chief Justice Wright came to the court in 1970, there were six short-term positions on the staff of the Chief Justice. These were reduced to four the next year, and to three in 1974. See note 5.76 supra. The additional long-term law clerk position was created by the Chief Justice in 1974 in order to give himself two full-time elbow clerks working exclusively on his personal assignments. Despite the apparent size of his staff of twelve (which increased to fourteen in 1975; see note 5.79 infra), these were the only two law clerks working with him personally on a continuing basis.

5.78. See generally Goodman & Seaton, supra note 2.71, at 313. For additional details on the use of externs at the Supreme Court of California, see notes 2.71, 2.74, & 2.77 supra. See also text accompanying notes 2.77–2.81 supra.

5.79. See Johnson, supra note 2.68, at 249 n.64. As of November 30, 1978, the Chief Justice of California had four short-term clerks and Associate Justices Mosk and Tobriner had one each. The rest of the legal staff of the court were long-term employees. All criminal petitions were reviewed by a pool of seven long-term clerks, nominally under the supervision of the Chief Justice but treated by her as functionally a central staff, with the Chief Justice's personal needs for legal staff assistance handled by a distinct group of six law clerks. Included within this personal staff of six were the four short-term clerks, who were hired without a definite termination date but on the understanding that they would move to other jobs within a year or two. The total number of staff attorneys of the Chief Justice, including the central staff and her Executive Assistant but excluding the court's Principal Attorney, was fourteen, the same size as the staff of the former Chief Justice after it was increased from twelve to fourteen in 1975. Buehl Interview, supra note 5.38.

5.80. Mosk, supra note 5.61, at 8. See also Discretionary Jurisdiction Note, supra note 5.65.

result of the screening of a petition by the staff of the judge to whom it has been assigned is a "conference memorandum," so called by reference to the weekly conference at which pending petitions are voted upon by the judges.[5.81] Because the court has not entirely forsaken an error-correcting function, and because the memoranda prepared by a particular judge's staff will be circulated to the court as a whole and will be the principal document by which most petitions are decided, these conference memoranda are generally more extensive than the "cert. memos" that are their counterparts at the United States Supreme Court.[5.82] Conference memoranda are generally self-contained documents reciting the facts of the case and summarizing the holding and reasoning of the decision below, if any. A memorandum is usually attributed not only to a particular judge but also to the particular law clerk responsible for its drafting. At least when the memorandum recommends an assertion of jurisdiction by the supreme court, its factual analysis and legal discussion may foreshadow in scope and tone that of an opinion. The more controversial the proffered reasons for asserting jurisdiction, the more likely it is that the memorandum will reflect the personal views of the judge in whose name it has been prepared, and that it will argue in the manner of a proposed opinion towards the outcome of the case after a hearing in the supreme court.

5.81. See generally Goodman & Seaton, supra note 2.71, at 312–13.

5.82. The phrase "cert. memo" refers to memoranda evaluating petitions for the writ of certiorari, which is the United States Supreme Court's mechanism for exercising its discretionary jurisdiction. See note 2.15 supra. Petitions for certiorari to the United States Supreme Court are thus analogous to petitions for hearing to the California Supreme Court.

Professor Wilkinson has described typical cert. memos as from one to five pages in length and produced at the rate of twenty to thirty memos per clerk per week. See J. WILKINSON, supra note 1.7, at 18, 20. It is unclear to what extent these figures typify cert. memos prepared solely for the use of one Justice, or cert. memos prepared for the common use of several Justices. See note 2.66 supra. We understand that some Justices who have had personal cert. memos prepared have expected them to be no more than one or two pages in length, and Justice Brennan has confirmed this publicly. See Brennan, supra note 1.7, at 836. Conference memoranda at the Supreme Court of California typically run from three to ten typewritten, double-spaced pages in length, and on rare occasions may exceed twenty pages in length. An actual California Supreme Court conference memorandum, of just under average length for a nonfrivolous petition for hearing, has been reprinted by permission of the court in J. POULOS, THE ANATOMY OF CRIMINAL JUSTICE 1101–03 (1976).

The court's weekly conference is generally held on Wednesday,[5.83] in the chambers of the Chief Justice. Clerical staff prepare carts laden with petitions and the accompanying briefs and opinions below, which are kept at hand for consultation in the course of the conference. Each judge brings to the conference a binder of all the memoranda on the pertinent cases; the memoranda have generally been circulated on the Friday preceding the conference. Using principally their notes on these memoranda, the justices confer in private on the disposition of the petitions. There is little incentive for delay in considering petitions; although petitions for original writs need not be acted upon immediately, the court has only 120 (and in some cases only 90) days after the decision of the court of appeal in which to reach its decision on whether or not to grant a petition for hearing.[5.84]

It has become commonplace over the last decade for there to be as many as one hundred petitions to be disposed of at a conference.[5.85] Some of these petitions, especially after appeals in criminal cases, are obviously lacking in merit, let alone public significance; in addition, many petitions protest the denial of pretrial writ review by the court of appeal in circumstances in which any error by the trial court will either be mooted by its final judgment or preserved for appeal from that judgment. Although the conference memoranda prepared in such cases are not abbreviated, rarely numbering fewer than three typed, double-spaced pages and sometimes running two or even three times that length, the court has evolved a procedure for giving each case abbreviated treatment at the actual conference. The cases are divided into an "A" and a "B" list in accordance with the disposition recommended by the conference memorandum for each petition. Cases on the "B" list are denied hearings without discussion at the conference. Recommended dispositions of "Grant" or "Submitted" (e.g., without recommendation either to grant or to deny) automatically place a case on the "A" list; a recommendation of "De-

5.83. See J. POULOS, supra note 5.82, at 1101; 1 B. WITKIN, CALIFORNIA PROCEDURE, supra note 2.52, Courts § 209, at 468.

5.84. See CAL. R. COURT 24(a), 28(a).

5.85. Five years ago, consideration of one hundred cases at a conference, if not commonplace, was not extraordinary either. See Goodman & Seaton, supra note 2.71, at 312. The volume of filings has, of course, risen since: by 16.7 percent in the four years between fiscal 1973 and fiscal 1977. See 1978 JUDICIAL COUNCIL OF CALIFORNIA REPORT 61 (Table I: Total filings by year since fiscal 1967).

nial" places a case on the "B" list. Occasionally, when denial is recommended but it is felt that the case merits discussion at conference, the recommendation "Denial-Submitted" will be used to route the case to the "A" list.[5.86]

All of the judges review carefully, either themselves or through a senior staff attorney, the recommendations made in conference memoranda assigned to them. As a practical matter, direct judicial participation is most extensive in those cases in which "A" list recommendations are made. This pattern of review is repeated in all the chambers to which a conference memorandum is circulated: a senior staff attorney and (by invariable practice in some chambers, occasional practice in others) the judge personally will review the "B" list and determine if any of the cases demand further consideration or active discussion at the conference.[5.87]

Any judge has the right to request elevation of a case from "B" list to "A" list status, either in advance or at the conference. This elevation is generally accomplished by deferring action upon or discussion of the case at its originally scheduled conference, and

5.86. Public disclosure of the court's "A" and "B" list system in a speech by author Oakley to the student body of the McGeorge School of Law, University of the Pacific, on September 25, 1974, was approved in advance by Chief Justice Wright, who was dedicated to improving lawyers' familiarity with supreme court procedures. The bifurcated system for managing conferences had earlier been discussed by the court's principal attorney at meetings with court of appeal judges, their staff, and others, pursuant to a memorandum on the operation of the supreme court which had been prepared on July 1, 1971, for the internal use of the court. The "A" and "B" list system became indisputably a matter of public record when it was described in testimony before special masters of the Commission on Judicial Performance in October and November of 1976, which testimony was released to the public in connection with the Commission's recommendation of the retirement of Justice Marshall F. McComb of the Supreme Court of California. *See High Court Relies Heavily on Staff*, Metropolitan News (Los Angeles), Nov. 29, 1978, at 3, col. 1. *See generally* Inquiry Concerning a Judge (No. 25, Comm'n on Jud. Performance, Dec. 30, 1976); McComb v. Commission on Judicial Performance, 19 Cal. 3d Spec. Trib. Supp. 1, 564 P.2d 1, 138 Cal. Rptr. 459 (Spec. Trib. 1977). *See also* J. POULOS, *supra* note 5.82, at 1101, for mention of the categories of recommended dispositions used in conference memoranda.

Justice Brennan has provided a detailed description of the similar system employed at the United States Supreme Court for limiting the number of cases actually discussed at their weekly Friday conferences. *See* Brennan, *supra* note 1.7, at 837.

5.87. *See generally* Goodman & Seaton, *supra* note 2.71, at 313.

having the case placed upon the "A" list of a subsequent conference, generally accompanied by a supplemental memorandum prepared by the staff of the judge who requested its elevation. All individual judges carefully review "A" list matters, and generally one or more of their staff attorneys will do likewise, to provide each judge with a preconference foil for discussion of the "A" list.

Once the supreme court has chosen to assert its jurisdiction, the Chief Justice assigns the case for precalendar preparation to one of the judges voting to hear the case, preferably the one responsible for preparation of the pertinent conference memorandum. The calendar memorandum which the assigned judge prepares and circulates in advance of oral argument generally assumes the form of a proposed opinion of the court.[5.88] Except in July and August, the court hears oral argument during one week each month.[5.89] About one week in advance, each judge is provided with a loose-leaf binder containing the calendar memoranda pertaining to the upcoming calendar of oral argument; unless there is a special request, the briefs and record of a case are not circulated among the judges prior to oral argument. These materials remain in the chambers of the judge responsible for the calendar memorandum, where they are often consulted informally by the staff of other judges. During the preparation and circulation of calendar memoranda, as during the week of oral argument, the weekly schedule of conferences to dispose of pending petitions continues inexorably.

The court confers after oral argument, customarily on the very afternoon of each day of argument, to decide if the views set forth in the calendar memoranda for particular cases command a majority of the court and to discuss matter raised at oral argument or by individual judges which is not covered by or is inconsistent with the calendar memoranda. The Chief Justice then assigns opinion preparation to a member of the majority, who will generally be the author of the calendar memorandum.[5.90] A draft opinion, ordinarily an edited and slightly revised version of the calendar memorandum, but sometimes either identical to or completely different from that document, is then circulated

5.88. *See* Johnson, *supra* note 2.68, at 249–50.

5.89. *See* 1 B. WITKIN, CALIFORNIA PROCEDURE, *supra* note 2.52, *Courts* § 209, at 468.

5.90. *See generally* Johnson, *supra* note 2.68, at 250.

around the court as part of the "box" of the case containing the briefs, the clerk's transcript, and, if not unduly voluminous, the reporter's transcript of any evidentiary proceedings. Generally the "box" is routed first to the members of the tentative majority, so that a loss of a majority can be discovered quickly and, incidentally if not intentionally, the writing of dissents discouraged. Most of the delays in the issuance of the court's opinions occur when a "box" gets stalled in the chambers of a dissenting judge, where it waits its turn as the judge sorts through the weekly flow of conference memoranda, the monthly flow of calendar memoranda, and prepares or reviews the tentative opinions in other cases in which that judge is aligned with the majority. Once the dissent is finished, the "box" must complete its initial circulation and then recirculate so that the dissent can be reviewed by the entire court. If any judge requires modification of an opinion as a condition of concurrence, and if the author agrees to the modification, the "box" must again make its rounds of the chambers of all the judges who had assented to the prior version of the opinion. When all disagreements have been aired and accommodated to the greatest possible extent, the opinion is filed.[5.91]

5. Composite Profile: Judge Beta

Judge Beta, our composite of the five justices of the California Supreme Court whom we interviewed, came to the supreme

5.91. Our description of the procedures for circulating draft opinions at the California Supreme Court, which was written on the basis of our own experience and our interview data, has received dramatic corroboration since its writing as the result of an apparent quarrel among the membership of the court. Charges that a politically unpalatable decision was being withheld by the court regrettably became public in connection with the 1978 general election, in which four members of the court, including its new Chief Justice, were before the voters for confirmation in office. In the aftermath of the election, in which all the justices were confirmed (but, in the case of the Chief Justice, by the narrowest margin in the history of the court), a detailed story was leaked to the press justifying the delay in the filing of the decision in light of the court's normal procedures for recirculating a proposed majority opinion after the preparation of a dissenting opinion. *See* Kang, *Behind that "Delayed Decision": Backstage at the High Court*, San Francisco Sunday Examiner and Chronicle, Nov. 19, 1978, § A, at 1, col. 2. Additional details on the supreme court's decision-making processes were revealed in Hager, *How Secret Should State High Court Decisions Be?* L.A. Times, Nov. 23, 1978, § 1, at 3, col. 1. The controversy leading to these disclosures was summarized in Endicott, *Personal Hostilities Tear at Supreme Court Fabric*, L.A. Times, Nov. 23, 1978,

court after about twenty years of private legal practice and fifteen years of judicial service on a superior court and a court of appeal. Like Judge Alpha, he knew little about law clerks when he was in law school and consequently gave little thought to seeking a clerkship upon graduation. He now recognizes that a clerkship is a very valuable opportunity indeed. This is one reason why he always has three externs working for him at any one time.[5.92]

When Judge Beta was on the court of appeal he started with a short-term law clerk, as was then the custom. Quality attorneys were simply unavailable for longer periods than a year or two at most. By the time he left, the court of appeal had acquired long-term clerks. Were he still on the court of appeal, he too would want a permanent clerk, although he might not be able to convince a good clerk to stay on indefinitely; ideally he would want two clerks, one long-term and one short-term. He has mixed feelings about the burgeoning central staffs of the court of appeal; they were in their infancy when he was promoted to the supreme court, and he sees them as a somewhat melancholy necessity.[5.93]

---

§ 1, at 1, col. 2, and led to the public release of a letter by the Chief Justice to the Commission on Judicial Performance requesting its investigation of the charges, accompanied by a 12-page typewritten "Description of California Supreme Court Procedures." *See* Stephen T. Buehl, Executive Assistant to the Chief Justice of California, News Release, Nov. 24, 1978, *reprinted in* Metropolitan News (Los Angeles), Nov. 29, 1978, at 1, col. 1. The Chief Justice's document describing the court's internal procedures is consistent with and corroborative of our account; not unexpectedly, in view of the circumstances of its release, the document discusses the procedures for granting hearings and petitions for original writs quite cursorily, and dwells extensively on procedures for circulating proposed majority and dissenting opinions. For details of the investigation and its aftermath, see Mosk v. Superior Court, 25 Cal. 3d 474, 601 P.2d 1030, 159 Cal. Rptr. 494 (1979); Kang, *The Decline of California's Vendetta-Ridden Supreme Court*, 10 CAL. J. 343 (1979). The Commission ultimately terminated its proceedings without filing formal charges against any member of the court, Order Terminating Proceedings (No. 30012, Comm'n on Jud. Performance, Nov. 5, 1979), but was prohibited by Mosk v. Supreme Court, *supra*, from issuing a public report. *See* Turner, *High Court on Coast Cleared by Inquiry*, N.Y. Times, Nov. 6, 1979, at A16, col. 5. *See generally Disorder in the California Court*, N.Y. Times, Nov. 10, 1979, at 22, col. 1 (editorial).

5.92. The major reason for Judge Beta's use of externs is, however, their assistance in reviewing petitions for hearing. *See* Appendix, Tables D & E.

We choose to refer to "Judge" rather than "Justice" Beta for the reasons set forth in note 5.3 *supra*.

5.93. *See* Appendix, Table J.

When he came to the supreme court, his colleagues were in the midst of a transition from a predominantly short-termed staff to a predominantly long-termed one. He started out with one career research attorney (who had been a short-term and then a long-term clerk with his predecessor) and two short-term law clerks. He now has two career clerks, the second being a former short-term clerk who, after a few years in practice, had indicated an interest in returning to the court for a career. His third clerk remains a short-term clerk, whom he picks annually from over a hundred applicants.[5.94] Although he might return temporarily to two short-term clerks were one of his current career clerks to quit, he imagines he would return ultimately to his present two-to-one mix of long- and short-term clerks. He enjoys the freshness of short-term clerks, but gets much of this flavor from his externs without the attendant burdens of selecting the clerk and later assisting him or her to find a subsequent job.

Judge Beta assigns to his personal research staff substantial initial responsibility for the preparation of conference memoranda. While recognizing his ultimate responsibility for the content of the memoranda, he also is aware that pressure of workload requires substantial delegation. Only one judge expressed concern over the extent to which caseload pressures compelled reliance upon staff-prepared conference memoranda.

Most judges rely heavily on their staffs for preparation of calendar memoranda, but beyond this we could not assemble a useful composite supreme court judge with regard to the writing of opinions. Work habits were too diverse, and even the attitudes of particular judges defy generalization.[5.95] Individual judges assign varying roles to their staffs from research and rough drafting to final composition. The degree to which a proposed opinion incorporates material from the underlying calendar memorandum varies not only from judge to judge but also from case to case. The single composite that emerges is that of a judge who is committed to the proposition that by whomever selected and arranged, the

5.94. It should be remembered that Judge Beta is based on interview data obtained in the summer of 1976. It appears that a representative judge of the California Supreme Court as of the fall of 1978 would have an entirely long-term personal staff. See notes 2.77 & 5.79 supra.

5.95. Note, as a consequence of internal conflicts in the statements of our subjects, our inability to quantify any attitudes regarding law clerk influence on the opinions of supreme court judges. See Appendix, Table H.

words of the opinion must reflect the judge's personal thought process.[5.96]

Judge Beta does not believe that supreme court supporting staff unduly intrude upon decision-making or the crafting of opinions. He views career staff as highly trained, experienced, and skilled technicians who are able to subordinate personal views to the judicial determination of the judge. He was pleasantly surprised at the ability of his inherited career clerk to adapt to the judge's social and political philosophy in light of the researcher's many years of prior service for Judge Beta's predecessor, whose social and political views were quite different from his own. Judge Beta believes that the combination of personal staff consisting of two career attorneys and one newly graduated short-term clerk plus externs represents the best possible mix to achieve the advantages of efficiency and experience leavened by the fresh approach and enthusiasm bred by recent exposure to law school.

With some dissent from colleagues, Judge Beta views the operation and impact of court of appeal staff in a different light.[5.97] Notwithstanding his admission that he too would have a permanent clerk were he still on the court of appeal, he is concerned that career researchers in that court may be exercising too influential a role. He is particularly worried that court of appeal central staff, however necessary it may be to accelerate the processing of routine cases, may be exercising too broad a function at the expense of necessary judicial input. While completely satisfied with career researchers operating in the supreme court, the composite judge

5.96. Because most of the supreme court judges were interviewed by author Oakley, a former law clerk at the court, the interviews display a general sense of the judges having assumed the interviewer's knowledge of the basic decision-making procedures of the court. This knowledge, compiled from personal experience and the available literature, has been incorporated into the discussion of the supreme court preceding the depiction of Judge Beta. *See* text accompanying notes 5.75–5.91 *supra*. The resulting paucity of decision-making data obtained from our interview subjects at the supreme court should not be seen as contradictory of or inconsistent with the prefatory description of the work of the court.

5.97. Because the initial motivation of our study came from our reaction to the trend toward permanent clerks at the courts of appeal, because most judges of the California Supreme Court have had extensive experience as counsel before or as judges of the courts of appeal, and because the decisions of the courts of appeal form the woof and warp of their own work, all of our subjects on the supreme court were principally interested in discussing the decision-making procedures of the courts of appeal.

would prefer substantially more turnover in court of appeal staff. This is due in part to his belief that law clerks willing to remain indefinitely at the court of appeal lack the quality of their counterparts at the supreme court.

Judge Beta makes no distinctions between short- and long-term law clerks in detailing the qualities most valuable to a judge: enthusiasm, diligence, legal and analytical skill, and the ability to write clearly and easily. For these reasons he thinks long-term law clerks are preferably people who were introduced to the supreme court as short-term law clerks and were later asked to remain at or return to the court. Career clerks of this type, who are characteristic of those at the supreme court, offer Judge Beta the best of both worlds. Law schools do a better job, he wryly notes, of training law students to be judges than of training them to be lawyers. This not only prepares the best law students to be good law clerks, but also may induce some of them to remain law clerks by allowing them to deal with law at a much purer level than practice would allow. Although Judge Beta is too modest to articulate it this way, he is at least intuitively aware that the seemingly paradoxical rapport between himself and clerks who may have much different political and social values is attributable to his status as a judge of a particularly powerful court of last resort. Even his long-term clerks pose little threat to his autonomy, because such clerks live to serve the law, and the judges of his court embody the law. Life is different on the court of appeal, where the law is as much a business as a calling, and where it is easy for both judges and clerks to become accustomed to sharing the task of judgment, which, however thankless, should be the judges' alone.

C. *United States Court of Appeals for the Ninth Circuit*

1. Jurisdiction and Organization

The United States Court of Appeals for the Ninth Circuit hears appeals and petitions for original writs concerning cases from the federal district courts in the states of Alaska, Arizona, California, Idaho, Montana, Nevada, Oregon, Washington, Hawaii, and the territories of Guam and the Northern Marianas.[5.98] Litigants are

---

5.98. 28 U.S.C. § 41 (1976). The District Court for the Northern Mariana Islands was created—and added to the Ninth Circuit—by the Act of Nov. 8, 1977, Pub. L. No. 95-157, 91 Stat. 1265 (codified at 48 U.S.C. § 1694 (Supp. I 1977)).

entitled by statute to appeal as of right from all "final decisions" of United States district courts not appealable directly to the United States Supreme Court;[5.99] in some circumstances, interlocutory decisions of district courts are also appealable.[5.100] As of June 1, 1976, there were twelve judges of the Ninth Circuit in regular active service and six other "senior" judges.[5.101] As of June 1, 1978, there were thirteen Ninth Circuit judges in regular active service and seven senior Ninth Circuit judges.[5.102] Legislation signed into law on October 20, 1978 has increased the authorized number of Ninth Circuit judges on regular active service to twenty-three, second only in size to the Fifth Circuit's twenty-six judges.[5.103] As a practical matter, the Ninth Circuit has for some time been operating as a court of over twenty judges, using senior judges, circuit judges assigned from other circuits, and district

5.99. 28 U.S.C. § 1291 (1976).

5.100. The most significant categories of appealable interlocutory orders are concerning injunctive relief, 28 U.S.C. § 1292 (a)(1)(1976), and orders which the district judge certifies in writing as involving "a controlling question of law as to which there is substantial ground for difference of opinion and that an immediate appeal from the order may materially advance the ultimate termination of the litigation," in which case the court of appeals may in its discretion permit the appeal, 28 U.S.C. § 1292(b)(1976).

5.101. See 525 F.2d XVIII–XIX (1976). "Senior" status is a device born of the Constitution's guarantee of life tenure to federal judges. U.S. CONST., art. III, § 1. Federal judges may retire at full pay at age 70 with at least ten years' service, or at age 65 with at least fifteen years' service, thereby freeing a position on their court for the appointment of a replacement judge in regular active service. 28 U.S.C. § 371(b) (1976). Disabled federal judges may also retire, at full pay if they have served ten years or longer, and otherwise at half pay. 28 U.S.C. § 372(a) (1976). On the assignment power, see note 5.104 *infra*. Some senior judges continue to render full-time service, maintaining working chambers and regularly-sized staffs. Many others continue working at a slightly reduced pace, and are afforded appropriate office space and staff. Thus the institution of the senior judge provides not only a graceful way of easing off the bench aging judges who can still render useful service when willing and able, but also a way of functionally augmenting the authorized strength of understaffed courts. A judge eligible for senior status can in effect create a new judgeship on his or her court by "retiring" and, while continuing to carry a full load at full pay with a full staff, acquiring for the court the services of the "retired" judge's successor in regular active service. Senior status also brings fewer administration responsibilities and some control over assignments of cases.

5.102. See 573 F.2d XVIII–XIX (1978).

5.103. Act of Oct. 20, 1978, Pub. L. No. 95-486, § 4, 92 Stat. 1629 (amending 28 U.S.C. § 44 (1976)).

judges sitting by assignment to augment the regular active judges of the court.[5.104]

2. Workload

Filings per judgeship have increased more rapidly in the Ninth Circuit than in any of the other federal courts of appeals.[5.105] In the period from fiscal 1961 to fiscal 1978, during which authorized judgeships increased only 44.4 percent from 9 to 13, the filings per judgeship increased 385.7 percent from 49 per judgeship to 238 per judgeship, the highest of any of the circuits. Although having the highest number of filings per judge, the Ninth Circuit is only the third among the circuits in usage of senior and other assigned judges, so that fiscal 1978's filings produced an adjusted total of 471 matters to be considered per judge.[5.106] As of

5.104. The assignment power is vested by statute in the Chief Justice of the United States and the chief judge of each circuit. See generally 28 U.S.C. §§ 291–96 (1976). The chief judge is responsible for the administration of the circuit. Unless declined, the chief judgeship of each circuit is vested in the most senior judge of that circuit still in regular active service and not yet seventy years of age. 28 U.S.C. § 45 (1976).

The common practice on the Ninth Circuit has been to have cases heard by panels consisting of two Ninth Circuit judges in regular active service and one assigned senior Ninth Circuit judge or judge of some other court. This is reflected almost exactly in statistics for the year ending June 30, 1978. (Throughout this book we use the terminology of the State of California and refer to this period as "fiscal 1978." The actual fiscal year for the federal courts ends on September 30th.) These statistics show that 66 percent of participants in cases heard by the Ninth Circuit were judges in regular active service, 13.4 percent were senior Ninth Circuit judges, and 20.6 percent were judges assigned from other courts. See 1978 AOC Report, supra note 5.27, at 50, Table 9.

5.105. Except as otherwise noted, all of the statistics in this paragraph were obtained from 1978 AOC Report, supra note 5.27, at 45, Table 3.

5.106. See id. at 50, Table 9. In the Ninth Circuit, only 66 percent of panel participants are Ninth Circuit judges in regular active service. See note 5.104 supra. The average for all circuits is 75.5 percent, the only circuits with lower percentages being the Second Circuit (59.6 percent) and the Seventh Circuit (65.7 percent), where filings per authorized judgeship are only 200 and 185, respectively. See 1978 AOC Report, supra note 5.27, at 50, Table 9. Multiplying the Ninth Circuit's 238 filings per judgeship by three to reflect the number of judges on each panel (see note 5.27 supra), yields a product of 714, which, when multiplied by .66 to reflect the percentage of panel participation by regularly authorized Ninth Circuit judges, yields a figure of just over 471 filings to be considered per Ninth Circuit judge in regular active service, after taking into account the assistance of other judges. Similar calculations with the averages for all circuits yield an assis-

the end of fiscal 1978, there were 277 cases pending per judgeship of the Ninth Circuit, which at the current rate of 209 dispositions per year per judgeship is a 16 months' backlog of pending cases alone.[5.107] The number of backlogged cases increased by 11.9 percent in fiscal 1978.[5.108]

3. Internal Procedures

Judges of the Ninth Circuit hear argument four days a month. Hearing panels of three are assembled weekly from the court's complement of regular and assigned judges, so that, in contrast to the California courts of appeal, the composition of the hearing panels constantly changes.

At the time of our interviews, the Ninth Circuit was experimenting with two procedures which it has since abandoned. One was an accelerated disposition procedure whereby counsel could stipulate that after oral argument the case might be decided from

---

tance-adjusted figure of just over 441 filings to be considered per circuit judge in regular active service, establishing that even with the extensive assistance they receive, Ninth Circuit judges are substantially more overworked than the average circuit judge. For the parallel statistic of the California courts of appeal, see text accompanying note 5.27 *supra*.

5.107. In fiscal 1978, a total of 2,715 cases in the Ninth Circuit were terminated, or 209 for each of the thirteen authorized judgeships. Of these cases, 447 were consolidated with other cases, leaving 2,268 to be disposed of by decision. Of these 2,268, memorandum opinions were issued in 1,633 (72 percent), and signed opinions were issued in 422 (19 percent), the remainder being disposed of by order. *See* 1978 AOC REPORT, *supra* note 5.27, at 51, Table 10. Reducing these figures by a factor of .66 to reflect assistance received by assigned judges (*see* note 5.104 *supra*) yields figures of 1,078 memorandum opinions, or 83 per authorized judgeship, and 279 signed opinions, or 21 per authorized judgeship. Thus, each judge is responsible for writing over 100 opinions per year, and for reviewing over 200 additional opinions per year prepared by other panel members. Even at this rate, new filings exceeded total terminations by 384 in the Ninth Circuit for fiscal 1978, adding 30 backlogged cases per authorized judgeship (or 19 backlogged cases per judge when allowance is made for assistance received from assigned judges). At the fiscal 1978 rate of 209 dispositions per authorized judgeship, this means that in fiscal 1978 alone an additional seven weeks' worth of cases was added to the court's backlog.

5.108. 1978 AOC REPORT, *supra* note 5.27, at 44, Table 2. At the time of our interviews, we were informed that the court had a backlog of 650 fully briefed cases which were simply awaiting their turn to be scheduled for oral argument. The judges attributed this accumulation not only to the increased rate of filings but also to the increased complexity of the cases themselves, especially those that survive screening procedures and call for full-dress treatment.

the bench with an oral statement of reasons for the decision in lieu of a written opinion. The second was the use of "washday calendars" in which ten to twelve routine cases, generally criminal appeals, were heard at a single session before a single panel of judges.

The accelerated disposition procedure sought to encourage cooperation from the bar by assuring that cases in which oral decision stipulations were received would be heard and decided within sixty to ninety days of such stipulation. The interest in speedy resolution of appeals among the bar was so great, however, that many of the cases heard under the procedure turned out to present complex issues unsuited to oral disposition; counsel were not so willing to accelerate the hearing of appeals of little substance, doubtless because in some cases appeal was taken only for the sake of delay. Washday calendars proved unpalatable to the judges, and the more or less routine cases on such calendars tended to be no more quickly decided than when they were included in the normal mix of cases for oral argument.

In most other respects, the Ninth Circuit's present procedures parallel those at the time of our interviews. Cases are assembled in clusters for oral argument according to the apparent degree of difficulty of the cases. The four degrees of difficulty in use in 1976 have since been increased to five: "one," the easiest; "three," "five," "seven," and "ten," the hardest. Each panel will hear one 16-point cluster of cases in one day of oral argument. In some cases, waiver of oral argument will be solicited in advance of argument; whether or not oral argument has been waived, all cases are assigned to a judge on the hearing panel for preparation of an opinion. Motion panels consisting of two judges, and a "tie breaker" if the two cannot agree, are periodically assembled to deal with petitions for habeas corpus and other pleadings calling upon the original jurisdiction of the court.

Routine cases, said in 1976 to be 40 to 45 percent of those in which an opinion is written, are decided by abbreviated opinions that are considerably shorter than the typical per curiam decision of the California courts of appeal. These opinions are sometimes no more than a half-page in length; a few cases are decided without opinion, by terse order of the court. The trend since 1976 has been towards a decline in the proportion of truly routine cases coming before the court, partly as a result of the sifting out of easy cases from the court's backlog by procedures such as washday calendars. In combination with the larger central staff available to deal with relatively simple cases since 1976 and the abandonment of washday calendars, this trend has led to somewhat longer opinions in the simpler cases. Virtually all opinions in "one" cases and a substantial proportion in "three" cases, however, are now prepared by judges in consultation with central staff attorneys, leaving the personal staff of judges free to deal with the more complex cases.[5.109]

4. Staff

At the time of our interviews, the chief judge of the Ninth Circuit had three elbow clerks, and the other judges two each.[5.110] The court is a recent convert to the use of central staff; as

5.109. Information as to current procedures was obtained in an interview with Arthur D. Hellman, Supervising Staff Attorney, United States Court of Appeals for the Ninth Circuit, in San Francisco, April 5, 1979 [hereinafter cited as Hellman Interview].

Regardless of whether cases are deemed routine or otherwise, the use of bench memoranda at the Ninth Circuit varies with the work habits of the individual judges. One of the court's most prominent former judges has characterized the temperature of the court at oral argument, measured in degrees of precalendar preparation, as varying from "cold" through "tepid" to "scorching." See Hufstedler, supra note 2.67, at 23–24. Occasionally panel members may be introduced to the case at oral argument, but generally they will have reviewed the cases carefully in advance of argument, either by dint of personal preparation or by review of law clerks' precalendar memoranda. See generally text accompanying note 5.116 infra.

5.110. Since 1974, circuit judges have had sufficient appropriations to hire three law clerks at somewhat reduced rates of pay (see note 2.53 supra); but so far as we could ascertain, none of the judges had sought to hire a third personal law clerk as of the time of our interviews, and some even complained that they could not afford to pay two law clerks at the maximum salary. We cannot account for the discrepancy between the statutory funding levels of circuit judge law clerks and the repeated assertions by our subjects that they had too little staff money to permit the hiring of three law clerks, or even to pay two law clerks at the highest legal level.

The general statutory scheme of limits on staff salaries and of the limitation of judicial staff to specified JSP grades keyed to the GS grades of the federal government's General Schedule is described in note 2.53 supra and Federal Funding Note, supra note 2.54. To be specific, the appropriations act in effect as of the time of our interviews was the Act of October 21, 1975, Pub. L. No. 94-121, § 401, 89 Stat. 611, which provided that, exclusive of step increases within grade, "the aggregate salaries paid to secretaries and law clerks appointed by each of the circuit . . . judges shall not exceed $60,902 . . . per annum"; the Act also limited secretaries to a maximum JSP grade equivalent to GS 10, and law clerks to a maximum JSP

of the summer of 1976, the size of its staff had just doubled from
ten to twenty attorneys. (By early 1979 the staff stood at thirty
attorneys, with no further growth anticipated in the near future.)
The court is experimenting with two innovations in the use of
central staff. Eight of the Ninth Circuit's twenty staff attorneys in
1976 had been hired on the same short-term, recently graduated
basis as traditional law clerks,[5.111] under the Ninth Circuit's

---

grade equivalent to GS 12. Under the then-applicable General Schedule, 5 U.S.C.
§ 5332 (1970), *as adjusted by* Exec. Order No. 11,883, 40 Fed. Reg. 47,092 (1975),
the basic salary (exclusive of step increases) at the GS 10 grade was $14,824, which
would leave $46,078 for law clerk salaries, more than enough to pay two law
clerks at the GS 12 level of $19,386 each, and even sufficient to afford two GS 10
law clerks at $14,824 and one GS 11 law clerk at $16,255. The three law clerks'
salaries could be adjusted upward somewhat if a less senior secretary were employed, but with only two law clerks there should have been no problem with
paying both the maximum permitted by law. It would appear that circuit judges
find the byzantine funding limitations on law clerk employment to be as confusing
as do district judges. See *Federal Funding Note, supra* note 2.54.

Some of our subjects complained of the inequity of Fifth Circuit judges being
allowed three law clerks to the Ninth Circuit's two. Fifth Circuit judges receive no
greater staff salary allowance than Ninth Circuit judges, however. We understand
that the third law clerk in the chambers of Fifth Circuit judges is not the result of
lower salary levels or additional funding, but rather reflects a policy decision at that
circuit to apportion among the individual judges staff attorney positions which the
circuit could otherwise use to augment the size of its central staff. Hellman Interview, *supra* note 5.109.

As explained in the addendum to *Federal Funding Note, supra* note 2.54, all
Federal circuit judges were provided with funds sufficient for three elbow clerks as
of October 1979.

5.111.   See Central Staffs Report, *supra* note 2.67, at 29. Most of the twelve
permanent staff attorneys are not nearly as highly paid as those of the California
state appellate courts, whose salary structure is discussed in note 5.41 *supra*. The
chief staff attorney for the entire circuit was limited by statute to no more than
$34,000 in fiscal 1978. Act of Aug. 2, 1977, Pub. L. No. 95-86, § 401, 91 Stat. 419.
This limitation was removed for fiscal 1979, and the position is now paid the JSP
equivalent of a GS 15 salary. *See* Act of Oct. 10, 1978, Pub. L. No. 95-431, § 401,
92 Stat. 1021. At the time of our interviews, the other staff attorneys were limited
to no higher than the JSP equivalent to GS 12, but five positions have since been
upgraded (two to JSP 14 and three to JSP 13). *See* 1977 REPORTS OF THE PROCEED-
INGS OF THE JUDICIAL CONFERENCE OF THE UNITED STATES at 56 [hereinafter cited as
1977 JUDICIAL CONFERENCE PROCEEDINGS]. For fiscal 1979, the pertinent salary
ranges were as follows:

JSP 12	$23,087–$30,017
JSP 13	$27,453–$35,688
JSP 14	$32,442–$42,171
JSP 15	$38,160–$47,500

"court law clerk" program.[5.112] (The 1979 proportions are approximately twenty-five "court law clerks" out of thirty staff attorneys.) To facilitate communication with the central staff, to maintain the morale of its members, and to make the "court law clerk" designation more than a euphemism, the program provides for central staff attorneys to be periodically rotated out to the chambers of cooperating judges. Each judge may have the use of central staff attorneys for periods aggregating up to one month per year.[5.113]

The central staff screens all cases coming to the court. It assigns degrees of difficulty to the cases, and these are utilized in determining the cases in which waiver of oral argument is solicited, in the grouping of cases for oral argument, and in assignment of opinions. Members of the staff prepare precalendar bench memoranda in cases of lesser difficulty, and inventory the issues presented in all fully briefed cases awaiting oral argument. The central staff also prepares motion calendars and pro se matters for judicial review and decision.[5.114]

5. Composite Profile: Judge Gamma

We interviewed five of the seven Ninth Circuit judges in regular active service who were then maintaining chambers in California; we also interviewed one of the four senior judges of the Ninth Circuit with chambers in California. Our composite, Judge Gamma, came to the bench between ten and fifteen years ago, following approximately twenty years of law practice. Some of Gamma's colleagues came to the Ninth Circuit with prior judicial experience; Gamma, too, had been a public servant prior to becoming a judge, his years of private law practice having been punctuated by periods as an attorney for the state or federal gov-

---

See the General Schedule, 5 U.S.C. § 5332 (Supp. I 1977), *as adjusted by* Exec. Order No. 12,087, 43 Fed. Reg. 46,827 (1978), *reprinted in* 5 U.S.C.A., following § 5332 (Supp. 1979). Virtually all the persons employed at JSP grades 12 through 15 are paid at the lower salary steps within those grades. Hellman Interview, *supra* note 5.109.

5.112. *See* note 2.69 *supra*. The data on 1979 staff size were obtained in the Hellman Interview, *supra* note 5.109.

5.113. This feature of the court law clerk program was described to us in our interviews. It appears that judges are using staff attorneys as elbow clerks principally in connection with cases for which staff attorneys prepared precalendar bench memoranda. *See* Central Staffs Report, *supra* note 2.67, at 31.

5.114. *See generally* Hufstedler, *supra* note 2.67, at 21–22.

ernment. Although his academic credentials might well qualify him for a clerkship were he graduating today,[5.115] Judge Gamma gave little thought to a clerkship upon his graduation, and knew little of the institution other than at the Supreme Court of the United States. He now regards clerkships as splendid opportunities for judge and clerk alike, and would desire to be one were he a contemporary law student.

We found great variation in the use of law clerks for precalendar preparation.[5.116] Two judges who formerly had law clerks prepare bench memoranda now regard that task as too unimportant for their law clerks, and perform that task themselves with some help from externs. Bench memoranda are not circulated among panel members by any institutional custom, but are pooled on an ad hoc basis among panel members with compatible styles of precalendar preparation.

Judge Gamma personally gives careful review to the circulating opinions of his fellow panel members, frequently employing his law clerks to assist him in reviewing particular points. A few of his colleagues, however, find that caseload pressures generally preclude using law clerk assistance in the review of circulating opinions. Only one judge found it useful to have clerks draft preargument memoranda in the form of draft opinions.[5.117]

Judge Gamma views the highest function of his personal law clerks as participation in the dialectic resolution of difficult legal issues,[5.118] which often call for sensitive policy determinations as well as technical virtuosity. He values vigorous presentation by the clerk of an independent position by which he can assess the merit of his own views, and feels this honing clash of ideas could not be duplicated were he dealing with a career retainer. Indeed, he is even reluctant to give way to the incipient trend among court of appeals judges to retain their clerks for two years each, with staggered terms so that there is always a senior and junior clerk in chambers. He recognizes clear advantages to productivity through such a system, but has been worried that a clerk will become stale during the second year, and that the best clerkship prospects will be deterred by a two-year requirement. The success of his colleagues in obtaining superior law clerks even for two-year terms and his continued receipt of a hundred or more

5.115. *See* Appendix, Table K.   5.116. *See id.*, Table F.
5.117. *See id.*, Table G.   5.118. *See id.*, Table I.

applications for highly qualified clerkship candidates each year are about to prompt him, too, to shift to a two-year system, but he has a nagging concern that even this modest departure from the traditional clerkship is a subtle compromise forced upon him by rising caseloads.

Judge Gamma treasures the traditional role of an appellate judge and the concomitant relationship with his clerks. Adoption of accelerated disposition procedures are easily justified if they will help preserve his generative function in the law. After routine cases are sifted out, and time for a brief vacation allowed, Judge Gamma finds himself assigned to author roughly one significant opinion per week, and he reserves his law clerks first and foremost for assistance in this task.[5.119]

He persists in the belief, somewhat stubbornly by his own admission and anachronistically by his own acknowledgment, that he must personally craft most of an opinion in order to properly monitor his thought processes as he reasons from principle to decision. With relatively few exceptions, he uses his clerks' draft opinions as working papers, rewriting them almost entirely even when the draft is excellent in its own right. A minority of Judge Gamma's colleagues feel more secure than he in editing a law clerk's draft opinion without fear of falling unduly under the analytical influence of the clerk. Such judges are more willing than Gamma to incorporate substantial portions of law clerk language into their own opinions.

In hiring his personal law clerks, Judge Gamma looks for a complex mix of talents and emotions: legal brilliance, assertiveness, diligence, exceptional writing ability, technical skill, meticulousness, creativity, "jurisprudential imagination," and common sense. He is convinced that he is much more likely to find those qualities in a short-term, newly graduated clerk than in a career court-employed lawyer, and that the new graduate will therefore be a markedly superior participant in the dialectic process of decision-making than his career counterpart.[5.120] Judge Gamma confesses candidly to a fear that if he employed career researchers as his elbow staff, he too would become overly dependent on the product of a trusted co-worker, and in turn the career researcher would tend too much to try to reach results which the staffer believed most acceptable to the judge—at the expense of

5.119. *See id.*, Table H.   5.120. *See id.*, Table A.

the value of a decision achieved through argument and counterargument. He accordingly regards it as virtually inconceivable that the Ninth Circuit will ever come to employ career research attorneys as personal law clerks. He is already concerned—indeed, one of his colleagues expressed "shock"—at the extent of the influence of the senior career clerks at the California Supreme Court, as perceived in that court's opinions and corroborated by his law clerks' peers at that court.

Although he feels vague qualms about its impersonality, Judge Gamma accepts the institution of central staff and his court's growing use of it as indispensable to preservation of his ability to handcraft the law in the face of the "crisis of volume."[5.121] He is not overly concerned about undue influence accruing to the career lawyers of the Ninth Circuit's own central staff, partly because of the limited role to which the court has consciously confined them. He has some worry that, after a period of four or five years of employment, the career staff attorneys may become overly bureaucratized. This concern leaves him somewhat torn in his attitude towards the generally low pay of the court's permanent staff attorneys;[5.122] while low pay means that the court cannot attract career employees of the caliber of the best senior research attorneys at the Supreme Court of California, it also encourages a high degree of turnover among the permanent staff, thereby mitigating the danger of bureaucratization, excessive influence, and gradual judicial dependence.

Judge Gamma believes he could put one more law clerk to good use, and would like to be able to employ a third clerk.[5.123] In the meantime, he generally has an extern on hand.[5.124] One judge opposes externs on grounds of principle, believing that the government ought not to accept free services and that externs threaten the confidentiality of the court. Other judges habitually have two and sometimes three externs assisting them. Given their intimate relationship with their law clerks, Ninth Circuit judges tend to employ externs only insofar as the externs contribute to their chambers' productivity; their varying views on that score accounts chiefly for their varying use of externs.[5.125] Active extern

5.121. See id., Table J.   5.122. See note 5.111 supra.
5.123. See note 5.110 supra; Appendix, Table B.
5.124. See Appendix, Table C.
5.125. See id., Table E. See also id., Table D.

users generally have institutional ties with particular law schools that supply externs, and sometimes clerks as well, on a regular basis. To the extent that favored institutions do not screen clerkship applicants for them, most judges have their present clerks pan the stream of applications for nuggets worthy of judicial appraisal.

D. United States District Courts

1. Jurisdiction, Organization, Workload, and Staff

The district court is the trial court of general jurisdiction in the federal system.[5.126] There are four United States district courts in California: the twelve-judge Northern District of California, headquartered in San Francisco; the six-judge Eastern District of California, headquartered in Sacramento; the seventeen-judge Central District of California, headquartered in Los Angeles; and the seven-judge Southern District of California, headquartered in San Diego.[5.127]

Besides supervising the trial of facts before juries, or acting as finders of fact themselves, federal district judges decide many questions of law upon motions to dismiss or for summary judgment. Such substantive motions are functionally similar to appeals on questions of law to an appellate court, and are commonly subject to quasi-appellate procedure, with full briefing, oral argu-

---

5.126. *See generally* 28 U.S.C. §§ 1331–62 (1976).

5.127. The size of the California districts is prescribed by the Act of October 20, 1978, Pub. L. No. 95-486, § 1, 92 Stat. 1629 (amending 28 U.S.C. § 133 (1976); their geographies are prescribed by 28 U.S.C. § 84 (1976). The sizes of the districts at the time of our interviews were as follows: eleven judges in the Northern District, three judges in the Eastern District, sixteen judges in the Central District, and five judges in the Southern District. *See* 28 U.S.C. § 133 (1976). According to 28 U.S.C. § 84 (1976), the Northern District "shall" hold court at Eureka, Oakland, and San Jose, as well as San Francisco. Regular sessions other than in San Francisco are held only at San Jose, however. *See* N.DIST.CA.R. 105–1. Also, according to 28 U.S.C. § 84 (1976), the Eastern District "shall" hold court at Fresno and Redding, as well as Sacramento. Regular sessions other than in Sacramento are held only at Fresno, however. *See* E.DIST.CA.R. 6. It is expected that one of the three judges just added to the Eastern District will sit in Fresno. Under the change of venue statute for civil actions, 28 U.S.C. § 1404(c) (1976), a district court may order any civil action to be tried at any place in the division within which it is pending. Since none of the California districts have been divided into formal divisions, the judges of each district have standing authority to sit wherever within the district they choose. *See also* N.DIST.CA.R. 105-2.

ment, and varying degrees of judicial pre-argument preparation.[5.128] Until the repeal in October, 1976 of most of the legislation requiring certain matters to be heard and decided by special
district courts of three judges,[5.129] district judges were often
called upon to sit on such courts to hear challenges to the constitu-
tionality of state and federal statutes.[5.130] In the Ninth Circuit,
willing and able district judges have been given frequent assignments on the chronically understaffed court of appeals,
where they join circuit judges to make up three-judge appellate
panels.[5.131]

The heavy workload of the California districts is typical of
federal district courts nationwide.[5.132] In the year ending June 30,
1977, California federal district courts averaged 382 filings, 385
terminations, and a year-end backlog of 376 pending cases.[5.133]
To assist them against this onslaught, district judges have at least
one law clerk, and generally two.[5.134] No districts have central
staffs as such, although some of the busier districts with substantial filings of petitions for habeas corpus, pro se civil rights suits,
and other prisoners' rights litigation have employed "writ clerks"

5.128. See S. Flanders, supra note 1.7, at 29–33, 62.

5.129. Act of Aug. 12, 1976, Pub. L. No. 94-381, 90 Stat. 1119 (repealing 28
U.S.C. §§ 2281–82 and amending 28 U.S.C. § 2284).

5.130. See generally 1977 REPORT OF THE DIRECTOR OF THE ADMINISTRATIVE
OFFICE OF THE UNITED STATES COURTS 227–30 [hereinafter cited as 1977 AOC
REPORT]; 1976 REPORT OF THE DIRECTOR OF THE ADMINISTRATIVE OFFICE OF THE
UNITED STATES COURTS 208–12.

5.131. See note 5.104 supra.

5.132. The Northern, Eastern, Central and Southern Districts of California
ranked respectively, in terms of total filings per judgeship in the year ending June
30, 1977, 69th, 29th, 62d, and 65th out of 94 district courts nationwide; within the
Ninth Circuit alone, parallel rankings were 8th, 2d, 6th, and 7th, respectively, out
of 14 district courts (not counting the newly established District Court for the
Northern Mariana Islands, discussed in note 5.98 supra). ADMINISTRATIVE OFFICE
OF THE UNITED STATES COURTS, 1977 MANAGEMENT STATISTICS FOR UNITED STATES
COURTS 101–04 [hereinafter cited as 1977 MANAGEMENT STATISTICS].

5.133. These statistics are derived from the figures for total filings, terminations, and pending cases per court listed in 1977 MANAGEMENT STATISTICS 101–04,
supra note 5.132, which were combined for the four California districts and divided by 34.51, a factor representing the total of thirty-five authorized judges for
the four districts as adjusted to reflect unfilled judgeships in the Northern and
Central Districts for part of the year in question.

5.134. See notes 2.49–2.54 and accompanying text supra.

or "pro se clerks" since the mid 1960s.[5.135] Although these law clerks for the court as a whole are not necessarily hired on a short-term basis, they generally remain with a court for a limited period.[5.136] An increasing amount of legal assistance, in some ways the functional equivalent of the work of central staffs and in many ways more explicitly quasi-judicial than the work of staff attorneys,[5.137] is being provided to district courts by federal magistrates.[5.138]

2. Composite Profile: Judge Delta

The fourteen federal district judges whom we interviewed were drawn from all four of the California districts. Three of our subjects were the chief judges of their districts; two subjects were senior judges.[5.139] Our composite, Judge Delta, has been a district judge in regular active service for about ten years, having come to the bench after fifteen to twenty years of extensive litigation experience with a mid-sized law firm engaged principally in civil practice. Several of his colleagues came to the district court bench by way of the California trial court bench.[5.140]

As a law student as well as a judge, Delta's interests have tended towards the practical rather than the academic aspects of the law.[5.141] When he was a law student, law clerkships were considered an academic institution; there was considerable prestige attached to clerkships at the United States Supreme Court, but little prestige and therefore little practical advantage attached to clerkships elsewhere.

5.135. *See* Zeigler & Hermann, *supra* note 1.7, at 176 ("pro se law clerk" at Southern District of New York since 1966). We learned from our interviews that the larger districts in California similarly employ "writ clerks."

5.136. The low salary ceilings on federal staff attorneys virtually assure considerable turnover even among "permanent" employees. *See* note 5.111 *supra*.

5.137. *See generally* Kaufman, *supra* note 2.85; Zeigler & Hermann, *supra* note 1.7, at 208 & n.219; S. Flanders, *supra* note 1.7, at 60–62. *See also* text accompanying note 2.85 *supra*.

5.138. *See* 28 U.S.C. §§ 631–39 (1976).

5.139. As previously noted, we interviewed one senior federal district judge through his proxy, the judge's law clerk. *See* note 4.20 *supra*; text accompanying note 4.22 *supra*.

5.140. Six of our fourteen subjects had served on a superior court, and three of those six had first served on a municipal court.

5.141. *See* Appendix, Table K.

Since taking the bench, Judge Delta has become firmly convinced that no experience can better prepare a law student for a life practicing law than a clerkship in a federal court: a district court for the litigation oriented, a court of appeals for the more academically inclined. Were he graduating from law school today, he would want very much to be a federal district court clerk, and he is conscious of the irony that were he among the applicants for a clerkship on his own court, his law school record would probably not qualify him for serious consideration. He is confident that he would have been a competent clerk, but he was not on his school's law review, and he has grown to regard law review experience as an essential qualification for a law clerk. There is no better guarantee that a law clerk will possess the qualities Judge Delta deems most important for the job: initiative, writing skills, and the ability to respond positively and productively to time pressure.

The judge started his career on the federal bench by employing a "court crier" or bailiff[5.142] and a single law clerk. He characterizes his initial conception of the judicial process as "naive" in its treatment of the law clerk as a relatively peripheral participant. Judge Delta had inherited from his predecessor judge a rather elderly bailiff whom he agreed to keep on the job and for whom he developed a great affection. He quickly realized, however, that he would benefit greatly from the services of a second law clerk. The utility of a bailiff as a sort of judicial retainer was anachronistic in the modern era of clogged calendars and increasing legal complexity. While declining to discharge his inherited bailiff, Judge Delta encouraged his early retirement and happily hired a second law clerk as his replacement.[5.143]

5.142. Although officially classified as a court crier, see note 2.54 supra, most judges referred to such a person as a "bailiff." Similar terminology is reported in S. Flanders, supra note 1.7, at 62.

5.143. An additional law clerk hired in lieu of a court crier or bailiff is officially classified as a "crier-clerk." See Federal Funding Note, supra note 2.54. Five of our fourteen subjects still had court criers instead of a second law clerk, but each indicated that he would hire a second law clerk upon the retirement of his crier. None of our subjects indicated that fewer than two clerks would be optimal. See Appendix, Table B. Only chief judges of districts with five or more judges are currently entitled to hire a third law clerk, see note 2.53 supra, and, indeed, 75 percent of our subjects felt that two rather than three clerks was the optimal number, doubting their own ability to effectively supervise more than two clerks at a time. It should be noted that the courtroom obligations of district judges severely limit their

For some time, Judge Delta functioned with two clerks selected annually. He hesitated at requiring two-year clerkships out of fear that the longer term would be unfair to the clerk and discourage the best applicants. He has recently overcome these qualms, however, and has begun to hire his clerks for two-year staggered terms, with one new clerk arriving each year. His burden of selection has been cut in half, and he will now always have one experienced clerk on hand to keep the work flowing as the new clerk gains a grasp of the job. Notwithstanding an inadequate first-year salary and the two-year commitment, the quality and quantity of clerkship applicants has not suffered from his new clerkship policy.[5.144]

Judge Delta uses his law clerks in a variety of ways, but their primary tasks arise in connection with substantive motions.[5.145] The judge has a weekly motion calendar, which sometimes may consume an entire court day. Civil and criminal motions are generally heard on alternating weeks. The clerks divide pending motions among themselves and review each, researching selected points very briefly. Generally, Judge Delta requests a single pre-calendar memorandum that collects and describes the pending

---

ability to monitor and coordinate the hour-by-hour activities of their clerks in chambers.

5.144. All five of our subjects with only one clerk hired that clerk annually, but six of the nine subjects with two clerks hired their clerks for staggered two-year terms. Of the three subjects with two annual clerks, two made it their practice to have one new clerk arrive a month or so earlier than the other, to allow some overlap between the outgoing and incoming clerks. The third judge accomplished the same objective by attempting to have both new clerks arrive several days before the departure of his old clerks.

5.145. As with our discussion of internal procedures of the Supreme Court of California, see note 5.96 supra, our paradigmatic presentation of the internal procedures associated with federal district court motion practice draws upon the personal knowledge of the authors as well as our interview data. The interviews were intended to produce data on departures from general practice: indirectly, however, the content of the interviews strongly corroborates that the details here depicted are an accurate account of the common knowledge shared by interviewer and subjects. For public corroboration of the validity of our composite judge's procedures for hearing and deciding motions, see S. Flanders, supra note 1.7, at 62. Flanders's account is consistent with our data except for the breadth of its generalizations as to law clerk practices in the Central District of California (e.g., Los Angeles), where we found somewhat greater diversity of law clerk use. See also Three Views, supra note 1.7, at 165–68 (procedures in Northern District of Alabama).

motions, noting troublesome issues in highly summary fashion; usually no more than a paragraph is devoted to each case. Most of the procedural motions are decided from the bench, as are some of the more substantive ones. Motions taken under submission are researched in accordance with the judge's instructions; since Judge Delta makes it his practice to decide submitted cases by written opinion, the postcalendar research memoranda of his clerks are usually prepared as draft opinions.

Within the parameters of Judge Delta's motion practice there are many individual variations by his colleagues. One judge generally reviews pending motions himself, preferring to save his clerks' time for substantive motions filtered out by the judge and assigned for special precalendar treatment, or for the drafting of opinions on motions taken under submission. Another judge encourages oral reports on pending motions when other duties prevent extensive law clerk precalendar preparation. Judges vary greatly in the frequency with which they decide motions by written opinions and in the frequency with which they submit their opinions for publication in the official reports; these variations affect their clerks' postcalendar activities.[5.146]

Judge Delta's clerks operate in conventional Ninth Circuit fashion when Judge Delta sits by assignment on the court of appeals. They prepare precalendar bench memoranda to Delta's specifications; these memoranda are much more detailed than those relating to pending trial motions. After oral argument at the court of appeals, Judge Delta's clerks prepare draft opinions in the cases assigned to him.

In addition to the precalendar activity and subsequent opinion preparation arising out of Judge Delta's motion practice and appellate assignments, Delta's law clerks perform a host of other chores ancillary to the trial of cases, such as advising the judge on jury instructions or procedural rulings and drafting decisional memoranda as outlined by the judge in cases in which he is the trier of fact. The mechanical aspects of operating the courtroom are handled by the judge himself, however, together with the administrative clerk and the stenographic reporter assigned to Judge Delta's courtroom. Judge Delta rarely requires his law clerks to be in the courtroom, although he welcomes them there and encourages their attendance when time permits.

5.146. *See generally* Appendix, Tables F & G.

Judge Delta frequently engages, at his own initiative, in discussion of problem cases with his clerks.[5.147] He believes that such dialectic argument contributes substantially to the sharpening of his own thought processes and to the quality of his decisions. He considers it the job of his law clerks to prevent him from making mistakes. It is inconceivable to him that the district court could operate effectively without these clerks; in a word, they are "indispensable."

He recognizes that his law clerks have considerable influence on his ideas and on the content of his opinions; indeed, he treasures the articulate clerk who can write well.[5.148] However, he does not fear ideological influence by his clerks; the mistakes they correct are misperceptions of law, not misconceptions of policy. A talented clerk is a valuable tool for communicating the ideas and decisions of the judge who is informed but not inveigled by the dialectic with his clerks. Occasionally, that dialectic leaves the judge and a clerk in irreconcilable positions; if this prevents the clerk from adequately drafting an opinion, the judge is quite prepared to produce the opinion on his own.

The judge has for the past few years had one or two externs working in his chambers during most of the year.[5.149] He has mixed feelings about externs, believing on balance that they contribute slightly to his ability to be productive.[5.150] Some of Judge Delta's colleagues believe that externs are a net burden on the court,[5.151] although they sometimes use externs nonetheless because of the value of the opportunity to the students.[5.152] Just as many of his colleagues, however, believe that externs are more than marginally helpful.[5.153] When at times Judge Delta has been on the point of personally dropping his extern program, a particularly adept student has made such a positive contribution, on a

5.147. *See id.*, Table I.   5.148. *See id.*, Table H.

5.149. *See id.*, Table C. We classified district judges who generally have at least one extern as making "moderate" use of externs. Two judges who frequently have two externs were classified as making "extensive" use of externs.

5.150. *See id.*, Table E.   5.151. *Id.*

5.152. One of the judges whom we classified as considering externs to be a burden to his productivity, *id.* at Table E, nevertheless uses two externs per semester because he enjoys providing such a valuable educational experience for them. The other judge classified as using externs because of the value to them of the experience, *see id.*, Table D, believes that he breaks even in terms of productivity so long as he confines himself to one extern at a time.

5.153. *See id.*, Table E.

par with a regular law clerk, that Delta has had to change his mind. He reduces the administrative burden of his extern program by leaving the selection process to one or more cooperating law schools.

Although he can imagine having a permanent law clerk, Judge Delta finds the prospect unpalatable.[5.154] Like all his colleagues, he believes that short-term clerks are of higher quality than career personnel and bring a greater degree of freshness of thought to the court. Through their freshness, short-term clerks provide an antidote to the professional isolation that Judge Delta has discovered to be an unfortunate consequence of taking the bench. He sees only one advantage in the use of long-term clerks: the practice would relieve him of the considerable administrative burden incident to culling long lists of outstandingly qualified clerkship candidates. However, his recent adoption of two-year, staggered terms for his clerks reduces this chore and also provides him each fall with a trained assistant of over one year's experience to share the arduous process of reviewing clerkship applications.

5.154. *See id.*, Table A. We found, somewhat to our surprise, that despite the budgetary disincentives, at least four judges within the memories of our subjects had employed long-term law clerks while on the district court. These judges sat on the Northern, Central, and Southern Districts of California and on the District of Hawaii; one was deceased and the other three were senior judges at the time of our interviews. One of the three was still active and still employed his career clerk at the time of our interviews, but was not among our subjects.

Two of the career clerks were described to us as "secretary–law clerks," but this position carries the same JSP 12 salary ceiling as a law clerk per se, which as of fiscal 1979 was $30,017. *See* notes 2.54 & 5.111 *supra*. It thus appears that the career clerks remained with their district judges, despite such an uncompetitive salary, because of either limited skills or second incomes. Of the two career clerks not classified as secretary–law clerks, we learned that one wrote books for supplemental income and may also have had private means; the other was a retired army officer.

Our subjects' knowledge of the use of career clerks by their colleagues tended to reinforce their preference for short-term clerks, regardless of budgetary constraints. One of our subjects recounted with evident distaste how it had been widely rumored among the bar that the decisions and opinions of one of the career-clerk-equipped district judges were the product of the clerk rather than the judge. One of the district judges' clerks with whom we spoke described his co-clerk—the one career clerk whom we knew was still active at a federal district court in California—as more concerned with "efficiency" and less inclined to "discursive discussion" than the other clerks at the court. The career clerk was also said to be very good at predicting the behavior of his judge.

Judge Delta can conceive of a proper role for long-term clerks at an appellate court, so long as short-term clerks are also present. If he were authorized to employ three law clerks, he might consider employing one on a long-term basis.[5.155] In such a hypothetical situation, however, he feels he would be nagged by misgivings that over time the career clerk would become his alter ego, subject to less supervision and acquiring by accretion greater and greater authority over the operation of his chambers. At the trial court level, the only justification for career clerks, as well as for central staff, is the development of judicial asssistants with special expertise.[5.156] This need is better filled, he believes, by the expanding use of magistrates.[5.157]

5.155. Only three of our subjects considered more than two clerks to be optimal, however. *See* Appendix, Table B.

5.156. Two of the three district judges shown in Table J of the Appendix as favoring the use of central staff were chief judges who endorsed the continued use of "writ clerks." *See* text accompanying note 5.135 *supra*. The third district judge whom we found to favor the concept of central staff appeared to contemplate a district court's central staff as performing the same function as writ clerks.

5.157. Although only three of our subjects directly expressed the point that magistrates were the proper means for performing a central staff function at the district court level, none of our subjects expressed or implied contrary sentiments. All of our subjects who mentioned magistrates, whether as a central staff or otherwise, took a very positive view of the expanding role of magistrates at federal district courts.

VI. COMPARATIVE ANALYSES OF COURTS AND COMPOSITES

Our four composite judges and our appended four-way tables of selected judicial attitudes invite comparative analysis. The structure of our analyses is patterned after the sequence of topics in Chapters II and III, above. First, we compare and contrast the duties of law clerks at the four courts we studied, using as a foil the idealized model of a traditional clerkship which we have derived from Samuel Williston's service with Horace Gray, and which we have defended as a worthy template for the institution. Second, we discuss the varying roles of central staff at our four courts. Third, we compare the use of externs at the four courts. Finally, we dwell at length on the relative hospitality of the four courts towards career clerks as opposed to short-term clerks, and we propose strategies for fostering the short-term law clerk usage which we believe essential if law clerkships at modern courts are to retain the essential attributes of the clerkship ideal.

A. *Limiting Considerations*

We wish to preface our analyses by noting, and then discounting, two potential caveats concerning the utility of our data for the purpose of comparative analysis between courts. First, our unstructured interviews produced inherently imprecise data, especially in the context of the aggregate attitudes of one court's judges versus another court's judges.[6.1] We have, however, kept this limitation uppermost in mind in processing our data and constructing our composites, leaving matters of detail undefined when the data are conflicting or unrevealing. Despite the caution

6.1. *See generally* text accompanying notes 4.7–4.15 *supra*.

with which our composites have been constructed, there may nonetheless be a tendency to regard each composite as representative of all the judges of that court, rather than just the judges who participated in our study. We do not mean to suggest that this tendency should necessarily be resisted. Nothing in our data or our personal experience leads us to believe that, in most respects, our composites are not representative of their courts as a whole, but it remains true that this assertion cannot provide its own corroboration.

Our second caveat calls attention to the tendency of most people accustomed to a particular behavior to view that behavior as the standard of propriety and to question the acceptability of behavior that deviates from their norm. Budgetary factors beyond the control of any of our judges have operated to afford federal judges little choice but to employ short-term elbow clerks, while encouraging state judges to hire career counterparts. This might lead us to expect unanimous disapproval of career clerks by federal judges, and similarly unanimous approval of career clerks by state judges—or at least approval of career clerks proportional to the number of state judges employing career clerks. However, we find that while federal judges do indeed abhor the idea of long-term clerks, their misgivings about career clerks are generally shared even by those state judges who choose to employ such clerks. Thus, we conclude that the influence of budgetary factors, like the unreliability of the fine points of our data, should be neither underemphasized nor overemphasized. Data such as ours can be compressed into nothingness by the sheer weight of qualifications or extrapolated beyond meaning if their limitations are ignored. In an effort at avoiding either extreme, we have presented our data in as raw a state as possible, given our promises of confidentiality. We have also described in detail the methods by which the data were gathered and processed, and we urge that the imprecision of these methods be remembered in evaluating the analyses that follow.

B. *Duties of Law Clerks*

Law clerk preparation of pre-argument memoranda is virtually universal at the state courts we studied, and is also the rule, with exceptions, at the federal courts.[6.2] Law clerks at the California

6.2. *See* Appendix, Table F.

courts of appeal have the preparation of "calendar memoranda" as their first priority;[6.3] at the Supreme Court of California, "calendar memoranda" compete with "conference memoranda" on pending petitions for discretionary review for first claim on law clerks' time;[6.4] at the Ninth Circuit, pre-argument memoranda are prepared with less regularity and formality, and are overshadowed by the clerks' role in formulating and articulating their judges' written opinions;[6.5] at federal district courts, all law clerks have a wide variety of tasks, but normally foremost among these are review and analysis of pending motions in advance of their argument.[6.6] Pre-argument memoranda are not typically in draft opinion form at any of the courts studied, but a significant proportion are prepared as draft opinions at all courts except the district courts.[6.7] At the California courts of appeal and supreme court, "calendar memoranda" significantly color the content of subsequent opinions at these courts, regardless of the format of the memoranda at the time of their circulation to other panel members.[6.8] However, there appears to be little variance in the ultimate influence of law clerks upon opinions at the four courts, regardless of their differences in pre-argument memoranda practice.[6.9]

There are notable differences in the frequency of discussion between judges and law clerks.[6.10] As might be expected, the federal courts, with their less systematic preconference memoranda practices, feature significantly higher degrees of discursive interaction between judges and law clerks. Unlike Judges Beta and Alpha of the California Supreme Court and courts of appeal, respectively, Judge Gamma of the Ninth Circuit and Judge Delta of the district court mention dialectic argument with their clerks as one of the most valuable results of the clerkship institution.[6.11]

The federal courts in general, and the district courts in particu-

6.3. *See* text accompanying note 5.49 *supra*.

6.4. *See* generally text accompanying notes 5.80–5.89 *supra*.

6.5. *See* text accompanying notes 5.116–5.119 *supra*.

6.6. *See* text accompanying notes 5.145–5.146 *supra*.

6.7. *See* Appendix, Table G.

6.8. *See* text accompanying notes 5.54, 5.90, & 5.95 *supra*. *See also* Appendix, Table H.

6.9. *See* Appendix, Table H.

6.10. *See id.*, Table I.

6.11. *See* text accompanying notes 5.118 & 5.147 *supra*.

lar, feature contemporary clerkship usage most similar to that of Horace Gray. Ninth Circuit judges most resemble Gray in their generally scholarly inclinations[6.12] and in the majority's penchant for rewriting opinions drafted by clerks.[6.13] District judges may rely more on clerks for opinion writing,[6.14] but in general follow Gray's model of getting the benefit of their clerks' advice largely by oral interaction, whether it be about pending motions, evolving opinions, or the day-to-day operation of the court.[6.15] Like Gray, district judges (and, to a varying extent, all the judges we studied who employed short-term law clerks) see their law clerks as talented apprentices with whom the judge can personally identify, and who provide the judge with the legal companionship that the judge lost from his contemporaries upon taking the bench.[6.16] These judges feel that they can attain and afford such intellectual intimacy with their clerks only because of the clerks' limited tenure; they regard the personalities of career clerks as less engaging, and they fear that a close relationship with a career clerk—judging from the examples known to them—breeds an atmosphere of too much equality and hence too much dependence on the clerk.[6.17] The paternalism inherent in the relationship between a judge and a short-termed, newly graduated law clerk is, for them, the sine qua non of proper judicial independence in the ultimate acts of decision-making by which the roles of judge and clerk are distinguished.

C. Central Staff

Of all the judges we studied, district judges were the least harried by an overwhelming caseload.[6.18] This not only maximizes their opportunity for close and personal interactions with their law clerks, but also leaves them, as a group, least sympathetic to the concept of central staff.[6.19] As a rule, district judges are like Justice Gray in having little discretion as to the exercise of jurisdiction. In

6.12. *See* Appendix, Table K.

6.13. *See* text accompanying notes 5.119–5.120 *supra*.

6.14. *See* text accompanying notes 5.145–5.148 *supra*.

6.15. Compare *id*. with text accompanying notes 2.25–2.31 *supra*.

6.16. *See generally* text accompanying notes 5.141 & 5.154 *supra*.

6.17. *See generally* text accompanying notes 5.97, 5.120–5.121, & 5.155–5.156 *supra*.

6.18. *See* text accompanying notes 6.55–6.58 *infra*.

6.19. *See* Appendix, Table J.

those fields in which district judges do have, in a functional sense, a considerable degree of discretion as to the exercise of jurisdiction—e.g., in deciding whether to order a return to a petition for a writ of habeas corpus or to appoint counsel for an indigent petitioner or civil rights complainant—district judges generally welcome the one-person central staff of a "writ" or "pro se" law clerk.[6.20]

At the Ninth Circuit and the California courts of appeal, judges lack discretion over their jurisdiction per se; but in order to avoid complete inundation by increasing caseloads,[6.21] they have devised tracking systems which do afford them considerable discretion over how much judicial time will be spent in reviewing and disposing of particular cases. The Ninth Circuit's tracking system has been engineered almost exclusively by judges, although its operation is left to central staff attorneys. For this reason, and because the staff attorneys are predominantly short-termed in tenure and are rotated out periodically to work in the chambers of individual judges, Ninth Circuit judges manifest little concern over central staff usurpation of judicial prerogatives. Ninth Circuit judges unreservedly allow central staff to screen routine cases and prepare cursory draft opinions disposing of them; together with a lower caseload and an additional clerk, this enables Ninth Circuit judges to spend a considerably greater proportion of their time personally crafting opinions than is the case with their California court of appeal counterparts.[6.22]

We received a different impression of attitudes toward central staff at the California courts. Judges of the courts of appeal generally felt that the central staff was under control in their division, but that undue delegation to both elbow clerks and central staff had occurred elsewhere at the courts of appeal and at the Supreme Court of California.[6.23] Our subjects at the supreme court, who generally had had experience as court of appeal judges, tended to suspect the central staffs of the courts of appeal of undue influence over the nominally responsible judges.[6.24] Moreover, there was a

6.20. *See generally* text accompanying note 5.135 *supra*.

6.21. *See generally* text accompanying notes 5.17–5.27 & 5.105–5.108 *supra*. *See also* text accompanying notes 6.49–6.55 *infra*.

6.22. *See generally* text accompanying notes 5.111–5.114 & 5.121–5.122 *supra*.

6.23. *See* text accompanying notes 5.58–5.59 *supra*.

6.24. *See* text accompanying note 5.97 *supra*.

distinct feeling manifested by many court of appeal judges whom we interviewed that the central staff was a judicial institution of somewhat remote judicial creation and only partially under judicial control. The principal attorneys of the two largest courts of appeal were repeatedly referred to by name with the greatest deference and respect; these men were clearly *éminences grises* that must be reckoned with, and, indeed, one was the brother of a sitting judge of the court that his staff served. At another of the courts of appeal, the judges acquiesced in a system under which all elbow clerk positions had been subsumed some years before into a central staff, notwithstanding that three of the five judges with whom we spoke at this court expressed a preference for returning to a conventional system of short-term elbow clerks responsible to each of them personally and exclusively.[6.25]

At the Supreme Court of California, we perceived little concern over the role of that court's central staff; indeed, there seemed to be a reluctance to acknowledge the extent to which the court's use of staff assistance in reviewing criminal petitions was procedurally similar to the screening function performed by the central staffs of the courts of appeal. This attitude appears to reflect the perception by our supreme court subjects that the central staffs at the courts of appeal were suspect institutions, largely autonomous and concerned primarily with quantitative output;[6.26] at the same time, these justices seemed to believe that the work of the Chief Justice's staff attorneys in screening criminal petitions not only reflected great concern for the quality of justice in the courts of appeal,[6.27] but also was closely monitored by the law clerks of the associate justices.[6.28] Thus, while the recommendations of the Chief Justice's specialists on criminal petitions were not in any real sense supervised by the Chief Justice personally— and hence were functionally the product of a central staff serving the court as a whole[6.29]—this central staff did not have the unsupervised aura of the central staffs of the courts of appeal. Although instances of ultimate disagreement were rare, the number of criminal petitions put over by the court for further review by

6.25. *See* note 5.39 *supra*; note 6.44 *infra*.

6.26. *See generally* text accompanying note 5.97 *supra*. *See also* Appendix, Table J.

6.27. *See generally* text accompanying note 5.82 *supra*.

6.28. *See* text accompanying note 5.87 *supra*.

6.29. *See* text accompanying note 5.77 *supra*.

the staffs of other judges was significant enough for the court as a whole to have little consciousness that the criminal petition staff was essentially a central staff. Indeed, it was somewhat paradoxical that while the perception of the criminal staff as something other than a central staff was reinforced by the practice of having the staff's work product issued in the name of the Chief Justice, there were nonetheless no inhibitions, to our knowledge at least, against disputing the staff's analysis on the ground that such analysis had been vouched for by the Chief Justice. Whatever its consciousness of the fact, the supreme court treated the criminal petition staff's work as that of a staff serving the court as a whole, and subject to the scrutiny of the court as a whole.

The Supreme Court of California's attitude thus approximates that of the Ninth Circuit, which presents a rather stark contrast to the California courts of appeal in its judges' control over central staff. Ninth Circuit judges appeared to us to monitor the work of central staff closely, not as observers but as supervisors. For example, several Ninth Circuit judges expressed dissatisfaction during our interviews with aspects of the central staff's work product. The following year, the supervising staff attorney of the circuit was replaced by a professor of law who took office with the mutual understanding that his tenure would be limited to the few years necessary to streamline the operation of the central staff to the court's satisfaction. Thus the court has cultivated a high degree of turnover among its staff directors as well as its junior staff attorneys. The result is a court that is confident in the clear subordination of its central staff to the commissioned judges whom they serve. As we have intimated, this confidence appears to underlie the court's acceptance of central staff treatment of its many routine cases as an appropriate means of conserving scarce judicial time for significant cases.

D. *Externs*

The Supreme Court of California stood out among our subject courts in its enthusiasm for externs.[6.30] A number of factors appear to account for this enthusiasm. The court's painstaking review of the huge number of petitions invoking its discretionary jurisdiction[6.31] creates a ready pool of work for externs, demand-

6.30. *See* Appendix, Tables C & E.
6.31. *See* text accompanying note 5.82 *supra*.

ing considerable energy and dedication but less sophisticated skills than the drafting of calendar memoranda or opinions. The fact that the court's employed staff consists predominantly of career law clerks encourages the judges to bring externs to the court for the benefit of their fresh thinking and as a line of communication to the latest law school theorizing, while also affording the judges the benefit of experienced subordinates to manage so much of the administration of extern programs as is not left to cooperating law schools, and to supervise the day-to-day activities of externs at the court. In most of the chambers of the Supreme Court of California, externs tend to function as the law clerks of the career clerk, dealing with the judge directly on some occasions but receiving most of their assignments and supervision from the career clerk.[6.32]

In this context, the judges of the supreme court see externs as very much pulling their own weight. Whatever the collateral benefits of extern programs, their principal justification is the contribution of externs to the processing of petitions for hearing.[6.33]

Ninth Circuit judges lack both the California Supreme Court's administrative infrastructure of career clerks and its overflowing reservoir of applications for discretionary review. Internal memoranda on undemanding cases, with resulting recommendations of accelerated-disposition treatment, are produced by central staff.[6.34] Moreover, Ninth Circuit judges relish the freshness of their employed law clerks,[6.35] and need not enlist externs as surrogates for this purpose. Ninth Circuit judges do feel understaffed, however, and generally use extern assistance in lieu of the third clerk they would prefer.[6.36] The productivity of externs is their key to continued employment by a given judge.[6.37] Those judges who save their clerks' time almost exclusively for opinion preparation find externs useful for pre-argument memoranda preparation;[6.38] to be more widely useful, externs must be of ex-

6.32. See note 2.77 *supra*.

6.33. See text accompanying notes 5.78–5.79 *supra*. See also Appendix, Table E.

6.34. See *generally* text accompanying notes 5.111–5.114 *supra*.

6.35. See text accompanying notes 5.120 & 5.125 *supra*.

6.36. See text accompanying notes 5.123–5.124 *supra*. See also text accompanying note 6.59 *infra*.

6.37. See text accompanying note 5.125 *supra*.

6.38. See text accompanying note 5.116 *supra*.

ceptional quality. Those judges who obtain externs by way of standing programs with cooperating law schools can place upon such schools the burden of ascertaining whether extern prospects have the ability to contribute to their chambers' productivity.[6.39]

Much more mixed patterns of extern use prevail at the federal district courts and the California courts of appeal. At both courts the judges vary widely in their assessment of externs' contributions to the courts' work, and at both courts some judges retain externs for altruistic reasons despite the lack of any perceived benefit—or even the occasional net detriment—to their chambers' output.[6.40] Generally, however, externs are used because they are useful. The way they are used, however, differs somewhat between the federal district courts and one faction at the state courts of appeal. Like Ninth Circuit judges, some California court of appeal judges use extern assistance in lieu of the additional law clerk they need.[6.41] These judges tend to have short-term law clerks;[6.42] like their federal district court peers, they generally give externs the same sort of assignments as their regular law clerks, and they rely heavily on cooperating law schools to relieve them of the burden of extern selection and administration. These judges frequently make their extern programs available to other judges of their courts of appeal, who enjoy the freshness of externs and retain them so long as they are provided by or through the efforts of their colleagues.[6.43] Such recipient judges generally leave the management of externs to their career clerks, while enjoying access to a fresh face when the spirit moves them. Federal district judges with two-year staggered clerkship programs also have the benefit of an experienced subordinate to assist in the care and feeding of externs; but even in these chambers, the role of externs at federal district courts more closely approximates the role of regular law clerks than is true at the chambers of the California court of appeal judges who employ long-term law clerks. As at the Supreme Court of California, court of appeal externs of judges with long-term law clerks are in many ways law clerks to the career clerks.

6.39. *See generally* text accompanying note 5.125 *supra*.

6.40. *See generally* Appendix, Tables C, D & E.

6.41. *See* text accompanying note 5.47 *supra*. *See generally* text accompanying note 6.59 *infra*.

6.42. *See* text accompanying note 5.58 *supra*.

6.43. *See id.*

E. *Deriving Coefficients of Short-Term Law Clerk Use*

A striking result of comparative analysis is that the contrast between the exclusive use of short-term law clerks by the federal judges and the general use of long-term law clerks by the state appellate judges is not mirrored by a similar division of attitude regarding the perceived qualities of law clerks as a function of their tenure. Judge Alpha of the California court of appeal and Judge Beta of the Supreme Court of California stand largely in agreement with Judge Gamma of the Ninth Circuit and Judge Delta of the federal district court concerning the lesser danger of undue judicial dependence on, and the greater intellectual assertiveness and general vivacity of, short-term clerks cut from traditional cloth, that is, from the uppermost ranks of the newly graduated students of major law schools. This poses the question of why state court judges tend to hire career clerks despite misgivings about their characteristics and effects on the judicial process.[6.44]

6.44. The misgivings to which we refer are those reflected in the assessments of the comparative qualities of long-term and short-term law clerks by our composite judges, Alpha of the California courts of appeal and Beta of the Supreme Court of California. *See* text accompanying notes 5.44–5.47 & 5.92–5.94 *supra*. These misgivings are just that and no more; they should not be supposed to be representative only of those judges who employ short-term clerks, or to suggest that judges with such misgivings are acting inconsistently if they nonetheless choose, all things considered, to hire long-term clerks.

Table A of our Appendix might appear to show such inconsistency, since it presents judges of the California courts of appeal as evenly divided over their preference for short-term, as opposed to long-term, law clerks, assuming (as is true at the California courts we studied) that their staff budget allows them to hire either sort. However, it must be remembered that while only seventeen out of forty-eight sitting judges of the California courts of appeal had short-term law clerks at the time of our interviews, sixteen out of our thirty-eight subjects (41.5 percent) were short-term clerk users. *See* note 5.39 *supra*. Of the eighteen court of appeal judges shown as favoring short-term law clerks in Table A, fifteen were short-term clerk users. (We classified the sixteenth short-term clerk user among our subjects as the one judge with "no preference" as to clerkship term.) The remaining three judges classified in Table A as preferring short-term clerks were judges of the Court of Appeal for the Third Appellate District, who by long-standing administrative arrangement in that district have no personal clerks at all. *See* note 5.39 *supra*. Thus, those judges of the courts of appeal whom we interviewed and classified as to law clerk tenure preference were completely consistent in their tenure preferences and elbow clerk hiring practices, insofar as they hired elbow clerks.

The answer appears to lie in a complex of factors, which may be summarized under the headings of caseload pressure, work-load per law clerk, clerkship prestige, and perceptions of law clerk productivity. The "coefficient of short-term law clerk use" for each court is a product of these factors (which vary significantly among the four courts we studied) and the more or less constant factor favoring short-term clerks on qualitative grounds. We believe that the variations in law clerk tenure among the courts may be accounted for by the negative coefficient which results, at the state appellate courts, from the negative force of factors other than the qualitative preference of judges for short-term clerks. These factors are less hostile to short-term law clerks at the federal courts, and result in a positive coefficient favoring short-term law clerks at federal courts.

1. Caseload Pressures

All of the courts we studied were extremely busy, and statistical intercourt comparison of caseloads is at best a dubious exercise in numerology. The types of cases and the manner of their disposition vary greatly by type of court. Like apples and oranges, cases before trial courts and appellate courts differ in ways that greatly limit the usefulness of comparison. Although cases before different appellate courts may seem more fungible, as with grapefruits, oranges, and tangerines, there remain important differences. At the Supreme Court of California, where all matters are considered *en banc*,[6.45] each of the seven justices was responsible

---

Because of the smaller numbers and greater prominence of the judges involved, we cannot be as specific as to the correlations between law clerk tenure preferences and hiring practices of the judges of the Supreme Court of California, except to note that the one judge we classified as having a weak preference for short-term law clerks had expressed interest in expanding his use of short-term clerks. This datum must be considered anomalous in view of the subsequent contrary trend at the supreme court. *See* notes 2.77, 5.79, & 5.94 *supra*.

6.45. Until 1966, the California Supreme Court was authorized to sit in departments of three judges each, with assignment of cases to departments or the court as a whole controlled by the Chief Justice or by vote of four judges. CAL. CONST. art. VI, § 2 (1879, repealed 1966). This provision was anachronistic after the creation of an intermediate appellate court in 1904. *See* CAL. CONST., art. VI, § 4 (1879, as amended 1904, repealed 1966). The present constitution states in pertinent part: "The Supreme Court consists of the Chief Justice of California and 6 associate justices. . . . Concurrence of 4 judges present at the argument is necessary for a judgment." CAL. CONST., art. VI, § 2. Four judges must also concur in a decision to assert jurisdiction. *See* text accompanying note 5.61 *supra*.

for consideration of all 3,665 matters filed in fiscal 1977. More meaningfully compared are the 610 and 471 filings to be considered per judge of the California courts of appeal and the Ninth Circuit, respectively, in each court's most recently reported year.[6.46] The 382 filings per judge of the California federal district courts in fiscal 1977 are of a wholly different genus.[6.47]

We would rank the caseload pressures of the four courts in the same order as the statistics just recited, but only after consideration of the practical effect of each case filed in the various courts, and with the caution that such a ranking is only roughly justified, if at all. Since our interest is in the effect of caseload pressure on law clerk tenure preferences, we cannot discount the incredible caseload facing each justice of the Supreme Court of California merely because the court is possessed of a large staff to share the burden. The size and type of staff at the supreme court reflect the justices' best efforts to cope with both the caseload and their own finite human capabilities. Nonetheless, the sheer weight of the numbers of cases which must be sifted through the mesh of the court's discretionary docket, let alone the burden of disposing of those cases over which jurisdiction is exercised, convinces us that the seven justices of the highest court of our most populous state face a burden rivaled only by their counterparts on the United States Supreme Court.[6.48]

6.46. *See* text accompanying notes 5.207 & 5.106 *supra*. In the profiles of the courts we studied, we have used the most current statistical data available as of April, 1979. Thus the data for the Ninth Circuit have been for the year ending June 30, 1978; data for the California courts of appeal have been for the year ending June 30, 1977. For direct comparability, Ninth Circuit data from fiscal 1977 (rather than fiscal 1978) should be compared with the contemporaneous California courts of appeal data. In fiscal 1977, there were 223 filings per judgeship in the Ninth Circuit, and active judges of the Ninth Circuit made up 64.5 percent of Ninth Circuit panel participants. *See* 1977 AOC REPORT, *supra* note 5.130, at 168, Table 3; *id.* at 178, Table 7. Processing this data (as described in note 5.106 *supra*) yields a figure of 432 filings per Ninth Circuit judge in fiscal 1977, the same year in which there were 610 filings per judge in the California courts of appeal.

6.47. *See* text accompanying note 5.133 *supra*.

6.48. During the 1976 term of the United States Supreme Court, which parallels the fiscal 1977 reporting year of the Supreme Court of California, *see* text accompanying notes 5.70–5.74 *supra*, the United States Supreme Court denied review in 3,633 cases and decided 373 cases on the merits. Furthermore, 203 of the cases decided on the merits were disposed of summarily; the remaining 170 were disposed of in a total of 142 opinions classified as containing "substantial legal reasoning." *See The Supreme Court, 1976 Term*, 91 HARV. L. REV. 70, 298, Table II & nn. e–f (1977). Counting concurring and dissenting opinions, the nine Justices

The California courts of appeal and the Ninth Circuit seem to us to face almost equal caseload pressures. Although the California court of appeal judge can summarily dispose of the 220 petitions for original writs out of the 610 cases that he or she faces annually, written opinions will issue in over 9 percent of these writ cases, and written opinions are constitutionally required in all 390 appeals which complete the figure of 610 cases to be considered.[6.49] Of the 471 cases per year confronting a judge of the Ninth Circuit,[6.50] 90 percent will be disposed of by opinion,[6.51] but four-fifths of these opinions[6.52] will be in memorandum form, often quite cursory in scope.[6.53] Both courts stand out as among the busiest of their types in the nation, and our ranking of the California courts of appeal as facing slightly greater caseload pressure than the Ninth Circuit is a product of the greater growth of the California courts' backlog in the most recent reporting year,[6.54] as well as the constraints on summary disposition imposed on the California courts by the constitutional requirement of written opinions; we place much less weight on the strict numerical difference in filings per judge.[6.55]

---

produced a total of 373 written opinions. *Id.* at 295, Table I. The workload of the United States Supreme Court has received extensive discussion in recent years. *See generally* G. CASPER & R. POSNER, *supra* note 2.56. *See also* authorities collected in *id.* at xi, n.2. The debate, simmering since 1976, over the propriety of changes in the Court's jurisdiction or internal processes as means of alleviating the Court's caseload pressure shows signs of again coming to a boil. *See* Brown Transport Corp. v. Atcon, Inc., 439 U.S. 1014 (1978) (opn. of White, J., dissenting from denial of certiorari); *id.* at 1025 (separate opn. of Burger, C.J.); *id.* at 1032 (separate opn. of Brennan, J.).

6.49. *See* text accompanying notes 5.18 & 5.27 *supra*.

6.50. *See* text accompanying note 5.106 *supra*.

6.51. *See* note 5.107 *supra*.   6.52. See *id.*

6.53. *See* text accompanying note 5.109 *supra*.

6.54. In fiscal 1977, the backlog of cases before the California courts of appeal increased by 13.6 percent (*see* text accompanying note 5.26, *supra*). In fiscal 1978, the Ninth Circuit's backlog increased by 11.9 percent (*see* text accompanying note 5.108 *supra*); and in fiscal 1977, the Ninth Circuit's backlog increased by only 8.3 percent (*see* 1977 AOC REPORT, supra note 5.130, at 167, Table 2).

6.55. Our ranking in terms of caseload pressure does not take account of the degree of difficulty of cases before the California courts of appeal in comparison with those before the Ninth Circuit. In the Ninth Circuit, it appears that no more than half of the cases are "routine." *See* text accompanying note 5.109 *supra*. By contrast, it appears that substantially more than half of the cases before the California courts of appeal are routine. In fiscal 1978, these courts deemed that only 16.9

The difficulty in comparing caseload pressures between appellate courts, arising out of differences in the courts' jurisdictions and decision-making procedures, is compounded when the comparison is between appellate courts and trial courts. Although appellate cases vary greatly in their complexity, almost all contested cases progress through the same steps of briefing, argument, and decision; and if litigated to judgment on appeal, they require only one decision prior to judgment (in addition to the decision to assert jurisdiction where jurisdiction is discretionary). In a trial court, contested cases are much more disparate in the degree of judicial attention that they demand. Cases vary greatly not only in the degree of difficulty of decision but also in the number of decisions required prior to a final judgment. A single complex case may engender dozens of motions, often calling for rulings on difficult and novel points of law, and yet may survive to consume days or even months of trial time. This feature of trial court practice is only slightly offset by a somewhat higher rate, in trial as opposed to appellate courts, of cases terminating without judicial action.[6.56]

---

percent of their opinions met the standards of public importance justifying publication in the official reports. *See* 1978 JUDICIAL COUNCIL OF CALIFORNIA REPORT 75, Table XV; CAL. R. COURT 976 (b). *See also* note 5.65 *supra*. Another investigator has found that California court of appeal judges consider that an "overwhelming" majority of the cases before them are "routine and repetitive," even after patently meritless appeals have been screened out by central staff. Wold, *supra* note 2.72, at 62–63.

In this light it seems that Ninth Circuit judges have more hard cases to resolve than California court of appeal judges, notwithstanding the slightly lower absolute numbers of cases considered by each Ninth Circuit judge. Moreover, it might fairly be assumed that the Ninth Circuit's hard cases are even more intractable than hard cases before the California courts of appeal, because of the greater body of precedent and institutional history that bears upon decisions of federal as opposed to state law. *See generally* Oakley, *Taking Wright Seriously: Of Judicial Discretion, Jurisprudents and the Chief Justice*, 4 HAST. CON. L.Q. 789, 790–809 (1977). Thus, our conclusion that the caseload pressure of the California courts of appeal exceeds that of the Ninth Circuit should not be mistaken as suggesting that the job of a Ninth Circuit judge is in any respect "easier" than that of a judge of a California court of appeal, except insofar as more hard cases make the lives of Ninth Circuit judges less boring than those of their California court of appeal counterparts. *Cf.* Wold, *supra* note 2.72, at 64–65 (boring effect of predominantly routine cases on judges of California courts of appeal).

6.56. We were somewhat surprised that the available statistics for comparing settlement and withdrawal rates of cases in trial and appellate courts failed to estab-

For this reason, we would not feel comfortable in concluding that California's federal district courts face somewhat less caseload pressure than the Ninth Circuit or the California courts of appeal simply because of the lower figure of 382 filings per year per district judge. More significant to us is the fact that, relative to other federal district courts, the California districts face only an average caseload.[6.57] The Ninth Circuit and the California courts of appeal are, by contrast, clearly among the most overburdened intermediate appellate courts in the country.[6.58]

2. Workloads per Law Clerk

Our interest in comparative workloads per law clerk is not in determining whether the law clerks of one court work harder

---

lish a significantly higher rate of settlement or withdrawal in trial, as opposed to appellate, courts. In the Ninth Circuit in fiscal 1978, some 45.2 percent of cases terminated (other than by consolidation) were terminated without hearing or submission to the court. The parallel figure for all circuits was 40.2 percent. These figures were derived from 1978 AOC REPORT, *supra* note 5.27, at A-3, A-5, & Table B 1. No directly comparable figures can be derived for district court cases terminated, because essentially uncontested criminal cases still require judicial action for the taking of pleas of guilty or nolo contendere. For a rough comparison, however, it is useful to note that nationwide 36.8 percent of civil cases terminated in fiscal 1978 in federal district courts were terminated without action by the court; the parallel figure for districts within the Ninth Circuit was 50.0 percent, and for the four districts within California it was 51.9 percent. These figures were derived from *id*. at A-28 & A-29, Table C 4A. As to criminal cases, roughly comparable data are provided by the percentage of total defendants who pleaded guilty or nolo contendere. For fiscal 1978 that percentage was 67.7 percent nationwide, 65.8 percent for all Ninth Circuit districts, and 70.4 percent in the four districts within California. These figures were derived from *id*. at A-84 & A-86, Table D-7. It does appear from these statistics that the California federal district courts benefit from a somewhat higher settlement or withdrawal rate than federal district courts nationwide.

6.57. *See* note 5.132 *supra*. In addition to comparatively moderate levels of filings per judgeship, the California districts benefit from a higher than average rate of termination of cases without judicial action. *See* note 6.56 *supra*.

6.58. On the Ninth Circuit's standing among the eleven federal circuits, see text accompanying notes 5.105–5.108 *supra*. Professor Meador has pointed out the modern trend of "radical increases in appellate business" far beyond contemporaneous increases in trial court filings. D. MEADOR, *supra* note 1.7, at 8. Although we are aware of no ranking of intermediate state appellate courts in terms of caseload per judge, the California courts of appeal obviously present a paradigm example of the "crisis of volume," *see* CAL. COURTS OF APPEAL, *supra* note 1.7, *passim*, and for the reasons already given, we rank the caseload pressure upon

than law clerks at another court, but rather in estimating whether the number of law clerks currently provided to a court is optimal in light of the caseload pressure upon that court and the ability of law clerks to ease the impact of excess caseload pressure at a particular court. To the extent that law clerks are really research assistants rather than para-judges, there are obvious limitations to their role in relieving caseload pressure; additional law clerks can draft additional opinions and evaluate additional briefs or pleadings, but if their recommendations are just that and thus are subject to more than pro forma review, the limit to the usefulness of additional law clerks will be determined by the demands of a court's caseload for research (which they can supply) as opposed to decisions (which should be left to judges). At the trial level, much of a judge's work is beyond the ken of law clerks, be it managing a jury, resolving disputes of fact placed at issue by motions for bench trials, or deciding such matters of "sound judicial discretion" as whether to grant probation or limit the number of plaintiffs' interrogatories. At the appellate level, law clerks are likely to be more pervasively useful, since even appeals to discretionary jurisdiction generally require careful legal analysis preliminary to the exercise of judicial discretion. Thus, as appellate caseloads rise, it should follow that the amount of the additional work that can be handled by law clerks will rise almost as fast, generating a condition in which judges with an impracticably low number of law clerks will demand productivity above all else from whatever law clerk assistance is at hand.

Table B of our Appendix shows great disparity in the satisfaction of our subject judges with the numbers of law clerks currently provided them for personal use. Seventy-five percent of responding federal district judges were happy with their current complement of two clerks; 25 percent would have preferred a third.[6.59] All responding California Supreme Court judges were happy with their current complement of three personal clerks.

---

judges of the California courts of appeal above that upon judges of the Ninth Circuit. *See* text accompanying notes 5.49–5.55 *supra*.

6.59. One of the three district judges indicating a preference for three rather than two law clerks was the Chief Judge of a district of five or more judges, who accordingly was equipped with three law clerks at the time of our interview. *See* note 2.53 *supra*. Thus the number of district judges dissatisfied with their current allotment of law clerks was actually two out of twelve, or 17 percent.

Sixty-one percent of responding California courts of appeal judges were dissatisfied with their current allotment of one elbow clerk each; 80 percent of responding Ninth Circuit judges would also have preferred additional elbow clerk support. On the basis of workload per law clerk, then, only the judges of the two intermediate appellate courts in our study tended to believe that there was more work suitable for law clerks to do than there were law clerks available to perform such work.

3. Clerkship Prestige

We learned of no recruitment problems at federal district courts or at the Supreme Court of California; judges of both courts had many highly qualified applicants for clerkship openings. The attractiveness of federal district courts varies somewhat with locale, but the nationwide uniformity of federal practice and the current interest of law students in trial litigation stimulates interest throughout the country in clerkships at California federal district courts. The Supreme Court of California offers not only the prestige of one of the nation's most respected and publicized state courts, but also the appealing environment of San Francisco.

The Ninth Circuit offers the prominence of a high court as well as the familiarity of federal practice, and has also served as a frequent stepping-stone to clerkships at the United States Supreme Court. Far less blessed are the judges of the California courts of appeal, save for those with chambers in San Francisco. The general view among these judges was that they had difficulty competing even with federal district courts for blue-chip clerkship candidates.[6.60]

4. Perceptions of Law Clerk Productivity

The final factor bearing on the coefficient of short-term law clerk use at a particular court is whether that court's judges view short-term law clerks as more or less productive than long-term law clerks. Judges of the Supreme Court of California rely heavily on law clerks for evaluation of petitions for discretionary re-

---

6.60. *See* text accompanying note 5.46 *supra*.

The prestige of the Supreme Court of California has declined somewhat since our interviews, *see generally* note 5.91 *supra*, but we doubt that the decline is permanent. In light of its historical stature and attractive location, the court should have no difficulty in continuing to attract highly qualified clerkship applicants.

view.[6.61] Although much of the research involved in preparing conference memoranda on these petitions is routine, there is a good deal of unwritten law surrounding the process of passing upon such petitions. Long-term law clerks, who can press externs into service for routine research, are highly productive in the preparation of conference memoranda; short-term law clerks of the quality attracted to the California Supreme Court could perform just as ably, but require constant retraining. Thus, Supreme Court of California judges view career clerks as more productive for administrative rather than intellectual reasons.

Federal district court judges can attract outstandingly productive short-term law clerks because of their access to the editorial boards of most of the nation's law reviews.[6.62] The productivity of federal district court law clerks has been further enhanced by the advent of staggered two-year clerkships, which has resulted in a reduction of the administrative burdens associated with short-term law clerks without any decrease in the quality of clerkship applicants.[6.63] Moreover, federal district judges treat their clerks as confidants as well as research assistants; part of the "productivity" they need is productive discussion with someone they can regard as following in their own footsteps, preparing for a life of litigation rather than a life as a law clerk.[6.64]

Ninth Circuit judges attract the best and the brightest law clerk candidates this side of the United States Supreme Court—which is where many of their clerks hope to go. Ninth Circuit judges tend to have an academic inclination, which allows them to take full advantage of their precocious clerks' abilities.[6.65] Moreover, as with federal district judges, Ninth Circuit judges can expect their ex–law review clerks to continue working law review hours, and so their clerks can more than outperform, in their prolonged work weeks, a more comfortably life-styled career clerk. Some Ninth Circuit judges also enhance their clerks' productivity by requiring staggered two-year clerkships.[6.66] Ninth Circuit judges recognize that career clerks could conceivably be as highly

6.61. *See* text accompanying notes 5.80–5.87 & 5.94–5.95 *supra*.

6.62. *See* text accompanying notes 5.141–5.142 *supra*.

6.63. *See* text accompanying note 5.144 *supra*.

6.64. *See generally* text accompanying notes 5.147–5.148 & 5.154 *supra*.

6.65. *See generally* Appendix, Table K.

6.66. *See* text accompanying notes 5.118–5.119 *supra*.

competent and motivated as they demand their short-term clerks to be, but they see no reason why such career clerks would want to work for the minimal pay available at the Ninth Circuit as opposed to the Supreme Court of California.[6.67]

Finally, judges of the California courts of appeal feel that the productivity of their short-term law clerks suffers from the loss of the best candidates to clerkship offers from other courts.[6.68] These judges feel blessed when they obtain law clerks of superior quality, and they are willing, despite misgivings in principle, to retain such clerks as long as they will stay. The cloistered atmosphere and substantial salaries that have allowed the Supreme Court of California to attract outstanding long-term law clerks are replicated in the somewhat less exalted circumstances of the courts of appeal. What is crucial to the assessment of the relative productivity of long-term and short-term law clerks at the courts of appeal, however, is not the type of work to be done, as at the Supreme Court of California, so much as the difference in quality of the short-term personnel generally available versus the occasional, exceptional person who can be induced to remain as a career law clerk.

F. *Comparing Coefficients of Short-Term Law Clerk Use*

1. Federal District Courts

The courts with the most positive coefficient of short-term law clerk use seem to us clearly to be the federal district courts. At least in California, these courts do not face extreme caseload pressure. Moreover, to the extent that cases pile up, there is little of a "routine" nature for clerks to do without judicial review; truly routine matters in a trial court are handled by the judge personally, from the bench or otherwise. Law clerk research is essential, but numerous law clerks producing voluminous research memoranda would exceed the reviewing capabilities of most district judges. Perhaps because of the nature of their work and their direct contact with litigants, as well as their lighter caseloads, district judges displayed to us no inclination to increase their produc-

6.67. *See* text accompanying note 5.122 *supra*.
6.68. *See* text accompanying note 5.46 *supra*.

tivity through the use of more clerks whose work was less thoroughly reviewed, or reviewed in depth only by a hierarchy of more senior clerks.

In such an environment, the outstanding short-term clerks attracted by the prestige of district courts offer superior productivity, especially when their administrative burden is reduced by staggering their terms. The potential advantages of long-term clerks are reduced by two distinct disincentives to attracting excellent long-term clerks to district courts. First, of course, are the limited salaries available;[6.69] more fundamental, perhaps, is the fact that district courts are not cloistered institutions of intrinsic appeal to law clerks-*cum*-scholars. District court law clerkships are invaluable apprenticeships for the practice of law, not for the study of law. This value is wasted on career clerks, who are likely to have little desire to put such practical wisdom to use.

2. Ninth Circuit

Only slightly less positive is the short-term clerk coefficient of the Ninth Circuit. This court surpasses all other courts we studied in prestige to clerkship candidates, with the possible exception of the Supreme Court of California in the eyes of strongly California-oriented clerkship candidates. Indeed, this prestige appears sufficient, together with the court's San Francisco headquarters, to attract excellent clerkship candidates even to the "court law clerk" program of the circuit's growing central staff.[6.70] As the growth of its central staff suggests, the capacity of the Ninth Circuit to shift some of its caseload pressure to staff attorneys makes the court potentially receptive to the employment of career clerks. The court already employs several long-term staff attorneys, although at salaries that suggest that the positions are unlikely to become truly "career" clerkships.[6.71] The predominant desire of Ninth Circuit judges for an additional elbow clerk indicates a high level of current workload per law clerk notwithstanding the growth in central staff, and therefore suggests that Ninth

6.69. See generally *Federal Funding Note*, *supra* note 2.54. *See also* note 5.111 *supra*.

6.70. *See generally* text accompanying note 5.112 *supra*. In the period since our interviews, the court law clerk program has proved quite popular with clerkship-minded students of our acquaintance.

6.71. *See* note 5.111 *supra*. *See also* text accompanying note 5.122 *supra*.

Circuit judges have a high interest in law clerk productivity. However, the prestige of the court, together with the nascent trend toward staggered two-year clerkships and the inadequate salaries that can be offered to long-term clerks, ensures that the most productive law clerks available to Ninth Circuit judges are still those cut from the traditional cloth of recent law graduates.

At the present time, Ninth Circuit judges are still able to devote substantial portions of their time to writing and refining opinions in important cases; to perform this creative task, the freshness and enthusiasm of short-term law clerks adds to their "productivity" in the eyes of Ninth Circuit judges. Should the Ninth Circuit's caseload pressure approach that of the California appellate courts, however, interest in long-term clerks would probably rise. Since the Ninth Circuit would be an attractive environment to prospective career clerks, given higher salaries, it is conceivable that long-term clerks may in time spread from the central staff to individual chambers of the Ninth Circuit. Peer pressure is likely to inhibit this development, however, as Ninth Circuit judges share a widespread suspicion that long-term clerks encourage judicial indolence. If the prestige of the court were to sink while caseload pressure rises, and if salaries competitive with those offered at the Supreme Court of California were to become available, such inhibitions might well be overcome.

3. Supreme Court of California

Were we not aware of the continued trend away from short-term law clerks,[6.72] we might have rated the coefficient of short-term law clerk usage at the California Supreme Court as slightly positive. On the face of our interviews, the supreme court would appear to be an environment favorable to successful use of short-term law clerks: the court's prestige is sufficient to attract law clerks of the same caliber as those at the Ninth Circuit and the most glamorous of the federal district courts. Such clerks have proven to be highly productive at the federal courts that we studied, meeting or surpassing any standard that more experienced but less driven career clerks would be likely to match over a career. Moreover, our subjects at the supreme court were generally satisfied with the number of law clerks currently provided them,

6.72. See note 5.94 supra.

suggesting that there was not more business at hand suitable for law clerk assignment than there were law clerks available. If this were the case, it might follow that concern over marginal advantages in quantitative productivity such as might be associated with experienced career clerks would not eclipse the general judicial preference, on qualitative grounds, for the fresh ideas and enthusiasm of the outstanding short-term law clerks whom the court could recruit.[6.73]

The factor missing from this analysis, which appears to be crucial to law clerk practices at the Supreme Court of California, is the magnitude of the caseload pressure felt by the court. It should be remembered that the court feels obliged to scrutinize its discretionary docket with elaborate care.[6.74] While the judges of the court do not feel that more law clerks would be useful in performing this chore to their satisfaction, this appears to be because of a feeling that more than three clerks could not effectively be controlled by a given judge.[6.75]

That the workload per law clerk is extreme, notwithstanding the lack of desire for additional law clerks, is demonstrated by the rise in extern use which has accompanied the decline, since our interviews, in the use of short-term law clerks.[6.76] Since externs are managed by the court's career law clerks, externs increase the

6.73. It should be noted that judges of the Supreme Court of California displayed to us little qualitative preference for short-term over long-term law clerks; yet the qualities that supreme court judges found most valuable to a judge were those that the entirety of our judges tended to attribute to short-term clerks. Supreme court judges found these favored qualities characteristic of their career clerks too, who had generally first come to the supreme court as short-term clerks. Only greater "freshness" seemed to distinguish short-term clerks as qualitatively superior in the minds of the judges of the California Supreme Court. *See generally* text accompanying notes 5.96–5.98 *supra. See also* text accompanying note 6.78 *infra.*

6.74. *See generally* text accompanying notes 5.80–5.87 *supra.*

6.75. It should be noted that the previously quoted comment of the former Chief Justice of California that he would have liked more than the twelve law clerks then authorized, *see* note 5.76 *supra,* referred not only to his personal staff but also to the de facto central staff of the supreme court. *See* text accompanying notes 5.76–5.77 *supra.* Although the Chief Justice's complement had increased to fourteen by the time of our interviews at the court, only two of these fourteen law clerks worked exclusively under the close personal supervision of the Chief Justice. *See* note 5.77 *supra.*

6.76. *See* note 2.77 *supra.*

productivity of a judge's staff, especially with regard to the preparation of conference memoranda, without a concomitant feeling by the judge that extern work product ought to be judicially reviewed. The externs are law clerks to the career clerks, who review the externs' work and are in turn responsible directly to the judge.[6.77]

Moreover, since the court has no central staff as such, except insofar as an echelon of career clerks of the Chief Justice processes all petitions in criminal matters, the screening function performed elsewhere by discrete central staffs is performed by the personal staffs of the judges.[6.78] This appears to place a premium on the experience of long-term clerks which outweighs the superior industry and enthusiasm of short-term clerks in assessing comparative productivity; the personal clerks of the judges of the supreme court must be able to sort the routine from the unusual with dispatch and without distraction, and without continual retraining. Although unwilling to dilute their personal control over their staffs by the employment of additional clerks, supreme court judges do rely heavily on the judgment of their present complement of clerks, both in the substantive sense of discerning routine issues from significant ones, and in the procedural sense of maintaining the overall pace of the processing of petitions in a fashion that comports with the court's jurisdictional deadlines. This unusual degree of reliance on law clerks' judgment in order to keep abreast of the court's workload does not mean that these law clerks operate without supervision. It does mean that the court is hampered if judges frequently disagree with the judgment of their clerks, and in this sense of "productivity"—the percentage of a law clerk's recommendations accepted by that clerk's judge—short-term clerks are hard put to match career clerks.

Finally, the characteristics of the career clerks at the court are close to those traditionally associated with short-term clerks, which most of the court's career clerks originally were.[6.79] Given the special sort of expertise demanded of the court's clerks and the caliber of clerk attracted to a career at the court in light of its prestige and salaries, the crucial factor in determining the comparative

6.77. *See* text accompanying note 6.32 *supra*.
6.78. *See* text accompanying note 6.78 *supra*.
6.79. *See* note 6.73 *supra*.

productivity of long-term and short-term clerks is the administrative burden of continual short-term clerk selection and training. Thus the qualitative preference for short-term clerks as opposed to long-term clerks is weakest at the Supreme Court of California of all the courts we studied, because the clerks of either tenure are not perceived by the judges as offering significant qualitative differences. This relatively weak predisposition toward short-term clerks on qualitative grounds pales beside the special features of productivity needed in light of the court's commitment to reviewing with extraordinary care all petitions for discretionary review.

4. California Courts of Appeal

Virtually all the factors that we have identified as bearing on the coefficient of short-term law clerk use, with the exception of a general judicial preference for short-term law clerks on qualitative grounds, combine to render that coefficient highly negative at the California courts of appeal. A court of appeal has an onerous caseload, which we have rated as more burdensome than that of the Ninth Circuit. The judges of the court generally feel that they are underequipped with personal clerks, and so must emphasize quantitative productivity in choosing the one clerk each is allowed. The court has little prestige among clerkship candidates, and so, except for San Francisco-based judges, the competence of available short-term clerks suffers in comparison to the skills of long-term clerks attracted by an appellate atmosphere and substantial career clerk salaries. The judges of the court do recognize qualitative distinctions between the career clerks and short-term clerks employed at the court, but the majority feel constrained to select a career clerk so long as only one clerk is allowed per judge.[6.80]

G. *Strategies for Fostering Short-Term Law Clerk Usage*

Our comparison of the dispositive factors at each court regarding the predominant tenure preferences of its judges suggests to us that policies of judicial administration can have a crucial impact on law clerk tenure choices. Insofar as budgetary limitations preclude paying competitive salaries to long-term clerks, this state-

6.80. *See* text accompanying notes 5.44–5.47 *supra.*

ment is no more than a truism. However, budgetary policies are maintained only when successful, and the success of budgetarily forcing judges to use short-term clerks is not foreordained. Our research suggests that some of the factors essential to successful short-term law clerk use can be identified and fostered so that judges may successfully use, whether by choice or budgetary compulsion, the short-termed law clerk whom tradition sanctions and whom judges themselves generally favor when their qualitative preferences are not overridden by other concerns.

1. Federal Courts

The existing success of short-term law clerk usage at federal courts can be summed up in two words: numbers and quality. Federal judges have generally been allowed to hire clerks in sufficient numbers to avoid judicial overemphasis on law clerk productivity in a quantitative sense; the prestige of federal courts has attracted law clerks of outstanding ability.

The prestige of federal courts is unlikely to decline, but this prestige does not translate directly into attractiveness to law clerks. What is important is that the task of law clerks at federal courts is largely to brief their judges on nonroutine matters. Routine matters are taken care of at the trial courts by the judges themselves and, increasingly, by parajudicial federal magistrates. While some routine inevitably accompanies the preparation of motion calendars, federal district law clerks and judges interact by and large over the resolution of difficult legal problems, where the attributes of recent law graduates are well and meaningfully employed. At the Ninth Circuit, routine matters are taken care of by the emerging central staff, which paradoxically makes elbow clerkships more attractive not only by the creation of the lower caste of "court law clerks," but also by freeing the upper caste of elbow clerks for cases in which the judges feel the need for extensive research and dialectic debate. This preservation of a generative and creative role for the judges and elbow clerks of the Ninth Circuit is facilitated considerably by the lack of stringent written opinion requirements, so that the court freely disposes of a substantial part of its caseload through summary procedures. Given the pool of talent available to Ninth Circuit judges, and given the diversion of routine matters to a central staff itself composed largely of talented and cheap short-term "court law clerks," it appears a false economy to restrict circuit judges to fewer than three law clerks each. To the extent that current budgetary practices do so restrict the judges, these practices should be changed, unless those responsible for the administration of the federal courts of appeal find the model of the California courts of appeal worthy of emulation.

2. Supreme Court of California

At the Supreme Court of California, part of the problem is the apparent suspicion of the work product of the courts of appeal. Were there greater confidence in the courts of appeal, the supreme court could be more cavalier in its selection of cases to review and more concerned with the optimal use of staff in the preparation of precalendar memoranda and opinions of the court. Aside from whatever improvement in the work product of the courts of appeal might result from our suggested doubling of the personal law clerks of court of appeal judges, the coefficient of short-term law clerk use at the supreme court would be made more positive if the processing of petitions for discretionary review at the supreme court were more rather than less centralized.

We feel that the experience of the Ninth Circuit could usefully be repeated at the Supreme Court of California. The present de facto central staff for criminal petitions should be expanded along the lines of the Ninth Circuit's court law clerk program, and should take over the initial processing of all petitions for discretionary review. The personal staffs of the individual judges of the supreme court should be involved, as they are now, in assisting the judges to review each agenda of conference memoranda, with special attention to "B" list cases that will not be discussed unless flagged for additional review. Personal staffs should not be involved in the production of conference memoranda except by special request of their judges.

The primary function of personal staffs should be, as at the Ninth Circuit, the preparation of their judges for oral argument and the articulation of their judges' views in resulting majority, concurring, and dissenting opinions. It can be expected that, should the elbow clerks of supreme court judges be emancipated from principal responsibility for detailed review of petitions for discretionary assertions of jurisdiction, the preference of the judges we interviewed for at least one short-termed law clerk in each chamber could be more generally indulged. This would, we hope, reaffirm one respect in which the qualitative benefit of short-term clerks cannot be replicated by the best and the brightest of career clerks: it would reintroduce to the supreme court, in a more influential role than that of externs rarely in contact with the judges, the short-termed law clerk as the messenger from academia, where criticism of the court's mistakes is less subdued than among the ranks of the court's career staff.

3. California Courts of Appeal

We thought at the outset of our research that an effective strategy for preserving short-term law clerks at the courts of appeal of California would be a system of "flexible funding" for law clerks: in effect, this would be a hybridization of the federal and state models of law clerk funding, affording court of appeal judges a pot of salary money as in the federal system, but allowing them to hire highly experienced career clerks at competitive salaries if they wished to expend their budget on one experienced career clerk instead of two short-termed and newly graduated clerks. While we found substantial support among our court of appeal subjects for such a proposal, which in more or less similar form had already been independently conceived and advocated by some of them, we also found considerable concern over the administrative burden associated with salary allocation. Moreover, in light of our subsequent conclusion that there is a highly negative coefficient of short-term law clerk use at the court of appeal because of extreme caseload pressure and low prestige among clerkship applicants, we doubt whether such a "flexible funding" proposal would be very efficacious. We have also come to realize that, within the current fiscal system of the state of California, such a budgetary proposal would be impractical to effectuate.[6.81]

6.81. In the course of our interview the Executive Assistant to the Chief Justice of California advised us of the administrative difficulties involved in requesting, contrary to the standard budgetary procedures of the state of California, that employee salaries be appropriated in a lump sum to be distributed among an uncertain number of employees. Buehl Interview, *supra* note 5.38. Standard practice is to budget for employees by the number of positions to be filled, rather than by the total salary that could be paid to an employee in a given position. Thus it would be consistent with standard practice to request that an additional law clerk be authorized for each judge of the courts of appeal, and to limit the salary which could be paid to that position.

We believe that a more aggressive way to assure the survival of short-term law clerks at the courts of appeal would also be more effective. The pilot project just begun by the Judicial Council of California at the urging of the Chief Justice, by which selected court of appeal judges are afforded an additional law clerk budgeted at a strictly short-term, newly graduated salary level,[6.82] should be expanded without delay to encompass every judge of the courts of appeal. This will meet the pressing need expressed by most of our subjects for additional law clerk assistance without forcing upon any judges a choice between retaining a single expert career clerk or attempting to attract two more-than-mediocre short-term clerks.

Allowing each judge of the courts of appeal to have an indefinitely tenured clerk as well as one clerk retained for just one year affords a clear choice of clerkship policies. Those judges who feel most pressed by the administrative burdens of law clerk selection and training can retain a career clerk to share the burden of replacing the short-term clerk on an annual basis. Other judges, especially those presently using short-term clerks, may wish to adopt the staggered two-year clerkship policy which has proved highly successful in the federal courts. This can be done by hiring one clerk each year and retaining that clerk's predecessor for an additional year as the judge's indefinitely tenured clerk. By this choice, judges could opt either for an entirely short-termed staff with their administrative burdens mitigated by staggered two-year terms, or for the administrative advantages of a permanent clerk assisted by an annually replaced short-term clerk.

An important result of expanding the Chief Justice's experiment into a systemwide regime of funding additional short-term clerks for every court of appeal judge would be a possible return, in time, of the California courts of appeal to parity with federal district courts in attractiveness to clerkship candidates, were it to become common knowledge that every court of appeal judge was fiscally committed to hiring a new short-term law clerk every

---

Whatever the impracticalities, it appears that our "flexible funding" proposal would not be impossible to implement. Such a system seems essentially similar to the Chief Justice's tactic, in fiscal 1979, of converting an experimental appropriation of one year's salary for six supplemental court of appeal law clerks into nine months' salary for eight such law clerks. *See id.*

6.82. See *id.*

year. We would hope that this influx of annual law clerks would be accompanied by a return among California court of appeal judges to more traditional relationships with their law clerks. At present, the degree of contact between judge and law clerk at the courts of appeal is significantly lower than at the federal district courts or the Ninth Circuit.[6.83] This reflects, in part, the predominant use of career clerks at the courts of appeal; the attractiveness of such clerks is precisely the lower level of supervision and interaction they require. But the conditions which make this an attractive quality of career clerks—the overloading and understaffing of the courts of appeal—would be alleviated by provision of additional law clerks. Given that, at least in our sample, California court of appeal judges were more academically oriented than federal district judges,[6.84] a by-product of committing the courts of appeal to a policy of additional, strictly short-term law clerks should be the rehabilitation of the reputation of the courts of appeal as fruitful places for talented law school graduates to gain insight into the appellate process. Indeed, if a substantial number of court of appeal judges should continue to retain one career clerk, hiring an additional clerk each year for an annual term, the courts of appeal might prove especially attractive to the occasional outstanding clerkship prospect who does not want to spend the extra clerkship year increasingly required by federal courts.

In sum, a clear and sustained institutional commitment by the courts of appeal to promoting short-term clerkships would bear the promise of attracting to the courts of appeal the sort of superior short-term law clerks who have convinced federal judges that career clerks are an unnecessary institution.

We disagree with the California Judicial Council's pilot project, however, insofar as it uses additional short-term law clerks as substitutes for central staff. While our research has not been directed to the proper organization and supervision of central staffs, we repeat here our advocacy of the Ninth Circuit's model for preserving traditional appellate judge–elbow law clerk relationships by diverting routine matters to central staffs. Whether, given the standing of the courts of appeal, their central staffs can attract short-term law clerks of the Ninth Circuit's caliber is debatable.

6.83. *See* Appendix, Table I.
6.84. See *id.*, Table K.

What remains established is the Ninth Circuit's ability to maintain substantial control over central staff work product through meaningful review of central staff work by individual judges, assisted by their law clerks. Given the crushing caseload of the courts of appeal, the laudable goal of ensuring that central staffs do not become brigades of headless horsemen is better met by putting judges in the saddle than by destroying the undeniable horsepower which central staffs do supply to busy courts. Doubling the law clerks of court of appeal judges will allow those judges to more systematically review the work product of their courts' central staffs. If those central staffs are eliminated, however, working conditions within individual chambers will likely deteriorate to the level now existing with one law clerk per judge, defeating the hoped-for renaissance of the courts of appeal as an environment attractive to outstanding clerkship candidates.

VII. CONCLUSION

A. Career Clerks

We undertook our study in order to inform ourselves of the reasons for the growing predominance of the career law clerk at California courts. Our findings suggest that most judges would prefer short-term clerks if their working conditions permitted it. Virtually all judges recognize the value of certain qualities generally associated with short-term clerks. Judges of the California Supreme Court have nonetheless retained a coterie of exceptional career clerks, who bring to the court many of the valued qualities of short-term clerks without the attendant administrative burdens and with advantages of experience critical to efficient management of the court's discretionary docket. Judges of the California courts of appeal recognize that their career clerks constitute more of a qualitative compromise, but justify their choice of career clerks on grounds of the excessive workload of their understaffed courts and the unattractiveness of their courts to superior short-term clerkship candidates. Federal judges face no such recruitment problems, and—at the trial level, at least—no such understaffing.

Our concern over the California state courts' trend toward exclusively career clerks has been tempered by our emphatic conclusion that there is nothing pernicious per se about the career law clerk. We agree with the consensus of the judges we interviewed that there are qualitative distinctions between the generality of short-term and long-term law clerks, but we recognize the great value to an overloaded judicial system of the exceptional career clerk who offers his or her judge the best qualities of both types of clerk. Nonetheless, we think it fantastic to suppose that such career clerks are the rule rather than the exception.

We accordingly think that judges and judicial administrators should pause before forsaking tradition by the wholesale hiring of career clerks. The ecology of each court will dictate what role, great or small, career clerks can usefully play without undue danger to the integrity of judicial decision-making. Quantitative analysis must not be overemphasized, however, in determining the appropriate mix of clerkship tenures. The consensus view of the judges we interviewed, that short-term clerks are qualitatively superior to long-term clerks, counsels restraint in prescribing heavy doses of permanent clerks as a miracle cure for court congestion.

In an era in which the pressure to obtain higher rates of dispositions per judge is unlikely to decrease, we expect career clerks to become more common at courts outside of California. We would hope that they become a little less common at the courts we studied. We suspect, for instance, that a small measure of career clerks, whether centrally organized or not, could help the United States Supreme Court manage its discretionary docket more efficiently, at little qualitative cost.[7.1] We also suspect that the California Supreme Court and courts of appeal have passed the point at which the quantitative benefits of career clerks are offset by qualitative costs.

Our vision is, then, that the age of the career clerk at American courts is just dawning. As to this, as with other cultural phenomena, California's experience may have foreshadowed the nation's. We propose no effort at turning the tide of history; but in light of our study of California courts, we think there are some lessons that can usefully be learned by those who would follow in California's path.

As courts increasingly resort to career clerks to remedy congested dockets, we recommend two forms of prophylaxis against the bureaucratization of justice. First, we urge that the qualita-

7.1. *See generally* note 2.66 *supra*. *See also* Cannon, *An Administrator's View of the Supreme Court*, 22 FED. B. NEWS 109, 111 (1975); Cannon, *Administrative Change and the Supreme Court*, 57 JUDICATURE 334, 340 (1974) (describing first steps toward a career legal staff at the United States Supreme Court, and pointing to the California Supreme Court as an example of sound use of career legal staff).

tive differences between long-term and short-term law clerks be minimized by recruiting long-term clerks from a court's short-term alumni. Second, we urge that, no matter how satisfied a court becomes with its complement of career clerks, it never permit its judges to insulate themselves from short-term clerks altogether. A court which forsakes the short-term clerk is a court which has forgotten—or worse, forsworn—the law clerk's highest purpose.

B. *The Fiddlers in the Woof*

"A fiddler on the roof. Sounds crazy, no?"[7.2] So opens the musical which reminds us that traditions keep cultures in balance. "Because of our traditions," Tevye tells us, "we've kept our balance for many, many years. . . . Because of our traditions, everyone knows who he is and what God expects him to do."[7.3]

We would, with some license, cast the classic law clerk as a fiddler in the woof. However poor a pun, the phrase has value as a metaphor. The lengthwise threads of a fabric are its warp, the crosswise threads its woof. The nature of the warp is thus fixed for the whole of the bolt; its threads run continuously throughout its length, giving the fabric its essential strength and continuity. If there are to be passing variations in texture and elasticity, they must be woven into the fabric by means of the woof.

We see law as the fabric of culture; to return to the poet whose vision we earlier credited, "Law is the clothes men wear / Anytime, anywhere."[7.4] Modern American culture demands law that is both ductile and durable; this demand has been met, we think, because the fabric of the law has been woven from the warp of the judiciary and the woof of their law clerks. In our ideal form, the law clerk is meant to fiddle with the law, to advocate innovation, to introduce to its inner sanctums the ideas of those outside. This gives the law needed play and capacity for change. So long as law clerks come and go in judicial chambers, so long as they are merely crosswise threads, their stimulus is no threat to the integrity of the law. But to let them run parallel to the commissioned

---

7.2. Stein, Bock, & Harnick, *Fiddler on the Roof*, act 1, Prologue, in BEST PLAYS OF THE SIXTIES, 243, 248 (ed. S. Richards, 1970).

7.3. *Id*.

7.4. W. H. AUDEN, *supra* note 1.2, at 154.

judiciary risks either the devolution of judicial power upon non-judicial officers or the evolution of stimulating law clerks into bureaucrats dedicated to continuity rather than variation.

So we end with a plea that most law clerks be and remain fiddlers in the woof of the law, respecting the traditions of their place, knowing who they are, and what the law expects them to do: to prod their judges, to expand their judges' awareness, to test their judges' conclusions, to color their judges' thinking and embellish their judges' writing, and then to go their separate ways. And may we mold our courts to meet this end.

Appendix

CONTENTS

Table A: Tenure Preference Independent of Financing

	California Courts of Appeal (Alpha)	California Supreme Court (Beta)	U.S. Court of Appeals (Gamma)	U.S. District Courts (Delta)
Firm short term	11	0	6	14
Weak short term	7	1	0	0
No preference	1	0	0	0
Weak long term	7	0	0	0
Firm long term	11	1	0	0
No response	1	3	0	0

Table B: Optimal Number of Personal Clerks

	California Courts of Appeal (Alpha)	California Supreme Court (Beta)	U.S. Court of Appeals (Gamma)	U.S. District Courts (Delta)
1	13	0	0	0
2	19	0	1	9
3	1	3	3	3
More than 3	0	0	1	0
No response	5	2	1	2

Table C: Present Use of Externs

	California Courts of Appeal (Alpha)	California Supreme Court (Beta)	U.S. Court of Appeals (Gamma)	U.S. District Courts (Delta)
None	12	0	1	3
Moderate	8	2	0	7
Extensive	10	3	2	2
No response	8	0	3	2

Table D: Motivation for Use of Externs

	California Courts of Appeal (Alpha)	California Supreme Court (Beta)	U.S. Court of Appeals (Gamma)	U.S. District Courts (Delta)
Aids Judge	6	4	1	5
Aids Extern	6	0	0	2
Aids Bar	1	0	0	0
Aids Judge and Extern	1	1	1	0
Aids Judge, Extern, and Bar	1	0	0	0
No response	23	0	4	7

Table E: Contribution of Externs to Productivity

	California Courts of Appeal (Alpha)	California Supreme Court (Beta)	U.S. Court of Appeals (Gamma)	U.S. District Courts (Delta)
Detriment	8	0	1	2
No effect	0	0	0	1
Moderate aid	13	3	1	3
Very helpful	1	2	1	2
No response	16	0	3	6

Table F: Law Clerk Preparation of Pre-Argument Memoranda

	California Courts of Appeal (Alpha)	California Supreme Court (Beta)	U.S. Court of Appeals (Gamma)	U.S. District Courts (Delta)
Never	0	0	1	1
Sometimes	9	0	1	3
Usually	2	0	1	3
Always	22	4	1	7
No response	5	1	2	0

Table G: Form of Pre-Argument Memoranda

	California Courts of Appeal (Alpha)	California Supreme Court (Beta)	U.S. Court of Appeals (Gamma)	U.S. District Courts (Delta)
Opinion	11	1	1	2
Memorandum	18	2	2	10
Varied	4	0	0	1
No response	5	2	3	1

Table H: Law Clerk Input to Written Opinions

	California Courts of Appeal (Alpha)	California Supreme Court (Beta)	U.S. Court of Appeals (Gamma)	U.S. District Courts (Delta)
None	1	0	0	1
Slight	2	0	0	1
Some	16	0	4	0
Considerable	10	0	1	7
No response	9	5	1	5

Table I: Frequency of Judge–Law Clerk Discussion

	California Courts of Appeal (Alpha)	California Supreme Court (Beta)	U.S. Court of Appeals (Gamma)	U.S. District Courts (Delta)
Rare	1	0	0	1
Some	9	2	0	1
Frequent	8	1	5	6
Constant	7	0	1	4
No response	13	2	0	2

Table J: Attitude re Central Staff

	California Courts of Appeal (Alpha)	California Supreme Court (Beta)	U.S. Court of Appeals (Gamma)	U.S. District Courts (Delta)
Firmly opposed	1	2	0	0
Opposed	3	0	0	4
Benefits equal burden	9	0	5	1
Favor	9	2	1	1
Strongly favor	13	0	0	2
No response	3	1	0	6

Table K: Academic Bent

	California Courts of Appeal (Alpha)	California Supreme Court (Beta)	U.S. Court of Appeals (Gamma)	U.S. District Courts (Delta)
Law review	3	0	2	1
Has taught	12	2	3	1
Both	2	3	1	0
Neither	21	0	0	12
No response	0	0	0	0

Note on the Supreme Court of California's Exercise of Discretionary Appellate Jurisdiction

Taken literally, CAL. R. OF COURT 29 authorizes the California Supreme Court to provide "review for correctness," *see* Hufstedler & Hufstedler, *Improving the California Appellate Pyramid*, 46 L. A. BAR BULL. 275, 278 (1971), when it declares that a hearing "will be ordered" when "necessary to secure uniformity of decision" or to "settle . . . important questions of law." This might be construed to give almost every individual litigant a right to supreme court review of a wrong decision, because such a decision is wrong only if it conflicts with settled law (thereby detracting from uniformity of decision) or decides a new issue the wrong way (which may present an important question of law for settlement by the supreme court, and in any event will create disuniformity when subsequent cases raising the same issue are decided the right way). Although there are strong arguments against construing Rule 29 this way, *see* Hufstedler & Hufstedler, *supra* at 296, there are frequent examples that the supreme court does not confine itself wholly to "institutional review," *id.* at 279, in determining whether to grant a petition for hearing.

Cases which reach wrong results but do not meet Rule 29's standards when construed to provide merely institutional review fall into three categories. The first category contains cases which concern issues that are novel but unimportant. Classification of a case in this category is inevitably contestable, given the vagaries of defining and discerning "important questions of law," but cursory review of a random recent volume of *California Reports, 3d*, suggests at least one instance of simple "review for correctness" in a case considering a novel but unimportant issue of law. *See* Post Bros. Construction Co. v. Yoder, 20 Cal. 3d 1, 569 P.2d 133, 141 Cal. Rptr. 28 (1977) (joint check rule relating to liabilities of owners and general contractors to subcontractors and materialmen paid by joint check applies when there are multiple joint payees and multiple job sites). In the same volume appear two cases which consider issues of law only in the attenuated sense of whether, under the particular facts of the cases reviewed, a finding of the trial court was supported by substantial evidence, Pasadena Unified School Dist. v. Commission on Professional Competence, 20 Cal. 3d 309, 572 P.2d 53, 142 Cal. Rptr. 439 (1977), and whether a conclusion of the trial court that the probative value of certain evidence outweighed its prejudicial effect was an abuse of discretion, People v. Anderson, 20 Cal. 3d. 647, 574 P.2d 1235, 143 Cal. Rptr. 883 (1978). The particular facts of any lawsuit are necessarily novel, but it is difficult to read anything of public importance into a supreme court decision applying familiar standards to novel facts.

One way to determine if the supreme court is simply reviewing cases to correct erroneous results is to compare the supreme court's disposition of a case with that of the court of appeal. This process is made difficult by the following facts: (a) only 16 or 17 percent of court of appeal opinions are published (*see* 1978 JUDI-

CIAL COUNCIL OF CALIFORNIA REPORT 75 [16.9%]; 1977 JUDICIAL
COUNCIL OF CALIFORNIA REPORT 195 [15.7%]; 1976 JUDICIAL
COUNCIL OF CALIFORNIA REPORT 97 [16%]; *see generally* CAL. R.
OF COURT 976); (b) the supreme court often grants a petition for
hearing after the court of appeal has summarily denied a petition
for an original writ, in which case the court of appeal will have
filed no opinion at all (*see* 1978 JUDICIAL COUNCIL OF CALIFORNIA
REPORT 64, Table V [37 out of 231 hearings granted in fiscal 1977,
or 16 percent, involved original proceedings in the court of ap-
peal]); and (c) even if the supreme court actually decides the case
itself rather than retransferring it to the court of appeal (*see* text
accompanying note 5.68 *supra*), it is asserting appellate jurisdiction over the trial court rather than the court of appeal, whose
opinion, whether published or unpublished, has been vacated and
is generally not mentioned by the supreme court (*see* Note, *supra*
note 5.63, at 268).

With regard to the three above-cited cases from 20 Cal. 3d, the
court of appeal's decision in People v. Anderson was unpublished.
(Although, overall, about one out of six court of appeal opinions
are published, a disproportionate number of the published opinions involve civil appeals. In fiscal 1977, 25 percent of all court of
appeal opinions in civil appeals were published, as opposed to
only 6.4 percent of court of appeal opinions in criminal appeals.
See 1978 JUDICIAL COUNCIL OF CALIFORNIA REPORT 75, Table
XV.) The court did publish opinions, however, in Post Bros.
Construction Co. v. Yoder, 66 Cal. App. 3d 21 (advance sheets),
135 Cal. Rptr. 730 (1977), and in Pasadena Unified School Dist. v.
Commission on Professional Competence, 70 Cal. App. 3d 899
(advance sheets), 139 Cal. Rptr. 236 (1977). Not surprisingly,
both of these opinions reached a result opposite to that reached by
a unanimous supreme court after its grant of a hearing. Ordinarily, the unpublished status of the court of appeal's opinion in
People v. Anderson would make impossible a determination of
whether the supreme court disagreed with the decision below.
Author Thompson having participated in and dissented from that
decision, however, it can be reported with particular relish that
the supreme court's unanimous opinion in People v. Anderson
reached a result opposite to that of the majority in the court of
appeal. Thus we know that in each of three "novel" cases of minor
importance decided by the supreme court in 20 Cal. 3d, the mem-

bers of the supreme court were in complete and unanimous disagreement with the decision below.

This is consistent with the findings of an empirical study undertaken by the *Stanford Law Review* in an era when all appellate opinions were published. By studying all cases decided in 1949 by a written opinion of the district court of appeal in which a petition for hearing was filed, the *Review* sought to ascertain the most significant factors associated with the supreme court's decision to grant a hearing in 100 of the 457 cases studied. The *Review* found that the most significant factor was simply whether the supreme court disagreed with the decision of the district court of appeal, as determined by comparison of the district court of appeal's opinions with those of the supreme court after the grant of hearings:

> Considering those cases which the Supreme Court takes because of maltreatment of its precedents as merely another aspect of the disagreement rule, eighty of the total of one hundred petitions granted can be explained on the basis of disagreement.
>
> . . . .
>
> Of the eighty cases in which the Supreme Court disagreed with the intermediate court, sixty-six present no novel question; of the fourteen in which there was no disagreement, ten presented no undecided question. The complete absence of significant correlation between novel points and hearings granted, coupled with the impressive majority of cases heard where the high court disagreed with reasoning or the conclusion of the intermediate court, is convincing evidence of the fact that disagreement, and not novelty, is the basis for a hearing in the Supreme Court.

Note, *supra* note 5.63, at 254–55.

A follow-up study covering the year 1950 reached a similar conclusion as to the primary importance of the supreme court's disagreement with the opinion below, while finding more evidence than in the prior study that novelty of issues presented was also an important factor in the granting of hearings, albeit one of considerably lesser statistical significance than disagreement. Note, *To Hear or Not to Hear: II*, 4 STAN. L. REV. 392, 397–98 (1952).

Although the great increase in the volume of petitions for hearing since the Stanford study, *see* text accompanying notes 5.70–5.73 *supra*, has inevitably decreased the supreme court's ability and inclination to function as a court of correction, there still appears to be a felt need to do so occasionally. Sometimes, as the Stanford study and our examples suggest, the supreme court will grant a hearing simply to correct the error of the court of appeal as to issues which are novel or even unique (because they arise upon the particular facts of a case) but which are of little public importance.

Of course, if a court of appeal reaches the wrong result in deciding an issue which is not novel, the court's error may well be said to threaten the uniformity of decision which Rule 29 seeks to preserve through the granting of hearings. However, in order for the granting of a hearing in the name of uniformity of decision to make any institutional sense, a court of appeal's wrong decision of a non-novel issue must have been published, so that if uncorrected the wrong decision will become precedent in conflict with earlier published decisions which rightly decided the same issue. Yet the supreme court sometimes grants hearings in two categories of cases in which there is no published decision: (a) cases in which the court of appeal's decision is not published; and (b) cases in which the court of appeal has summarily refused to grant a petition for an original writ. Such cases are most easily identified in two circumstances. First, when the supreme court grants a petition for hearing and immediately retransfers the case to the court of appeal to be reconsidered in light of authority cited to the court of appeal in the supreme court's minute order. *See*, *e.g.*, People v. Murphy (4th Crim. No. 8731, June 29, 1978) and People v. Mendoza (4th Crim. No. 9636, July 5, 1978), Supreme Court Minutes at 3, 9, 1978 Cal. Official Reports Adv. Sh. No. 20 (July 27, 1978). Second, as more commonly happens, when the supreme court grants a petition for hearing and retransfers the case to the court of appeal with the instruction simply to reconsider in a written opinion whether to grant a petition for an original writ. *See*, *e.g.*, Level v. Superior Court (5th Civ. No. 3997, May 25, 1978), Supreme Court Minutes at 2, 1978 Cal. Official Reports Adv. Sh. No. 17 (June 27, 1978).

Of course, there may well be an institutional function served in cases in which the court of appeal's error leads to imposition of some serious deprivation upon the losing party, if one views it as a matter of public importance to avoid a miscarriage of justice. Certainly in criminal cases there is a strong compulsion for the supreme court to correct mere error, even when an unpublished opinion conceals the error's existence and prison walls conceal its effect. Whatever its motivation, the Supreme Court of California clearly does review petitions for hearing for more than the institutional effect that the underlying decisions may have on other litigation, and this searching scrutiny greatly compounds its burden of processing petitions for hearing.

Note on Funding of Law Clerks at Lower Federal Courts

Circuit and district judges are currently authorized to "appoint necessary law clerks and secretaries." 28 U.S.C. §§ 712, 752 (1976). For the evolution of these provisions, see notes 2.48–2.49 *supra*. The Director of the Administrative Office of the United States Courts is authorized to fix the compensation of these law clerks, as well as all other court employees not otherwise funded. 28 U.S.C. § 604 (1976). However, the appropriations acts have, since at least 1950, contained provisions limiting the compensation of circuit and district court secretaries and law clerks to certain grades of the General Schedule of Salaries for the federal civil service. *See, e.g.*, Act of Sept. 6, 1950, ch. 896, § 401, 64 Stat. 595. *See also* note 2.53 *supra*. As of the summer of 1979, the current limitation provision was set forth in the Act of Oct. 10, 1978, Pub. L. No. 95–431, § 401, 92 Stat. 1021. The General Schedule, updated yearly, appears as 5 U.S.C. § 5332 (Supp. I 1977). Thus a circuit or district judge is effectively limited in the appointment of law clerks to as many as can be fit within the judge's staff salary limitation, which must cover the salaries not only of the law clerks, but also of the judge's secretary.

As if this were not complicated enough, the appropriations acts provide that only the base salary for an employee must conform to the stipulated general schedule level, and only this base salary counts toward the aggregate salary limitation; thus, step increases within grade are not subject to the limitation. The 1965 amendment allowing district court judges to choose to have an additional law clerk added the following perturbation: "A crier designated to serve as a crier–law clerk shall receive the compensation of a law clerk, but only so much of that compensation as is in excess of the compensation to which he would be entitled as a crier [as set by the Director of the Administrative Office of the Courts pursuant to 28 U.S.C. § 604] shall be deemed the compensation of a law clerk for the purposes of any limitation imposed by law upon the aggregate salaries of law clerks and secretaries appointed by a district judge." 28 U.S.C. § 755 (1976) (as amended by Act of Oct. 21, 1965, Pub. L. No. 89–281, 79 Stat. 1012).

It will come as no surprise that our study revealed that virtually no district judges understood just how they came to have a choice between hiring one law clerk and a court crier, or hiring two law clerks; they simply got the message from their chief judge, who in turn got word from the Administrative Office through a personnel manual. (Although this manual is presumably a public document, we were unable to find a copy that was available for public reference. None of the district court chief judges with whom we spoke regarded it as confidential, and our references to it are based upon notes taken from an examination in chambers of one chief judge's personal copy.)

Based on our 1976 notes and subsequently published details on changes in the maximum JSP grades for secretaries and crier-law clerks, see 1977 JUDICIAL CONFERENCE PROCEEDINGS, *supra* note 5.111, at 7–8; 1978 REPORTS OF THE PROCEEDINGS OF THE JUDICIAL CONFERENCE OF THE UNITED STATES 12 [hereinafter cited as 1978 JUDICIAL CONFERENCE PROCEEDINGS], the pertinent provisions of the Administrative Office's personnel manual are as follows (all dollar amounts have been adjusted to reflect the salary levels and aggregate salary limitations effective in the summer of 1979, pursuant to the Act of Oct. 10, 1978, Pub. L. No. 95–431, § 401, 92 Stat. 1021, and the General Schedule, 5 U.S.C. § 5332 (Supp. I 1977), *as adjusted by* Exec. Order No. 12,087, 43 Fed. Reg. 46,823 (1978), *reprinted in* 5 U.S.C.A., following § 5332 (Supp. 1979)):

The aggregate salary allowances for law clerks and secretaries are:

Chief Judge of Circuit	$91,747
Circuit Judge	73,489
Chief Judge of District (five or more judges)	57,608
District Judge	45,272

The entrance salaries, upon which aggregate salary computations are based without regard to periodic step increases, are set in terms of "JSP" grades equivalent to "GS" grades from the General Schedule, as follows:

JSP 5	$10,507
JSP 6	11,712
JSP 7	13,014
JSP 8	14,414
JSP 9	15,920
JSP 10	17,532
JSP 11	19,263
JSP 12	23,087

The JSP levels to which a judge may appoint secretaries and law clerks are at the judge's discretion, subject to the statutory aggregate salary levels and certain standards set by the Judicial Conference. Secretaries may be appointed to JSP 5 through JSP 11, based on experience. A crier–law clerk or junior law clerk is at least a JSP 9, and should have graduated from law school or completed law school studies. Little or no experience is expected. An associate law clerk is a JSP 10 or 11, at the judge's discretion. One year of experience in practice is expected, or a law school class standing in the upper third, or law review experience, or an L.L.M. degree from an ABA or AALS accredited law school, or proficiency in legal studies deemed equivalent to these exceptions by the appointing judge. A senior law clerk is a JSP 12, and should be a member of the bar, qualified for appointment as an associate law clerk, and have one year of experience in practice, legal research or administration, or the equivalent. Crier–law clerks with similar qualifications may, since 1977, also be appointed to JSP 10 or 11. Finally, a judge may appoint as a JSP 12 a secretary–law clerk, which requires professional training in the law equivalent to graduation from law school, membership in the bar, one year of legal experience, and five years of secretarial experience, including three years as a legal secretary. (This classification is rarely used by district judges today, but was apparently introduced as a form of overscale appointment for the secretaries of some judges who had paralegal skills and were able to obtain admission to the bar.)

Pursuant to the Administrative Office manual, if a district judge elects to have a crier–law clerk instead of a court crier, only the difference between the JSP 5 salary grade of a court crier and the JSP 9 to 11 salary grade of the crier–law clerk is charged to the judge's aggregate salary limitation of $45,272. Thus a district judge with a court crier and a JSP 10 secretary could hire a JSP 12 law clerk: the court crier's salary is not subject to the aggregate limit, and the secretary's $17,532 base salary would leave $27,740 of the aggregate limit available for the law clerk—well over the JSP 12 salary level of $23,087. Should this judge elect to have a second law clerk, however, he or she would encounter a problem. By not hiring a crier, the judge gets a credit of $10,507—the GS 5 salary of a crier. But adding this figure to the $27,740 left over after payment of a GS 10 secretary produces only $38,247—not enough for two GS 11 law clerks. One clerk must be paid as a GS 10, at a salary differential of $1731 per year. Both law clerks could be paid at the GS 11 only by reducing the secretary—generally a long-time associate of the judge—to the GS 8 level.

Judges unable to pay equal salaries to their law clerks solve the problem either by reclassifying their clerks at midyear so that each receives the lower salary for half a year, or by appointing one clerk as a senior clerk by virtue of experience or other qualifications. Salary parity has not been a problem for judges who use two law clerks and hire them for staggered two-year terms; such judges uniformly pay the lesser salary to the junior law clerk, regardless of how they otherwise allocate duties among the clerks.

Addendum

As this book was in press, the staff salary allowances for federal circuit and district judges were significantly increased by the Act of Sept. 24, 1979, Pub. L. No. 96-68, § 401, 93 Stat. 416. For the federal fiscal year beginning October 1, 1980, circuit judges can afford to hire three law clerks without paying any clerk less than a JSP 12 salary. District judges would have to limit their clerks to JSP 10 and 11 salaries in order to hire three, but can now hire two clerks at equal JSP 12 salaries. *See generally* Exec. Order No. 12,165, 44 Fed. Reg. 58,671 (1979) (setting General Schedule and hence JSP salary levels for fiscal 1980). We understand that most Ninth Circuit judges are planning to hire a third law clerk now that they can do so without underpaying any of them. *Cf.* text accompanying note 5.123 *supra* (desire for third clerk); note 5.110 *supra* (concern over adequate salaries). We do not know of any district judges who anticipate hiring a third law clerk, although we expect more district judges to employ "court criers" or bailiffs now that they can do so without necessarily sacrificing a second law clerk. *Cf.* text accompanying notes 5.143–5.155 *supra* (use of bailiffs declining because of need for second clerk); note 1.555 *supra* (two clerks sufficient). Although the liberal funding provided by the fiscal 1980 appropriations act has alleviated most of the immediate administrative problems concerning staff assistance for judges of the lower federal courts, the act did not reform in any way the accounting complexities of the staff salary allowance system. Judges with atypical staff arrangements will continue to face confusion, and most judges will be uncertain of just how atypical they can afford to be.

The fiscal 1980 appropriations act is also significant for its implementation of the September 1978 recommendation of the Judicial Conference that the salary ceiling for law clerks be raised from the JSP 12 to the JSP 13 level. *See* 1978 JUDICIAL CONFERENCE PROCEEDINGS, *supra*, at 49. Although this measure was specifically intended to permit federal judges to retain career law clerks, the Judicial Conference recommended it only to accommodate a small minority of federal judges, and explicitly endorsed the preferability of short-term law clerks. In response to a committee report that the number of career law clerks in the federal judiciary had dwindled from 36 to 24 in the 10 years preceding September 1978, the Judicial Conference adopted the following resolution:

> It is the sense of the Conference that the best interests of the judiciary are better served through continuation of the traditional practice of appointing recent graduates as law clerks for periods of one to two years. In recognition of unusual situations, the Conference approves changes in the qualification standards for law clerks on the personal staffs of federal judges to provide that, after five years of experience as a law clerk to a federal judge, a grade JSP-12 law clerk may be considered qualified for promotion to grade JSP-13 upon recommendation by the judge, subject to the availability of funds.

Id.

Even as increased for fiscal 1980 the staff salary allowances are not sufficient for federal judges to pay JSP 13 salaries to all their law clerks. A circuit judge could hire one JSP 13 career law clerk along with two JSP 12 short-term clerks, and a district judge could hire one JSP 13 career law clerk along with a short-term crier-clerk. We do not expect any rush to career law clerks by the federal judiciary, however. Not only does the great majority of federal judges remain lukewarm to the idea, see note 5.154 supra, but also the salaries available even at the JSP 13 level are unlikely to induce many short-term federal law clerks to make clerking a career. For fiscal 1980 the JSP 13 salary range is $29,375 to $38,186, depending on years of service. By comparison, the JSP 15 salary range for fiscal 1980 of the senior staff attorney for each circuit is $40,832 to $53,081, which is competitive with the salaries paid staff attorneys at the Supreme Court of California. See notes 5.41 & 5.111 supra.

The possibility of a trend toward greater use of career law clerks at federal courts nonetheless bears watching. The looser purse strings of the fiscal 1980 appropriations act certainly encourage federal judges to reconsider their clerkship tenure policies. Experimentation with career clerks continues at the United States Supreme Court, see note 2.56 supra, and may be encouraged by the publication of an instantly notorious journalistic study of Supreme Court decision-making, see B. Woodward & S. Armstrong, supra note 2.46. Much of the material for this book came from interviews with former law clerks, leading one knowledgeable reviewer to predict that the Justices, their confidence in short-term clerks shaken, might hire "older and more experienced attorneys" in their stead. See Murphy, Spilling the Secrets of the Supreme Court, Wash. Post, Dec. 16, 1979, Book World, at 1, 11. But cf. Barbash, Five 'Brethren' Helped Authors, Wash. Post. Dec. 9, 1979, at A1, col. 1 (some Justices encouraged clerks to talk to Woodward and Armstrong); Frank, The Supreme Court: The Muckrackers Return, 66 A.B.A.J. 161, 164 (1980) (Justices may simply have too many law clerks). If a trend toward use of career law clerks does develop at the Supreme Court of the United States, history certainly teaches that, like the institution itself, it will in time spread to the lower federal courts.

Bibliography

Abraham, Henry J. *The Judicial Process: An Introductory Analysis of the Courts of the United States, England and France.* 3d ed., rev. and enl. New York: Oxford University Press, 1975.

Acheson, Dean. "Recollection of Service with the Federal Supreme Court." *Alabama Lawyer* 18 (1957): 355–366.

Administrative Office of the United States Courts. *Annual Report of the Director, 1978.* Washington, D.C.: U.S. Government Printing Office, 1978.

————. *Annual Report of the Director, 1977.* Washington, D.C.: U.S. Government Printing Office, 1977.

————. *Annual Report of the Director, 1976.* Washington, D.C.: U.S. Government Printing Office, 1976.

————. *Management Statistics for United States Courts, 1977.* Washington, D.C.: U.S. Government Printing Office, 1977.

Advisory Council for Appellate Justice. *Appellate Justice: 1975— Summary and Background,* vol. 1. Edited by P. Carrington. Denver: National Center for State Courts, 1975.

"Alabama Appellate Court Congestion: Observations and Suggestions from an Empirical Study." *Alabama Law Review* 21 (1968): 150–163.

Alaska Judicial Council. *First Annual Report.* Anchorage: Alaska Judicial Council, 1960.

Aldisert, Ruggero J. "Duties of Law Clerks." *Vanderbilt Law Review* 26 (1973): 1251–1257.

American Bar Association Commission on Standards of Judicial Administration. *Standards Relating to Appellate Courts.* Chicago: The Commission, 1977.

American Bar Association Section of Judicial Administration. *Internal Operating Procedures of Appellate Courts.* Los Angeles: American Bar Association, 1961.

————. "Methods of Reaching and Preparing Appellate Court Decisions." Report of a committee to gather information concerning methods of reaching and preparing appellate court decisions, 1942.

American Judicature Society. "Law Clerks in State Appellate Courts." Report No. 16, January 1968.

————. "Solutions for Appellate Court Congestion and Delay, Analysis and Bibliography." American Judicature Society Information Sheet No. 24, 17 September 1963.

Association of American Law Schools and the Law School Admission Council. *Pre Law Handbook 78–79*. Princeton, N.J.: Association of American Law Schools and the Law School Admission Council, 1978.

Association of the Bar of the City of New York. *Bad Housekeeping: The Administration of New York Courts*. New York, 1955.

Auden, Wystan H. "Law Like Love." In *Collected Shorter Poems 1927–1957*. New York: Random House, 1966.

Austen, Jane. *Pride and Prejudice*, with an introd. by W. D. Howells. New York: Scribner's, c. 1918.

Baier, Paul R. "The Law Clerks: Profile of an Institution." *Vanderbilt Law Review* 26 (1973): 1125–1177.

Baier, Paul R., and Lesinski, T. John. "In Aid of the Judicial Process: A Proposal for Law Curricular and Student Involvement." *Judicature* 56 (October 1972): 100–107.

Baker, David H.; Watkins, W. David; and Tardy, Thomas W. "Appellate Court Reform." *Mississippi Law Journal* 45 (1974): 121–161.

Barbash, Fred. "Five 'Brethren' Helped Authors." *Washington Post*, 9 December 1979, p. A1.

Barnett, Peter. "Law Clerks in the United States Courts and State Appellate Courts." Chicago: American Judicature Society, 1973.

Barrett, Edward R.; Feeney, Floyd; and Mayhew, Leon. "The National Conference on Appellate Justice: An Evaluation." Report to the National Center for State Courts, June 1976.

Benthall-Nietzel, Deera. "Staff Attorneys and Kentucky Courts in Transition." *Kentucky Bench and Bar* 41 (1977): 27–29.

Bickel, Alexander M. *The Caseload of the Supreme Court—And What, If Anything, To Do About It*. Washington, D.C.: American Enterprise Institute for Public Policy Research, 1973.

————. "The Court: An Indictment Analyzed." *New York Times Magazine*, 27 April 1958, p. 16.

————. *Politics and the Warren Court*. New York: Harper and Row, 1965.

Biddle, Francis B. *Mr. Justice Holmes*. New York: Scribner's, 1942.

Bird, Rose E. "The Hidden Judiciary." *Judges' Journal* 17 (Winter 1978): 4–6, 46.

Blume, William W. "California Courts in Historical Perspective." *Hastings Law Review* 22 (1970): 121–195.

Bogdan, Robert, and Taylor, Steven J. *Introduction to Qualitative Research Methods.* New York: Wiley, 1975.

Boskey, Bennett. "Mr. Chief Justice Stone." *Harvard Law Review* 59 (1946): 1200–1202.

Braden, George D. "The Value of Law Clerks." *Mississippi Law Journal* 24 (1953): 295–299.

Breen, Fred E. "Solutions for Appellate Court Congestion." *Journal of American Judicature Society* 47 (1964): 228–235.

Brennan, William J. "Justice Brennan Calls National Court of Appeals Proposal Fundamentally Ill-Advised." *American Bar Association Journal* 59 (1973): 835–840.

"The Bright Young Men Behind the Bench." *U.S. News & World Report*, 12 July 1957, pp. 45–48.

Brudney, Victor, and Wolson, Richard F. "Mr. Justice Rutledge —Law Clerks' Reflections." *Indiana Law Journal* 25 (1949–50): 445–461.

Buehl, Stephen T. "Description of California Supreme Court Procedures." News Release by the Executive Assistant to the Chief Justice of California, 24 November 1978.

California. *West's California Rules of Court 1975–76.* St. Paul, Minn.: West Publishing Co., 1976.

California Commission on Judicial Performance. "Inquiry Concerning a Judge." Commission on Judicial Performance Report No. 25, 30 December 1976.

California. Governor. *Budget Message, 1978–79.* Sacramento, 1978.

———. "Salaries and Wages Supplement." In *Budget Message, 1978–79.* Sacramento, 1978.

California. Supreme Court. *California Reports 3d.* Vol. 20. San Francisco: Bancroft-Whitney, 1977.

———. *California Reports 3d.* Vol. 18. San Francisco: Bancroft-Whitney, 1977.

———. *California Reports 3d.* Vol. 17. San Francisco: Bancroft-Whitney, 1976.

———. *California Reports 3d.* Vol. 15. San Francisco: Bancroft-Whitney, 1976.

——. *California Reports 2d*. Vol. 65. San Francisco: Bancroft-Whitney, 1967.

——. *California Reports 2d*. Vol. 34. San Francisco: Bancroft-Whitney, 1950.

——. *California Reports 2d*. Vol. 16. San Francisco: Bancroft-Whitney, 1941.

——. *California Reports 2d*. Vol. 15. San Francisco: Bancroft-Whitney, 1940.

——. *California Reports 2d*. Vol. 14. San Francisco: Bancroft-Whitney, 1940.

Cameron, James D. "The Central Staff: A New Solution to an Old Problem." *UCLA Law Review* 23 (1976): 465–479.

——. "Judges' Fears and Central Staff." *Judges Journal* 17 (Spring 1978): 27.

Cannon, Mark W. "Administrative Change and the Supreme Court." *Judicature* 57 (1974): 334–341.

——. "An Administrator's View of the Supreme Court." *Federal Bar News* 22 (1975): 109–113.

Carrington, Paul D. *Accommodating the Workload of the United States Court of Appeals*. Chicago: American Bar Foundation, 1968.

Carrington, Paul D.; Meador, Daniel J.; and Rosenberg, Maurice. *Justice on Appeal*. St. Paul, Minn.: West Publishing Co., 1976.

Casey, Gregory. "The Supreme Court and Myth: An Empirical Investigation." *Law and Society Review* 8 (1974): 385–419.

Casper, Gerhard, and Posner, Richard A. *The Workload of the Supreme Court*. Chicago: American Bar Foundation, 1976.

"Chief Justice Vinson and His Law Clerks." *Northwestern University Law Review* 49 (1964): 26–35.

Chilton, Jan T. "Appellate Court Reform: The Premature Scalpel." *California State Bar Journal* 48 (1976): 392.

Christian, Winslow. "Delay in Criminal Appeals: A Functional Analysis of One Court's Work." *Stanford Law Review* 23 (1971): 676–702.

——. "Using Prehearing Procedures to Increase Productivity." *Federal Rules Decisions* 52 (1971): 55–78.

Clark, Tom C. "Internal Operation of the United States Supreme Court." *Journal of American Judicature Society* 43 (1959): 45–51.

Cohen, William. "Justice Douglas: A Law Clerk's View." *University of Chicago Law Review* 26 (1958): 6–8.

Council of State Governments. *State Court Systems: A Statistical Summary Prepared for the Conference of Chief Justices*. Lexington, Ky.: Council of State Governments, 1974.

Cuomo, Mario M. "The New York Court of Appeals: A Practical Perspective." *St. John's Law Review* 34 (1960): 197–218.

Curran, Edward, and Sunderland, Edson. "The Organization and Operation of Courts of Review, Chapter VI: Providing the Judges with Trained Assistants." *Third Report of the Judicial Council of Michigan*. Lansing, 1933.

"Dedication." *Southern California Law Review* 46 (1973): 227–228. (In Honor of Justice Raymond E. Peters of the California Supreme Court.)

DiLeo, Anthony M., and Rubin, Alvin B. "Law Clerk Handbook." Federal Judicial Center FJC-M-1 (looseleaf), September 1977, revised March 1978.

"Disorder in the California Court." *New York Times*, 10 November 1979, p. 22 (editorial).

Dolbeare, Kenneth M. "The Public Views the Supreme Court." In *Law, Politics, and the Federal Courts*. Edited by Herbert Jacob. Boston: Little, Brown, 1967.

Dorsen, Norman. "Law Clerks in Appellate Courts in the United States." *Modern Law Review* 26 (1963): 265–271.

"Douglas: Personal View of Impersonal Judge." *Sacramento Bee*, 24 November 1975, p. B 2.

Douglas, William O. *Go East, Young Man: The Early Years*. New York: Random House, 1974.

Edwards, George. "The Avoidance of Appellate Delay." *Federal Rules Decisions* 52 (1971): 61–70.

Endicott, William. "Personal Hostilities Tear at Supreme Court Fabric." *Los Angeles Times*, 23 November 1978, section 1, p. 1.

English, Robert E. "Crisis in Civil Appeals." *Chicago Bar Record* 50 (1969): 231–237.

Farer, Tom J., and Jacob, Cynthia M. "The Appellate Process and Staff Research Attorneys in the Appellate Division of the New Jersey Superior Court." Report of the Appellate Justice Project of the National Center for State Courts, Publication No. W0011, May 1974.

Federal Judicial Center. "Central Legal Staffs in the United States Courts of Appeals." Federal Judicial Center Report FJC-R-78-3, April 1978.

"Federal Order Lifts Ban on Importing 'Tropic of Cancer.'" *New York Times*, 11 August 1961, p. 25.

The Federal Reporter. Second series. Vol. 573. St. Paul, Minn.: West Publishing Co., 1978.

———. Second series. Vol. 525. St. Paul, Minn.: West Publishing Co., 1976.

Fite, Arthur; Potts, Robert L.; and Sweeney, Donald B., Jr. "Law Clerkships: Three Inside Views." *Alabama Lawyer* 33 (1972): 156–179.

Flanders, Steven. "District Court Studies Project Interim Report." Federal Judicial Center, June 1976.

Flanders, Steven, and Goldman, Jerry. "Screening Practices and the Use of Para-Judicial Personnel in a U.S. Court of Appeals: A Study in the Fourth Circuit." *Justice System Journal* 1 (1975): 1–16.

Francis, John J. "Post-Argument Procedures." *Federal Rules Decisions* 52 (1971): 70–76.

Frank, John P. "Fred Vinson and the Chief Justiceship." *University of Chicago Law Review* 21 (1954): 212–246.

———. *The Marble Palace*. New York: Knopf, 1958.

———. *Mr. Justice Black: The Man and His Opinions*. New York: Knopf, 1949.

———. "The Supreme Court: the Muckrakers Return." *American Bar Association Journal* 66 (1980): 161–164.

Frankfurter, Felix, and Landis, James M. *The Business of the Supreme Court*. New York: Macmillan, 1927.

Freund, Paul A. "Why We Need the National Court of Appeals." *American Bar Association Journal* 59 (1973): 247–252.

Glaser, Barney G., and Straus, Anselm L. *The Discovery of Grounded Theory*. Chicago: Aldine, 1967.

Goldberg, Irving L. "Preparation for Hearing Oral Argument." *Federal Rules Decisions* 63 (1974): 499–507.

Goodman, William M., and Seaton, Thomas G., "The Supreme Court of California, 1972–73—Foreword: Ripe for Decision, Internal Workings and Current Concerns of the California Supreme Court." *California Law Review* 62 (1974): 309–364.

"Great Saving Through Use of Supreme Court Clerks." *Journal of the American Judicature Society* 16 (1932): 63.

Griswold, Erwin N. "Appellate Advocacy, With Particular Reference to the United States Supreme Court." *The Record of the Association of the Bar of the City of New York* 26 (1971): 342–357.

Gustafson, Roy A. "Some Observations About California Courts of Appeal." *UCLA Law Review* 19 (1971): 167–208.

Hager, Philip. "How Secret Should State High Court Decisions Be?" *Los Angeles Times*, 23 November 1978, section 1, p. 3.

Hamley, Frederick G. "Law Clerks for Judges of the Ninth Circuit Court of Appeals." *Vanderbilt Law Review* 26 (1973): 1241–1250.

Haworth, Charles R. "Screening and Summary Procedures in the United States Courts of Appeals." *Washington University Law Quarterly* 1973: 257–326.

Hazard, Geoffrey C., Jr. "After the Trial Court—the Realities of Appellate Review." In *The Courts, The Public, and the Law Explosion.* Edited by N. Jones. Englewood Cliffs, N.J.: Prentice-Hall, 1965.

Heineman, Benjamin W., Jr. "Book Review: J. Harvie Wilkinson, *Serving Justice.*" *Harvard Law Review* 88 (1975): 678–685.

Hellman, Arthur D. "The Business of the Supreme Court Under the Judiciary Act of 1925: The Plenary Docket in the 1970's." *Harvard Law Review* 91 (1978): 1709–1803.

"Henry Miller Ban to be Defied Here." *New York Times*, 25 April 1961, p. 37.

Herman, Michael J. "Law Clerking at the Supreme Court of Canada." *Osgoode Hall Law Journal* 13 (1975): 279–292.

Heydebrand, Wolf V. "The Context of Public Bureaucracies: An Organizational Analysis of Federal District Courts." *Law and Society Review* 11 (1977): 759–821.

"High Court Relies Heavily on Staff." *Metropolitan News* (Los Angeles), 29 November 1978, p. 3.

Hills, Roderick M. "A Law Clerk at the Supreme Court of the United States." *Los Angeles Bar Bulletin* 33 (1958): 333–338.

"Historical Note[s]." In *West's Annotated California Code*, vol. 37 (following Government Code §§ 69101 through 69105). St. Paul, Minn.: West Publishing Co., 1976.

"Historical and Revision Notes." In *United States Code Annotated,*

Title 28, Judiciary and Judicial Procedure, §§ 171 to 1250 (following § 604). St. Paul, Minn.: West Publishing Co., 1968 [and 1979 Pocket Part].

Hopkins, James D. "The Winds of Change: New Styles in the Appellate Process." *Hofstra Law Review* 3 (1975): 649–661.

Hufstedler, Shirley M. "The Appellate Process Inside Out." *California State Bar Journal* 50 (1975): 20–24.

Hufstedler, Shirley M., and Hufstedler, Seth M. "Improving the California Appellate Pyramid." *Los Angeles Bar Bulletin* 46 (1971): 275.

Jaffe, Louis L. "An Impression of Mr. Justice Brandeis." *Harvard Law School Bulletin* 8 (April 1957): 10–11.

Johnson, Nicholas. "What Do Law Clerks Do?" *Texas Bar Journal* 22 (1959): 229.

Johnson, Phillip E. "The Supreme Court of California 1975–1976—Foreword: The Accidental Decision and How It Happens." *California Law Review* 65 (1977): 231–254.

Judicial Conference of the United States. *Reports of the Proceedings of the Judicial Conference of the United States*. Washington, D.C.: U.S. Government Printing Office, 1978.

———. *Reports of the Proceedings of the Judicial Conference of the United States*. Washington, D.C.: U.S. Government Printing Office, 1977.

Judicial Council of California. *1978 Judicial Council of California Report*. Sacramento, 1978.

———. *1977 Judicial Council of California Report*. Sacramento, 1977.

———. *1976 Judicial Council of California Report*. Sacramento, 1976.

———. *1970 Judicial Council of California Report*. Sacramento, 1970.

———. *1968 Judicial Council of California Report*. Sacramento, 1968.

Judicial Council of Kansas. *Second Annual Report*. Topeka, 1928.

Kang, K. Connie. "Behind that 'Delayed Decision': Backstage at the High Court." *San Francisco Sunday Examiner and Chronicle*, 19 November 1978, p. A 1.

———. "The Decline of California's Vendetta-Ridden Supreme Court." *California Journal* 10 (1979): 343–347.

Karlen, Delmar. *Appellate Courts in the United States and England.* New York: New York University Press, 1963.

Kaufman, Irving R. "The Judicial Crisis, Court Delay, and the Parajudge." *Judicature* 54 (1970): 145–148.

———. "The Pre-Argument Conference: An Appellate Procedural Reform." *Columbia Law Review* 74 (1974): 1094–1103.

Kidney, James A. "Anonymous Clerks Serve Justices, Gain Experience." *Washington Post,* 16 June 1974, p. L 6.

Klecka, William R.; Nie, Norman H.; and Hull, C. Hadlai. *SPSS Primer.* New York: McGraw-Hill, 1975.

Kocourek, Albert. "Relief for the Appellate Courts: The Referendary System." *Journal of American Judicature Society* 7 (1923): 122–130.

Kurland, Philip B. "Book Review: C. Herman Pritchett, *Civil Liberties and the Warren Court.*" *University of Chicago Law Review* 22 (1954): 297–303.

———. "Jerome N. Frank: Some Reflections and Recollections of a Law Clerk." *University of Chicago Law Review* 24 (1957): 661–665.

Lake, James A. "The Appellate Process and Staff Research Attorneys in the Supreme Court of Nebraska." Report of the Appellate Justice Project of the National Center for State Courts, Publication No. W0009, May 1974.

Lash, Joseph P. "A Brahmin of the Law: A Biographical Essay." In *From the Diaries of Felix Frankfurter.* Edited by J. P. Lash. New York: Norton, 1975.

Leach, W. Barton. "Recollections of a Holmes Secretary." Unpublished, September 1940. Archival Collection, Harvard Law School Library.

Lee, Joe, and Moloney, R. P., Jr. "The Kentucky Court of Appeals Apprentice Law Clerk Program." *Kentucky State Bar Journal* 21 (1957): 90–91.

Leflar, Robert A. *Appellate Judicial Opinions.* Edited by R. A. Leflar. St. Paul, Minn.: West Publishing Co., 1974.

———. *Internal Operating Procedures of Appellate Courts.* Chicago: American Bar Foundation, 1976.

Lesinski, T. John. "Judicial Research Assistants: The Michigan Experience." *Trial Judges Journal* 10 (1971): 54–55.

Lesinski, T. John, and Stockmeyer, N. O., Jr. "Prehearing Research and Screening in the Michigan Court of Appeals: One Court's Method for Increasing Judicial Productivity." *Vanderbilt Law Review* 26 (1973): 1211–1240.

Lilly, Graham C. "The Appellate Process and Staff Research Attorneys in the Supreme Court of Virginia." Report of the Appellate Justice Project of the National Center for State Courts, Publication No. W0008, May 1974.

Lilly, Graham C., and Scalia, Antonin. "Appellate Justice: A Crisis in Virginia?" *Virginia Law Review* 57 (1971): 3–64.

Llewellyn, Karl N. *The Common Law Tradition: Deciding Appeals.* Boston: Little, Brown, 1960.

Lofland, John. *Analyzing Social Settings—A Guide to Qualitative Observation and Analysis.* Belmont, Calif.: Wadsworth, 1971.

Lucas, Jo Desha. "The Appellate Process and Staff Research Attorneys in the Illinois Appellate Court." Report of the Appellate Justice Project of the National Center for State Courts, Publication No. W0010, May 1974.

McCormack, Alfred. "A Law Clerk's Recollections." *Columbia Law Review* 46 (1946): 710–718.

McCormick, Mark. "Appellate Congestion in Iowa: Dimensions and Remedies." *Drake Law Review* 25 (1975): 133–160.

Mars, David, and Kort, Fred. *Administration of Justice in Connecticut.* Edited by I. Davis. Storrs: Institute of Public Service, University of Connecticut, 1963.

Mason, Alpheus T. *Harlan Fiske Stone: Pillar of the Law.* New York: Viking Press, 1956.

Meador, Daniel J. *Appellate Courts: Staff and Process in the Crisis of Volume.* St. Paul, Minn.: West Publishing Co., 1974.

———. "Justice Black and His Law Clerks." *Alabama Law Review* 15 (1962): 57–63.

———. "Professional Assistance for Appellate Judges: A Central Staff of Lawyers." *Federal Rules Decisions* 63 (1974): 489–499.

Medina, Harold R. "The Decisional Process." *Bar Bulletin of the New York County Lawyers' Association* 20 (1962): 94–103.

———. "Some Reflections on the Judicial Function at the Appellate Level." *Washington University Law Quarterly* 1961: 148–156.

"Methods of Work in the Appellate Courts of the United States." *Journal of American Judicature Society* 10 (1926): 57–63.

Molinari, John B. "The Decisionmaking Conference of the California Court of Appeal." *California Law Review* 57 (1969): 606–614.

Morris, Thomas R. *The Virginia Supreme Court: An Institutional and Political Analysis.* Charlottesville: University Press of Virginia, 1975.

Mosk, Stanley. "The Supreme Court of California 1973–1974—Foreword: The Rule of Four in California." *California Law Review* 63 (1975): 2–8.

Murphy, Walter F. "Spilling the Secrets of the Supreme Court." *Washington Post,* 16 December 1979, Book World, p. 1.

Naff, John M., Jr. Letter sent, as Supervising Staff Attorney, United States Court of Appeals for the Ninth Circuit, to "All Placement Directors," undated, circa summer 1976.

National Center for State Courts. *The California Courts of Appeal.* Denver: National Center for State Courts, 1974.

———. *Parajudges: Their Role in Today's Court Systems.* Denver: Research and Information Service, National Center for State Courts, 1976.

Newland, Chester A. "Personal Assistants to Supreme Court Justices: The Law Clerks." *Oregon Law Review* 40 (1961): 299–317.

Nie, Norman; Hull, C. Hadlai; Jenkins, Jean G.; Steinbrenner, Karin; and Bent, Dale H. *SPSS: Statistical Package for the Social Sciences.* 2d ed. New York: McGraw-Hill, 1975.

Noble, M. E. "The Law Clerk." *Trial Judges Journal* 7 (October 1968): 4.

Oakley, John B. "Taking Wright Seriously: Of Judicial Discretion, Jurisprudents and the Chief Justice." *Hastings Constitutional Law Quarterly* 4 (1977): 789–854.

O'Connell, Kenneth J. "Streamlining Appellate Procedures." *Judicature* 56 (January 1973): 23–239.

Parness, Jeffrey A. "The Expanding Role of the Parajudge in the United States." American Judicature Society Research Project, preliminary draft, 1973.

Pickering, John H.; Gressman, Eugene; and Tolan, T. L., Jr. "Mr. Justice Murphy—A Note of Appreciation." *Michigan Law Review* 48 (1950): 742–744.

Poulos, John W. *The Anatomy of Criminal Justice.* Mineola, N.Y.: Foundation Press, 1976.

"Proceedings of the Annual Meeting of the Association." *Connecticut Bar Journal* 26 (1952): 428–460.

Ragatz, Thomas G., and Shea, Jeremy C. "Supreme Court Law Clerks." *Wisconsin Bar Bulletin* 35 (August 1962): 33–38.

Rehnquist, William H. "Another View: Clerks Might 'Influence' Some Actions." *U.S. News & World Report*, 21 February 1958, p. 116.

———. "Who Writes Decisions of the Supreme Court?" *U.S. News & World Report*, 13 December 1957, pp. 74–75.

"Relief for Appellate Courts." *Journal of American Judicature Society* 15 (1931): 175–178.

"Report and Recommendations on Improvements of Appellate Practices, Topic IV: Central Staff." In *Appellate Justice: 1975— Supplement, Proceedings and Conclusions*, vol. 5. Advisory Council for Appellate Justice. Edited by P. Carrington. Denver: National Center for State Courts, 1975.

"Report of the Study Group on the Caseload of the Supreme Court." *Federal Rules Decisions* 57 (1973): 573–612.

"Report on Group Discussions, Topic II: Responsibility for Decisions." In *Appellate Justice: 1975—Supplement, Proceedings and Conclusions*, vol. 5. Advisory Council for Appellate Justice. Edited by P. Carrington. Denver: National Center for State Courts, 1975.

Roche, John P. "The Utopian Pilgrimage of Mr. Justice Murphy." *Vanderbilt Law Review* 10 (1957): 369–394.

Rogers, William D. "Clerks' Work Is 'Not Decisive of Ultimate Result.'" *U.S. News & World Report*, 21 February 1958, pp. 114–116.

Rutzick, Mark C. "Gerald Gunther: A Man Who Enjoys an Occasional Brief Constitutional." *Harvard Law Record*, 2 March 1973, pp. 8–9.

Sacks, Albert M. "Felix Frankfurter." In *The Justices of the United States Supreme Court 1789–1969*, vol. 3. Edited by L. Friedman and F. Israel. New York: Chelsea House in association with Bowker, 1969.

Salzman, Ed. "Why Brown Jumped into the Budget Inferno." *California Journal* 10 (1979): 289–291.

Sarat, Austin. "Studying American Legal Culture: An Assessment of Survey Evidence." *Law and Society Review* 11 (1977): 427–488.

Schatzman, Leonard, and Strauss, Ansel L. *Field Research: Strategies for a Natural Sociology*. Englewood Cliffs, N.J.: Prentice-Hall, 1973.

Schick, Marvin. *Learned Hand's Court*. Baltimore: Johns Hopkins University Press, 1970.

Schroeder, Mary M. "Judicial Administration and Invisible Justice." *University of Michigan Journal of Law Reform* 11 (1978): 322–335.

Schubert, Glendon. *Judicial Policy Making: The Political Role of the Courts*. Rev. ed. Glenview, Ill.: Scott, Foresman, 1974.

Schwartz, Mortimer. "Interview with William W. Oliver, Professor of Law, Indiana University." Unpublished interview conducted for the Earl Warren Oral History Project of the Bancroft Library, University of California, Berkeley, 17 May 1972.

"Screening of Criminal Cases in the Federal Courts of Appeals: Practice and Proposals." *Columbia Law Review* 73 (1973): 77–105.

Shafroth, Will. "Survey of the United States Courts of Appeals." *Federal Rules Decisions* 42 (1968): 243–315.

Shakespeare, William. *Romeo and Juliet*. Edited by J. D. Wilson. Cambridge, England: Cambridge University Press, 1955.

Shapiro, Robert A., and Osthus, Marlin O. "Congestion and Delay in State Appellate Courts." American Judicature Society Research Project, December 1974.

Smith, George R. "A Primer of Opinion Writing for Law Clerks." *Vanderbilt Law Review* 26 (1973): 1203–1210.

Spector, Sidney. "Staffs of State Courts of Last Resort." *Journal of American Judicature Society* 34 (1951): 144–148.

Stein, Joseph; Bock, Jerry; and Harnick, Sheldon. "Fiddler on the Roof." In *Best Plays of the Sixties*. Edited by S. Richards. Garden City, N.Y.: Doubleday, 1970.

Stern, Robert L., and Gressman, Eugene. *Supreme Court Practice*. 4th ed. Washington, D.C.: Bureau of National Affairs, 1969.

Stockmeyer, N. O., Jr. "Rx for the Certiorari Crisis: A More Professional Staff." *American Bar Association Journal* 59 (1973): 846–850.

Stockmeyer, N. O., Jr.; Borst, Jack L.; Stenger, John H.; and Reid, Joseph G. "The Office of the Commissioner of the Michigan Court of Appeals and Its Role in the Appellate Process." *Federal Rules Decisions* 48 (1970): 355–364.

Stuart, William C. "Iowa Supreme Court Congestion: Can We Avert a Crisis?" *Iowa Law Review* 55 (1970): 594–613.

"The Supreme Court, 1976 Term." *Harvard Law Review* 91 (1977): 70–301.

Supreme Court of California. "Summary of Comments Received by the Chief Justice's Special Committee to Study the Appellate Practices and Procedures in the First Appellate District." San Francisco, Calif., 21 August 1978.

Tamura, Stephen K. "What Everyone Wants to Know About the Courts of Appeal But Were Afraid to Ask." *L.A. Daily Journal*, 17 October 1973, pp. 25–29.

Texas Bar Association. "Proceedings of the Thirty-Third Annual Session held at Dallas, July 7–8, 1914." Dallas, 1914.

Theodorson, George A., and Theodorson, Achilles G. *Modern Dictionary of Sociology*. New York: Crowell, 1969.

Thompson, Robert S. "Mitigating the Damage: One Judge and No Judge Appellate Decisions." *California State Bar Journal* 50 (1975): 476.

"To Hear or Not to Hear: A Question for the California Supreme Court." *Stanford Law Review* 3 (1951): 243–269.

"To Hear or Not to Hear: II." *Stanford Law Review* 4 (1952): 392–400.

Traynor, Roger J. "Justice Raymond E. Peters." *California Law Review* 57 (1969): 559–562.

Turner, Wallace. "High Court on Coast Cleared by Inquiry." *New York Times*, 6 November 1979, p. A16.

United States Court of Appeals for the Third Circuit. "Internal Operating Procedures." *Federal Rules Decisions* 63 (1974): 319–359.

Weinstein, Jack B. "Proper and Improper Interactions Between Bench and Law School: Law Student Practice, Law Student Clerkships, and Rules for Admission to the Federal Bar." *St. John's Law Review* 50 (1976): 441–462.

Weinstein, Jack B., and Bonvillian, William B. "A Part-Time Clerkship Program in Federal Courts for Law Students." *Federal Rules Decisions* 68 (1975): 265–280.

West's California Reporter. Vol. 150. St. Paul, Minn.: West Publishing Co., 1979.

————. Vol. 145. St. Paul, Minn.: West Publishing Co., 1978.

Wilkinson, J. Harvie. *Serving Justice: A Supreme Court Clerk's View*. New York: Charterhouse, 1974.

Williams, Richard L. "Justices Run 'Nine Little Law Firms' at Supreme Court." *Smithsonian*, February 1977, pp. 84–93.

Williston, Samuel. "Horace Gray." In *Great American Lawyers*. Edited by W. Lewis. Philadelphia: J. C. Winston Co., 1907–09. South Hackensack, N.J.: Rothman Reprints, 1971.

————. *Life and Law*. Boston: Little, Brown, 1940.

Witkin, Bernard E. "Appellate Court Opinions—A Syllabus for Panel Discussion at the Appellate Judges Conference of the Section of Judicial Administration, American Bar Association." Montreal, 1966.

————. *California Criminal Procedure*. Supp. 1978. San Francisco: Bender-Moss, 1978.

————. *California Criminal Procedure*. San Francisco: Bender-Moss, 1963.

————. *California Procedure*. 2d ed. Vol. 5. San Francisco: Bancroft-Whitney, 1971.

————. *California Procedure*. 2d ed. Vol. 1. San Francisco: Bancroft-Whitney, 1970.

————. *Manual on Appellate Court Opinions*. St. Paul, Minn.: West Publishing Co., 1977.

————. "New California Rules on Appeal." *Southern California Law Review* 17 (1944): 232–301.

Wold, John T. "Going Through the Motions: The Monotony of Appellate Court Decisionmaking." *Judicature* 62 (August 1978): 58–65.

Woodward, Bob, and Armstrong, Scott. *The Brethren*. New York: Simon and Schuster, 1979.

Wright, Eugene A. "Observations of an Appellate Judge: the Use of Law Clerks." *Vanderbilt Law Review* 26 (1973): 1179–1196.

————. "Selection, Training and Use of Law Clerks in United States Court of Appeals." *Federal Rules Decisions* 63 (1974): 457–488.

Zeigler, Donald H., and Hermann, Michele G. "The Invisible Litigant: An Inside View of Pro Se Actions in the Federal Courts." *New York University Law Review* 47 (1972): 157–257.

TABLE OF CASES
AND STATUTES

All citations to cases and statutes, here and in the footnotes, conform to *A Uniform System of Citation*, 12th edition (1976), published by the Harvard Law Review Association. The following explanations of the more commonly used abbreviations should allow readers unfamiliar with legal citations to locate most of the cited material at any substantial law library. The more arcane citations should prove intelligible to any experienced legal reference librarian.

Cases

Cases in the United States Supreme Court are cited to the official case reporter, the *United States Reports* (U.S.), published by the United States Government Printing Office.

Cases in the federal courts of appeals are cited to the *Federal Reporter, 2d* (F.2d), published by the West Publishing Company.

Cases in the federal district courts are cited to the *Federal Supplement* (F. Supp.), also published by the West Publishing Company.

Cases in state courts are cited to the official state reporter as well as, where applicable, the regional and state reporters of the West Publishing Company. For example, a case cited as 18 Cal. 3d 660, 557 P.2d 106, 143 Cal. Rptr. 815 (1976) refers to a 1976 decision of the Supreme Court of California, and is published in the following three places:

1. At page 660 of volume 18 of the *California Reports, 3d*, published by the Bancroft-Whitney Company. This is the official reporter for the Supreme Court of California.

2. At page 106 of volume 557 of the *Pacific Reporter, 2d*, published by the West Publishing Company.

3. At page 815 of volume 143 of *West's California Reporter*, published by the West Publishing Company.

If a reporter's title includes an ordinal number, the number refers to the series of that reporter within which the case appears.

Each series of a reporter has a separate sequence of volumes beginning with volume 1. Thus, a citation to 18 Cal. 3d 660 refers to page 660 of volume 18 of the third series of *California Reports*.

Certain material which does not appear in the permanent, bound copies of the reporters is cited to the paperbound "advance sheets" that are issued by all the systems of reports as preliminary printings of cases later collected in the bound volumes. These advance sheets are preserved only by the larger law libraries.

Statutes

Whenever possible, federal statutes are cited to the official code, the *United States Code* (U.S.C.), published by the United States Government Printing Office. When the citation is to other than the current official code, the following information is given: the name of the statute (generally "Act of [full date of enactment]"), the public law (Pub. L.) or chapter (ch.) number, the number of a particular section of the statute as enacted (§), if relevant, and the location of the statute in the *Statutes at Large* (Stat.) published by the United States Government Printing Office. Citations to the *Statutes at Large* consist first of the volume number and then of the page number, so that 41 Stat. 209 refers to a statute published at volume 41, page 209 of the *Statutes at Large*. Statutes are published in *Statutes at Large* in chronological order of enactment. The unofficial code of the West Publishing Company, the United States Code Annotated (U.S.C.A.), is cited when it contains information not available elsewhere. Executive Orders are cited by number, as well as by the volume and page of publication in the *Federal Register* (Fed. Reg.), published by the United States Government Printing Office.

State statutes are usually cited by the name of the codification, the subdivision (ch. or §), and a parenthetical reference to the publisher of the code and the date of publication. Thus, Cal. Gov't Code § 68541 (West 1976) refers to the West Publishing Company's 1976 edition of the volume containing section 68541 of the California Government Code. The full names of the cited California codes are indicated in square brackets in the following table of statutes. The final three entries in that table refer to rules of practice before particular courts, and are explained in the appended brackets.

Citations to state or federal constitutions are to the current version unless otherwise indicated. By convention, no publisher is indicated in constitutional citations; the text of current as well as superseded constitutional provisions can be most easily obtained from the annotated constitutions that are included in the West Publishing Company's annotated versions of the federal and various state codes.

Table of Cases

Table of Statutes

Act of Sept. 24, 1979, Pub. L. No. 96-68, § 401, 93 Stat. 416.

Act of Oct. 20, 1978, Pub. L. No. 95-486, § 4, 92 Stat. 1629 (amending 28 U.S.C. §§ 44 and 133 (1976)).

Act of Oct. 10, 1978, Pub. L. No. 95-431, § 401, 92 Stat. 1021.

Act of Nov. 8, 1977, Pub. L. No. 95-157, 91 Stat. 1265, codified at 48 U.S.C. § 1694 (Supp. I 1977).

Act of Aug. 2, 1977, Pub. L. No. 95-86, § 401, 91 Stat. 419.

Act of Aug. 12, 1976, Pub. L. No. 94-381, 90 Stat. 1119 (repealing 28 U.S.C. § 2281–82 and amending 28 U.S.C. § 2284).

Act of Oct. 21, 1975, Pub. L. No. 94-121, § 401, 89 Stat. 611.

Act of Oct. 5, 1974, Pub. L. No. 93-433, § 401, 88 Stat. 1187.

Act of Dec. 24, 1969, Pub. L. No. 91-153, § 401, 83 Stat. 403.

Act of Aug. 9, 1968, Pub. L. No. 90-470, § 401, 82 Stat. 666.

Act of Sept. 1, 1959, Pub. L. No. 86-221, 73 Stat. 452.

Act of Sept. 6, 1950, ch. 896, § 401, 64 Stat. 595.

Act of June 25, 1948, ch. 646, 62 Stat. 869.

Act of June 28, 1941, ch. 258, 55 Stat. 265.

Act of May 14, 1940, ch. 189, 54 Stat. 181.

Act of Feb. 17, 1936, ch. 75, 49 Stat. 1140.

Act of June 17, 1930, ch. 509, 46 Stat. 774.

Act of Feb. 13, 1925, ch. 229, 43 Stat. 936.

Act of May 29, 1920, ch. 214, 41 Stat. 631.

Act of July 19, 1919, ch. 24, 41 Stat. 163.

Act of March 1, 1919, ch. 86, 40 Stat. 1213.

Act of Aug. 4, 1886, ch. 902, 24 Stat. 222.

Exec. Order No. 12,165, 44 Fed. Reg. 58,671 (1979).

U.S. Const. art. III, § 1.

5 U.S.C. § 5332 (Supp. I 1977), *as adjusted by* Exec. Order No. 12,087, 43 Fed. Reg. 46,827 (1978).

5 U.S.C. § 5332 (1970), *as adjusted by* Exec. Order No. 11,883, 40 Fed. Reg. 47,092 (1975).

20 U.S.C. § 42 (1976).

28 U.S.C. § 41 (1976).

28 U.S.C. § 45 (1976).

28 U.S.C. § 84 (1976).

28 U.S.C. § 133 (1976).

28 U.S.C. §§ 291–96 (1976).

Index

Designer:	Peter Koch
Compositor:	G & S Typesetters
Printer:	McNaughton & Gunn
Binder:	McNaughton & Gunn
Text:	VIP Bembo
Display:	VIP Bembo
Cloth:	Holliston Roxite B51508
Paper:	50 lb. P&S offset